PRAISE FOR **WE'RE IN AMERICA NOW:** A SURVIVOR'S STORIES

"This beautiful memoir touches my heart. Fred Amram writes eloquently of his childhood in Nazi Germany: being born in a Catholic infants' home because Jews were banned from the public hospital; the narrowing of his world as Jews were banned from radios, park benches, trolleys, and schools; opening the door to the Gestapo; and, ultimately, the extermination of nearly all his relatives and his new life in America. But he didn't leave the war behind him in Europe. He writes about how it continues to touch his life and the lives of his children and his grandchildren, not only through the generations' commitment to social justice, but in their very DNA that was shaped by the trauma of the Holocaust."

—*Ellen J. Kennedy*, Ph.D., Executive Director, World Without
Genocide at Mitchell Hamline School of Law

"Fred Amram has given us something very precious. A lively, eclectic and moving memoir of his life as a Jewish child in Nazi Germany, and as a émigré in the US. Sensibly written and full of illustrative anecdotes these stories provide a unique vantage point into the early stages of the Holocaust, when a community of mutual acceptance has been destroyed. But the primary function of this book is to keep the Holocaust—not only the event in history, but also the potential for its repetition—before everyone's eyes. Fred Amram writes with the hope that his readers become also witnesses—to the lost world of European Jewry, to the fate of other children in his family who did not survive the Nazis, and thus to the past's unrealized possibilities. Amram invites us to remember and to assume responsibility for the world we live in."

—*Alejandro Baer*, Chair and Director of the Center for Holocaust
and Genocide Studies at the University of Minnesota

FRED AMRAM

WE'RE IN AMERICA NOW:
A SURVIVOR'S STORIES

Holy Cow! Press
Duluth, Minnesota
2016

Author photographs (pages 10, 247, and back cover)
by David Sherman.

Book and cover design by Anton Khodakovsky.
Printed and bound in the United States of America.

First printing, 2016

ISBN 978-0-9864480-2-7

10 9 8 7 6 5 4 3 2 1

This project is supported in part by grant awards
from the Ben and Jeanne Overman Charitable Trust,
the Elmer L. and Eleanor J. Andersen Foundation,
the Cy and Paula DeCosse Fund of The Minneapolis
Foundation, the Lenfestey Family Foundation, and
by gifts from individual donors.

Holy Cow! Press books are distributed to the trade
by Consortium Book Sales & Distribution,
c/o Ingram Publishing Services, Inc.,
210 American Drive, Jackson, TN 38301.

For inquiries, please write to:
HOLY COW! PRESS, Post Office Box 3170, Mount
Royal Station, Duluth, MN 55803.

Visit www.holycowpress.org

CONTENTS

DEDICATION

I'M AN ONLY CHILD.

It was customary for young Jewish German adults during the Holocaust to have only one child—often none at all. "Why bring more Jewish children into a world like this?" my mother often asked. Why, indeed.

Papa had an older sister, *Tante* Beda, who married Ernst Lustig. No children. Papa's younger brother, roly-poly *Onkel* Max, my favorite relative, married Jenny late in life. No children. They all died of natural causes in the United States.

Mutti (German for mommy) was the oldest of three girls. The second, Karola, married Jakob Stern. No children. She died in the Riga (Latvia) ghetto on January 6, 1945. Perhaps Onkel Jakob did, too.

The youngest sister, Käthe—Mutti called her the baby—moved to Amsterdam and married a Dutch man, Isaak Wurms. Their only child, my only first cousin, Aaltje, was born in Holland on August 21, 1939, when Holland still seemed like a safe country for Jews.

At the end of October 1939, shortly after Aaltje's birth, Mutti, Papa and I, a six-year old "adventurer," escaped from Germany. We stayed with Tante Käthe and Onkel Isaak where I met Aaltje for the first and only time. I held the baby with great love. Everyone reminded me often that this was my only cousin. I couldn't really play with this babe of two months. How does one "play" with a newborn? At best, one shakes a rattle in hopes of eliciting a gurgle. Did I sit on the carpet with her nestled in my arms? Did I sing to her? Surely, it was the clichéd love at first sight.

Cousin Aaltje Wurms

The Nazis invaded Holland on May 10, 1940. We don't know the details of the family's suffering. Years later, however, while studying records at Yad Vashem in Jerusalem, I learned that on April 30, 1943, Onkel Isaak died in the Auschwitz concentration camp. He outlived cousin Aaltje by a few months. On February 19, 1943, Aaltje, with her 29-year old mother, was killed in an Auschwitz gas chamber. The Nazi executioners scrupulously documented their evil in a clear script. Aaltje's age at the time of her murder: 3½.

What can I tell about Aaltje Wurms? All I remember is that she was small, an infant, when I saw her last. I can only imagine her life story; what might have been. Might she have become a Pulitzer Prize recipient? A Nobel laureate scientist? Or, might she have become a housewife caring for her own children and grandchildren? She might have grown old, just as I did. She might have grown old with me, my only cousin—just six years my junior.

Parents gone. Uncles and aunts gone. Cousin Aaltje gone. I am an only child. All I have left is the photograph of a child who did not survive the Holocaust.

This book is dedicated to my cousin Aaltje and all the children butchered in genocides.

PROLOGUE

> "When I was younger, I could remember anything, whether it had happened
> or not; but my faculties are decaying now and soon I shall be so I cannot
> remember any but the things that never happened."
>
> *Mark Twain's Autobiography*

PAPA LIKED TO TELL how he met Mutti. In 1930, he and a friend
each brought a girlfriend on a Sunday afternoon date to Café
Kröpke in Hannover, Germany. Sometime before sunset, Papa
and his friend traded dates. Papa claimed he took home the prettier
girl—the woman who became my mother. One day when he wasn't
nearby, I asked Mutti how she met Papa. She told the same story—and
allowed that Papa took home the prettier girl.

The story of how my parents met illustrates how I learned about
many of the events in this book. For example, I write about my *bris*, my
circumcision ceremony. Only eight days old at the time, clearly I don't
really remember the details. However, if Mutti and Papa separately told
the same story and it was corroborated by my Uncle Max and my Aunt
Beda, surely it must be true—or so I believe. And so, many events were
told and retold around the dinner table until I can't be sure what I remember and what I was told and only think I remember.

Do I tell the truth? Only as much as I am able. My favorite poet,
Dylan Thomas, wrote in 1954, "I can never remember whether it
snowed for six days and six nights when I was twelve or whether it
snowed for twelve days and twelve nights when I was six." Memory,
Thomas and I agree, is unreliable.

In *Memories of a Catholic Girlhood*, American author Mary McCarthy writes, "I remember we heard a nightingale together, on the bou-
levard near the Sacred Heart convent. But there are no nightingales in
North America." The "memory" becomes part of McCarthy's memoir
and we believe it even if the "memory" might have come from reading

Elderly Fred Amram

London-dwelling T.S. Eliot's poem about the convent of the Sacred Heart. And so my perceptions are my perceptions. In a memoir one should not take liberties with the truth. This is my world as I believe it to be true—today.

I tell the truth as I remember events filtered through my feelings as a youngster and, again, filtered through the memory of a nostalgic old timer. Twice-baked potatoes. I have changed a few names to protect the innocent—or because my memory hit a blank.

And forgive me if I interrupt myself or become sidetracked. Isn't that the way we tell a story? Ultimately the truth lies in the interruptions. Ask any psychiatrist.

As much as we like to generalize, each Holocaust survivor describes a unique experience. Each Auschwitz survivor tells a different story as does each survivor who spent the war in hiding or who, like me, was lucky enough to leave before the worst of times. This book tells my story and focuses, in part, on the events that led up to the worst of the genocide, led up to Auschwitz and the other death camps.

Every genocide creates displaced persons—refugees. All of us, no matter from which genocide we escaped, bring memories that shape our assimilation

In this collection of stories—and it is a collection—I share my experiences and feelings as a child survivor. It is my truth of being an outsider, a Jew in Nazi Germany, and then a foreign Jew growing up in America, still an outsider—a stranger in a strange land.

My life in Germany is written in the past tense. As I step off the boat I enter the present tense. What's past is past and...

I. TWO BUTCHERS

"Throughout all generations, every male shall be circumcised when he is eight days old... This shall be my covenant in your flesh, an eternal covenant."

Genesis 17:1-14

HITLER BECAME CHANCELLOR OF GERMANY on January 30, 1933. I was born September 19 of that year. I was born in a Catholic infants shelter. My birth certificate has the signature of a nun. Not just any run-of-the-mill nun. The illegible signature shows a clear title underneath: Mother Superior.

Why would a Jewish baby have his birth certificate certified by a nun? Because the Nazis, led by Adolf Hitler, had already closed Jewish hospitals and had prohibited Jews from using public hospitals. *Juden Verboten*. Jews Forbidden.

A few Catholic orders were prepared to stand up to Hitler. My Mother Superior allowed Mutti to use her facilities and encouraged her nurses to serve Jews. Surely they had taken a risk on my behalf.

Eight days later, as prescribed by Jewish law, I was circumcised. Two butchers attended my circumcision.

My family had scheduled the entire day as a celebration of this special event. Ashkenazi Jews call it a *bris*. Sephardic Jews call it a *brit* or more formally a *brit milah*, a ritual circumcision. Either way it's a big deal and a party was planned in our fourth-floor apartment.

Nowadays circumcisions are commonplace and they're usually performed in hospitals shortly after birth. However, for many Jews a special ceremony is involved and certainly, when I was a tad in Hannover, Germany, a *bris* involved relatives, dinner, drinking—a major celebration. After all, one is celebrating the birth of a male child.

My parents told and retold the story of my circumcision a hundred times. The relatives arrived for the party. Uncle Max came from Hamburg. Aunt Beda, whose hugs I adored during my adolescence because of her substantial bosom, came from Berlin with her husband, Uncle Ernst. My widowed grandmothers, of course. My mother's sister Karola and her husband Kurt, who never had children of their own and doted on me, drove all the way from Kassel. Friends from the synagogue were there. And then entered our local kosher butcher, Herr Mandelbaum.

Theological regulations "circumscribe" the ritual for circumcisions. A professional is hired. In Hebrew he's called a *mohel*, in Yiddish a *moyl*. Although the butcher Mandelbaum was not a rabbi, he had the special training of a *moyl*. He knew the ritual, the prayers, the cutting technique and he had a sharp knife.

Moyl Mandelbaum, a small, heavily bearded man in his mid-forties, began by blessing the wine. Almost all Jewish ceremonies begin by sanctifying wine. It's a marvel that we're sober most of the time. Papa placed a few drops on my lips, presumably as an anesthetic. I was expected to join in blessing the wine. I gurgled my best imitation of a Hebrew prayer. When the moyl became serious I let out a bellow.

I've been asked by friends to provide more details about the event. Unfortunately, three factors interfere with my memory. First, expert as old Mandelbaum was, the pain was excruciating. Second, in some Jungian flashback, I was reliving Everyman's fear of losing his manhood. And third, I was drunk.

I've been told that Mandelbaum washed his hands in a special bowl and said the blessing for washing the hands. Jews have a blessing for everything. After more prayers and blessings, he cut.

Papa paid Herr Mandelbaum who then returned to his kosher butcher shop.

Next the dinner. Mutti was ushering the guests to a fine buffet when we heard music. A marching band. Uncle Max, the family tease, announced that there was to be a parade in honor of my manhood. Several guests believed Uncle Max could pull off such a trick. Imagine, celebrating a Jewish babe in Nazi Germany with a parade.

As the music became louder, everyone rushed to the windows. Our apartment had a small balcony and Papa carried me outside to see my first parade. We could see men, women and children gathering on the sidewalks.

There were soldiers in khaki uniforms and shining leather boots. There were drums and clarinets and all the wonderful brass instruments one expects in a marching band. And between platoons of more soldiers we could see a long black open car. The man standing near the back of the car had dark hair and a mustache. Just as he drew even with our balcony he saluted with an outstretched arm at a 45-degree angle. At that sign the spectators raised their arms and, with one voice,

Mutti with baby

shouted, "*Heil* Hitler." The platoons of German military might echoed in unison, "Heil Hitler." Mutti pulled us inside. Adolph Hitler was not a welcome guest at my bris. He was, however, the second butcher to attend.

Is there a blessing for two butchers at a bris?

II. THE CHANUKAH MAN

UNCLE MAX ALWAYS spent the first night of Chanukah with us. Our large apartment in Hannover had space for overnight guests. Uncle Max, Papa's brother, was a bachelor living in Hamburg. He visited often. Like most bachelor uncles, he doted on his nephew—in this case his only nephew, an only child. Uncle Max was short like papa. However, unlike Papa who was thin and fit, even a little muscular, Uncle Max was round. After the Chanukah dinner and the lighting of the first candle and the singing of songs, Uncle Max lay on the couch, lit a cigar and relaxed. His round belly created a mountain on which my few lead soldiers could climb. Just when Uncle Max lit his cigar, my father announced that he had to go to the post office for business—weekday or weekend.

Even before *Kristallnacht*, Crystal Night, the night of broken glass, the Gestapo came to search Jewish homes. Sometimes they took the men with them. The men never returned. Later they came for the families, but in 1937 it was mostly men who disappeared. Papa was never home when the gruff uniformed men, with their "Heil Hitlers" and their pistols knocked on *our* door. He was out "on business"—perhaps he had gone to the post office—just as he was out each year on the first night of Chanukah.

And on the first evening of every Chanukah—every Chanukah before Kristallnacht—after the first candle was lit, the electric lights turned low and round Uncle Max on the couch blowing huge round clouds of cigar smoke, Papa announced that he needed to go to the post office for business. After a short while, a man with a deep voice would

Papa's childhood Chanukiah

ring the doorbell. Mutti would let him in and announce with great surprise that the Chanukah man had come. He was wearing a hooded green Mackinaw which he never opened. I sat on this stranger's lap, almost as frightened as when the Gestapo came to our house.

"Have you been a good boy during the past year?"

I assured the Chanukah man that I had been as good as I could be—allowing some room for error. Uncle Max laughing aloud on the couch, with his jelly belly rocking, assured me that I was safe.

"Do you deserve coal for Chanukah?"

"No," I whimpered. I was too well-behaved for that. In the end, the Chanukah man produced a small toy—once a lead ambulance that would ride on my uncle's belly when we played together or on my blanketed legs when I was sick. And then the stranger was gone.

When Papa arrived home, I complained that he was always at the post office when the Chanukah man visited. Surely, I must have been the only Jewish boy in history who had a personal Chanukah man.

We arrived in New York City just before Chanukah of 1939, too poor to have a Chanukah that first year. Too poor even for a Chanukah man.

III. NUR FÜR JUDEN

MUTTI AND I PEEKED INTO the ice cream shop window as we did each time we passed on our way to Goethe Platz, an island of trees and flowers at the end of Goethe Strasse—our busy commercial street. We lived on Goethe Strasse, shopped on Goethe Strasse and caught the trolley right in front of our house on Goethe Strasse.

"Will we stop in for ice cream on the way home?" I asked. We almost always did.

"If you're a good boy," was Mutti's answer. That meant I had to hold her hand all the way to the park and all the way home.

I held Mutti's hand tight and we walked to a corner, watched for traffic, crossed the street and walked another block and then another. Mutti liked to window shop and so did I. We checked for new displays.

"Look. There's a new black hat we could get for Papa to wear to the synagogue."

"Would your father like that striped tie for his birthday?"

But we never bought anything.

There were a few dress shops with manikins. Once we saw a bright red dress that I promised to buy Mutti with my first earnings. She said she hated the color. She wanted the burgundy colored one to wear to the opera.

We always stopped at WMF, an elegant cutlery shop. When we had company for dinner we used knives and forks and spoons from the WMF store. We also owned one of the store's silver butter dishes and a candy dish. These only came out for visitors.

Manfred (Freddy) at Goethe Platz

"Can you read the letters on the sign," Mutti asked, pointing at three big letters over the shop.

"W—M—F."

"And they stand for...," Mutti began.

I interrupted. "F is for *Fabrik*. M is for *Metallwaren*. W is for..." I made some funny sounds and Mutti laughed. I couldn't pronounce the six-syllable word so I faked it.

"Good boy," she *kvelled*. "Can you say *Wurtemburgische*?"

I couldn't and we walked on.

A few stores had the letter J painted on them. Others spelled out *JUDE*. People were supposed to boycott those stores. I didn't know why and Mutti always evaded my questions about the J. She just walked faster.

We crossed the last street and just as we stepped into Goethe Platz I let go of Mutti's hand and ran. I hid behind a fat bush twice my size and watched Mutti walk by. She was supposed to look for me as she did on most of our outings. But this time she pretended to ignore me. I knew she was only pretending to ignore me because she always whistled songs when we played "Find Me." Her whistling said, "I'm looking for you" so I knew she really was. Mutti was a really good whistler. She could whistle a whole song and then sing it in French or in German.

When Mutti was a few steps past my hiding place I jumped out behind her and hollered, "Boo."

"Oh, you frightened me. I may faint." Mutti fainted sometimes but this time I knew she was teasing.

I ran ahead to my favorite bench. It was hidden in an alcove surrounded by tall trees. I liked it because it was shady and lots of birds lived in the trees. Mutti sometimes pointed to the nests and identified many types of birds. I gave them individual names like Suzie or Hannelore. There was one bird that came often and Mutti identified it as a boy bird. I named it Little Manfred because it was smaller than me and I really liked it. Sometimes Mutti called and Little Manfred came and tilted his little yellow head.

Sitta (Mutti) at Goethe Platz

The birds whistled songs and Mutti whistled back at them. I think they liked Mutti's whistles.

On this day I ran ahead and when I reached my bench I jumped up and sat as if I'd been waiting there for hours. "Oh, you're here, finally."

"Thank you for waiting for me," Mutti said with a big smile. Then her face changed. Her mouth opened and her eyes darted around nervously. "We have to go now." She emphasized "now."

"Why? We just arrived. I want to play with the birds."

"We must go."

I caught her looking past my head so I turned around to see some letters printed on the top board of the bench. Words that had not been there before.

I had never been to school. Nevertheless, I could read pretty well unless the words were too big—and some German words have many syllables. When the words were too long, I'd forget the beginning before I reached the end, like the W word in WMF.

I sounded out the short words printed on the bench. "N-u-r f-ü-r J-u-d-e-n," I said slowly. Then I put the words together in a sentence. "*Nur für Juden.*" Only for Jews.

"Wow! Boy! A bench just for me." I was so excited that I jumped up and down on the bench. Mutti looked to see if we were being observed. No. No one was near. I loved the bench and the new sign.

"Are we so special that we can have our own bench? Are the Nazis apologizing for telling people to boycott stores with the J mark? Whoopie! My own bench. They can't use it." I said all these things to Mutti and to the birds. I wasn't sure who *they* were, the people who couldn't use my bench, but I was too happy to care.

Mutti wasn't happy at all. She was even paler than usual and she was leaning against a tree. Perhaps she would faint. Tears were coming from her eyes and she was dabbing at her face with the little lace hankie she always carried around. It had her initials: SA.

"Perhaps I should take Mutti home after all," I thought. I took her hand and we started walking away from my bench. I picked a few yellow flowers that smelled especially sweet even from a distance of several feet. I gave them to Mutti. She started crying harder and sat on a bench that didn't say, "Nur fur Juden." It didn't have any words printed on it. Only my bench had that sign.

Suddenly she jumped up as if she remembered something. She pulled me off the bench even hurting my arm a little. She started walking toward home really fast and we didn't stop at the ice cream store even though I'd been a very good boy. But Mutti was not herself that day.

When we arrived home, Mutti went to her bedroom and closed the door. I went to my room to play with my lead soldiers. I didn't know what had come over my mommy, but I knew that I needed to be especially well behaved until Papa came home to fix what was broken.

Papa finally arrived several hours later, I told him about Mutti's crying. He went to the bedroom and ten minutes later, Mutti came out saying that she would cook supper while Papa washed up. While eating, they discussed the day's events but no one could or would explain to me why we Jews were allowed to have our very own bench.

Papa and Mutti argued about leaving the country. Mutti wanted to leave as soon as possible. She said this often, especially after reading a newspaper or hearing a radio news program.

"Bad things are happening in the country. I saw more broken store windows today. The Jewish paint store, for example."

"Everything will be better soon. This can't last," Papa reassured.

"Today the milkman said he had to give his Jewish customers less milk because there is a shortage. The boy needs his milk. And each week we have fewer ration stamps. Even fewer than they get. We'll starve. Manfred is a growing boy and needs good food."

"All this will change at the next election. I still have my business and it's going very well. I can always trade fabric for food if we need to." Truly Papa's textile business was going well. His storeroom, which was also my playroom, was filled with many beautiful fabrics. His daily sales trips to the farms and suburbs around Hannover made him happy and each evening he counted out a bundle of money.

But Mutti wasn't satisfied. "Perhaps we could go to Holland for a while to visit my sister. Perhaps we could even go to America."

Papa, as usual, assured us that everything would be fine. "This too will pass," he said.

A week later, Mutti and I were both tired of being cooped up in our apartment. I finally persuaded her that it was time to return to the park. I wanted to play on my bench. At several dinners during the week, Papa had joined me in arguing that we should go back to Goethe Platz to visit the bench that welcomed me. So one morning Mutti and I dressed for the park and off we went. Papa went to his business.

On the way we looked into the shop windows, just like always. Mutti promised ice cream if I were a good boy. Everyone had to limit their shopping and Jews received fewer stamps than others. I asked why, but no one gave me an answer. On the radio an official delivered a speech that explained that the food shortage was the fault of the Jews. Papa said, "Nonsense!" Ice cream certainly would make me feel better.

When we arrived at the park I ran directly to my bench. It still had its sign, "Nur für Juden." It was the only bench in the park reserved for me. But then I noticed that today all the other benches had words printed on them too. I walked close to one bench and sounded out the words. "Nur für Arier." Only for Arians. When Mutti reached our bench I saw that her fists were clenched, her lips were tight and she looked angry—the way she looked when I broke a favorite vase.

"What's Arier?" I asked.

"The Nazis," she answered brusquely.

"Why do we have only one bench and they have all the rest?"

"I can't understand it either. They hate us."

On the way home we saw a trolley stopped on busy Goethe Strasse. The conductor was letting off passengers at the back door and the driver was helping an old man on at the front door. Proud of my recent reading successes, I slowly sounded out a sign I had never before seen on the trolley, "*Für Juden Verboten.*" I read it aloud to Mutti. "Für Juden Verboten." To Jews Forbidden.

I loved trolley rides to the countryside on Sunday with Papa or with one of my grandmothers. I had been such an extraordinarily good boy and I was being punished. No more trolley rides. Why? I put my face into Mutti's skirt and sobbed. I could hear Mutti crying too. We watched a few more trolleys. They all had the same lettering.

"We need a treat," Mutti announced.

Holding hands, we stepped into the ice cream store and sat at one of the little tables. Ice cream was served in a little glass dish with a wafer standing in its middle. Mutti said she would order coffee-flavored ice cream. I wanted chocolate.

The owner, a tall, fat, jolly man knew us from our many previous visits. He tried to make all the children believe that he was Kris Kringle. No one believed him but we all called him Herr Kringle. He always called me *Struwwelpeter* because I once stumbled into his shop during a rainstorm looking very wet and windblown. Struwwelpeter was a messy looking boy in a story that my *Oma*, Papa's mother, used to read to me. Mutti sometimes called me the same name because I hated to have my fingernails cut.

On this day, Herr Kringle didn't look jolly. He came to our table with a long face looking as if he, too, were about to cry. Very quietly, so that the other customers wouldn't hear, he said, "I'm very sorry. We can't serve Jews."

IV. THE RELUCTANT GROWN-UP

A LOUD, DEMANDING KNOCK frightened Mutti. Her face tightened and she pursed her lips. The Victorian pallor, in which she prided herself, seemed especially white. We both looked at the door as if awaiting a miracle.

An even louder, more insistent knock caused Mutti to jump. She sprang to the door, inhaled and turned the doorknob. The push from the other side knocked her to the floor. "I want Meinhardt Amram," demanded the handsome man. To me he looked like a uniformed giant. Mutti at 5'2" made everyone look like a giant.

"Gestapo," announced the officer in his intimidating black uniform and calf-high leather boots. His visor cap displayed an eagle and a death mask—or was it a skull? On his left arm he wore a red band emblazoned with a swastika. A holstered pistol rode on his right hip.

Mutti grasped the door handle and slowly pulled herself to a standing position. "Meinhardt Amram is my husband," she responded, trying to stand tall.

"I want him at once," demanded the officer.

"He's out on business," Mutti said almost belligerently.

"Have him report to Gestapo headquarters as soon as he returns." It was clear that the officer was finished. He clicked his heels, gave an almost imperceptible bow, raised his right arm to a 45-degree angle and with a "Heil Hitler," he was gone.

It was 1938 and such unwanted visits were not unusual at the homes of Jews living in Hannover, Germany. Gestapo officers would knock and take the Jewish men. To where? No one knew for sure in those early days, although there were stories. I was too young to be told all the details.

I think the kosher butcher, Mandelbaum, disappeared first. A youngster remembers a name like Herr Mandelbaum: Mr. Almond Tree. Ironic that this man with his sharp knives and so popular in the community would be the first to go. Mutti and Papa talked about him lovingly. He was the moyl at my bris.

Whenever the tall uniformed men in their shiny boots and gruff tones knocked on *our* door, Papa wasn't home. Youngster that I was, no one trusted me with information. He was simply "out on business."

The truth, learned much later, was that he had "ways of knowing." He would disappear "downstairs." We lived on the fourth floor of a five-story apartment building. "Downstairs," he went to the apartment of some gentiles who found a hiding place for him. I can't shake the image of this tiny man fitting comfortably under a bed. I was never told the names of the righteous Christians who sheltered my Papa. Even when I questioned him directly in his later and more comfortable years, he wouldn't reveal their names or their apartment number. They were simply "downstairs." Decades later, on a continent far away, Papa was still protecting these good people.

Papa returned in time for supper. As we sat around the kitchen table, Mutti described what had happened that day. Papa asked if his son had cried. "No," said Mutti. "At least not while the swine was here." In conversation, Jews referred to all Nazi officials as swine.

I told Papa about the black uniform and the death mask and the red arm band and the gun. Papa's training in textiles showed when he explained that the uniform was a low quality gabardine. He was unable to satisfy my obvious interest in pistols.

Papa did not report to the Gestapo. "They'll be back," he announced with certainty. And they were.

In 1939 the Gestapo—in fact all SS officers—who visited our apartment wore the new wartime stone gray uniforms. The gray was not nearly as terrifying as the black they had worn earlier. Papa was always "out on business" when they came.

One day we heard the insistent knock. No matter which officer came, the knock was always the same. By now we assumed that the knock was part of the SS training. My mother had learned to step away from the door so that she would not be thrown over.

This time three officers entered, all in shiny boots and all carrying drawn pistols. One officer told my mother and me to stand in a corner, pointing with his gun to the preferred spot. The other two holstered their guns and started searching. I held tight to Mommy's skirt.

"Radios. Where are your radios?"

Mommy explained that we owned only one. "It's in the living room."

The truth wasn't enough. The gangsters emptied every wardrobe and every cabinet. When the search was over, our guard announced, "Jews will not listen to radios. Never! We will check." As if it were rehearsed, the three thieves gave us a "Heil Hitler" in perfect unison, and they were gone with our radio.

At supper, Mutti told Papa that we should all go into hiding. "They will kill you. They will kill our son." Papa, ever hopeful, gave his usual biblical assurance. "This too shall pass." They argued.

Knock! Knock! Knock! Always that triple knock.

"Meinhardt Amram."

Mutti's response never wavered. "Meinhardt Amram is my husband and he is out on business." Was he really out on business or was he downstairs? No one trusted me with such information. Perhaps his business was downstairs.

"What business does he do?"

Mutti explained that he drove around suburban Hannover where he sold fabric by the yard to the housewives who make clothing for themselves and their families. Unfortunately, Mutti glanced at a closed door near the entryway. The SS officer saw the glance and was suspicious. "Kranz," he hollered down the stairs. "I need help."

Another officer bounded up to our apartment on the fourth floor with pistol drawn.

"Kranz, open that door."

My favorite room in the apartment was Papa's storage room. Perfectly white walls with perfectly white shelves showed off bolts of fabric in every imaginable color and texture. I loved the colors from pastel pink to glowing red, from aqua to royal blue, from lemon yellow to grass green. Sometimes Papa let me stand on his ladder so that I could feel the different textures: wool and silk, cotton and linen. He explained "quality" by discussing the different weaves. I learned about dyeing techniques and why colors sometimes run. He suggested which fabric would make a fine woman's skirt, which would make a man's dress shirt and which should be used as a dish towel. I loved Papa's fabric room better than going to the park, even better than eating ice cream. The colors made my heart beat faster.

Finding the cloth, the two officers talked quietly, both with their guns drawn and aimed at Mutti and me. Kranz left and was gone almost half an hour. While we waited, Mutti and I didn't dare say a word. Each of us knew what was about to happen. Even as a five-year-old, I had seen the police and civilians smash Jewish shop windows. Looting Jewish stores was by now common. Jewish shopkeepers were beaten, humiliated and then hauled away.

Kranz returned with three additional men. When the gang, all uniformed officers with leather calf-length boots, had finished hauling away the last bolt of fabric they looked at my mother, clicked their heels, gave a small bow and, in unison, shouted a "Heil Hitler." Mutti locked the front door and we went into Papa's storage room. The glass chandelier made the white walls even whiter. All white! No color anywhere. We both cried. I think that was my last cry for many years.

That night, Papa didn't come home until well after supper. He was dirty and tired. Papa explained that the SS had traced him through his automobile license plates. They arrested him, confiscated his car and brought him to a construction site. There he worked with other Jewish slave laborers under the supervision of armed guards. He had a choice. He could live in a barracks set up near the construction site or he could go home. If he chose to go back to his apartment, he must return in the morning or he and every member of his family would be executed. Papa described how workers at the site had been shot because they fainted from the hot sun and the heavy work.

Papa now had no income and would be forced to work as a slave seven days each week. He returned home after my bedtime and he left before I awoke. I had no Papa.

I was six years old the next time the men in uniform returned with their terrifying knock. I went to the door, unlocked it and sprang out of the way as it was pushed open. They had come to search, although they refused to tell us what contraband we might be hiding. This time I stood in front of my mother—not behind. I looked straight at the lead officer with my arms crossed. I guessed that was the proper posture for a grown-up.

I never regained my childhood.

V. KRISTALLNACHT, THE NIGHT OF SHATTERED GLASS

THOUGH I WAS ONLY FIVE YEARS OLD, I remember November 8, 1938 quite clearly. Any Jew, no matter how young or old, living in Nazi Germany on that day will have clear memories of the night of shattered glass, Kristallnacht, Crystal Night.

On November 9 and 10, Jewish shop windows were smashed. Others have described how men and women were humiliated and beaten on the streets, how Jews were kicked while forced to clean streets with toothbrushes. However, for me the night of shattered glass began in the evening of November 8, a Tuesday, as we

Bergstrasse Synagogue in Hannover before Kristallnacht

stood on our balcony terrified by the sky's fiery glow. All the synagogues in my city of Hannover were looted and burned. The synagogue where we worshipped, our neighborhood synagogue, had flames shooting out of every window.

Watching the fires, we knew that this was not a good night to be out.

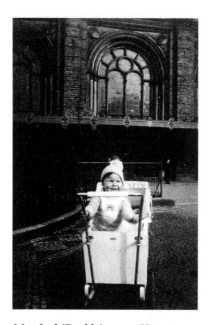

Manfred (Freddy) at our Hannover synagogue

Yet Papa disappeared again. I was told that he was going out "on business," just as he did whenever the Gestapo came knocking.

Papa missed supper. When he finally came home, he reported that this time he had not been at the post office or "downstairs." He was carrying a huge bundle covered with large rags and blankets. Was it a body?

When the wrappings were removed, I could see that they had sheltered a *torah* almost as big as my Papa. He had rescued the holy scroll from our local synagogue while the building was aflame. "Why take the risk?" my mother scolded. "One should take precautions. And why bring a torah into an apartment where even radios are forbidden?"

Radios! Just recently the Gestapo had come to all Jewish homes hunting for radios. The men in shiny black boots searched every room. Radios were verboten. Contact with the outside world was forbidden.

"Why bring a torah into an apartment where even radios are forbidden?" Mutti asked again. A meaningful question! A full-sized torah on the fourth floor of an apartment building would put all the residents at risk. "Hero" was not a word that entered the evening's conversation. I didn't hear talk of "hero" until years later when we were safely settled in the United States.

Papa had no plan for the torah. He trusted that the rabbi would know what to do. "Wait until after midnight," he said. Of course, no one told this five-year-old where one would find a rabbi on Kristallnacht.

When I awoke the next morning, the torah was gone. Apparently the rabbi did know what to do. Papa was quite pleased with himself.

VI. BOMBS BURSTING IN AIR

AFTER HITLER INVADED POLAND, much of Europe readied for war. The British responded by sending RAF fighter planes over much of Germany. At first they dropped leaflets warning us that they would send bombs if Germany didn't stop its aggression. Each morning I chased the windblown leaflets, captured a few and brought them home. My parents, of course, were already persuaded that Hitler should stop his crazy path of destruction. Hitler, however, didn't heed the messages from England. He marched into Austria and then into Czechoslovakia. Next he attacked Poland. So the English sent bombs as well as leaflets.

Sirens signaled lights out. Every sturdy structure, including our five-story apartment building at 25 Goethe Strasse, had a designated bomb shelter in the basement. Each night the shrill sirens woke us and, enveloped in darkness, we rushed to our refuge.

Our bomb shelter was cold, damp and gloomy. Sometimes I gagged from the smell of urine and sweat. A few cranky residents railed against two ten-year-olds, Walter and Rolf, who roared around the crowded shelter with arms outstretched, pretending they were Messerschmitt airplanes shooting down the RAF fighters. Nonetheless, most neighbors were cheered by the opportunity to chat about their fears and about the news they heard on the radio. Papa provided encouragement to the fearful and walked around cuddling frightened children. Old Mrs. Wassermann, although well into her 80s, was more afraid to die than the rest of us. I held her hand and played with the jeweled ring on her finger to console her. I had too little light to see the colors of the jewels but counting the reflections kept me busy. Sometimes I put my head in Mrs. Wassermann's lap and fell asleep.

One night when the sirens whined, my parents scooped up their "one and only" to join the others in the race to the basement. This time we saw a new sign on the door, "Juden Verboten." Jews Forbidden! Now we were to experience the RAF airplanes without the protection of the basement shelter and without the camaraderie of neighbors. Night after night we watched the RAF sky show from our windows. Papa sometimes sat with me under a table.

The roaring planes, whistling bombs and explosions in my mind were far more frightening than the leaflets and the occasional real bomb. My small boy imagination was far more dramatic than reality.

Papa believed that God would protect the Jews, believed it deep in his soul. Mutti had less faith. Her rage at "Juden Verboten" increased each day as neighbors, understanding the message, stopped talking to us—even avoided us. One night, she cracked. As the planes came directly over our building, she stepped onto our little balcony, looked up into the blackness and cried out, "Dear God, please let the bombs destroy this building and these people. I will be content to die with them."

Quietly she added, "If they won't live with Jews, let them die with Jews."

VII. A FREEDOM CRUISE

SUDDENLY I WAS NO LONGER sleeping in my own bed in Hannover. Grownups talked about being refugees from Nazi Germany. Here in free Amsterdam we saw no Gestapo, no burned synagogues, no Star of David armbands and no food shortages. But I missed our own apartment.

We were visiting Mutti's youngest sister Käthe, her husband Isaak Wurms and their new baby, my only cousin, Aaltje. I can't explain how we got there. Events happened quickly and no one trusted me with information. I do remember some packing. However, having never taken a trip anywhere, packing had no significance for me. Mutti, in her super orderly manner, was always moving things from one box to another to assure absolute cleanliness, household purity. However, these new boxes—Mutti called them suitcases—were different. They had handles.

In Amsterdam I played with my new cousin as much as one can play with an eight-week old baby. Aaltje slept in her cradle most of the time. When awake, she cooed or cried. Her smell often reminded me of toilets when someone is sick. When she cried or stank, I left the room to play with Onkel Isaak.

Sometimes Mutti made me sit in a rocking chair. Then she'd place Aaltje on my lap with her little head in the crook of my arm. "You should be good to your little cousin," Mutti instructed. "Sing her some of the songs you make up. One day you'll be like a big brother to her."

I had no idea what "big brother" meant nor had I ever met one. I am an only child and all my relatives were childless or had only one child.

Mutti liked to create titles for me. She often told me to act like a "man" and that I was her *kleiner Mann*, her "little man." I hated that even more than "big brother." I didn't want to be a man. I wanted to be cuddled like Cousin Aaltje. Life had been pretty scary for the past three years and now we were in a strange land with a language that I didn't understand. Didn't Mutti understand that Papa was no longer in slave labor and he was again the man of the house? I wasn't ready for the responsibility of being a big brother or a man—even if it was only a *little* man.

Early one morning I was told to dress in my *Lederhosen* and a white shirt. While eating my oatmeal, I watched Mutti and Tante Käthe cry a lot. Mutti, who considered herself perfect in every way, dropped a teacup. Shards slid all around the kitchen. Hysterical sobs.

After a round of hugs, Mutti, Papa and I left the Wurms household with our three little brown suitcases. The shiny golden locks glistened in the sun. Mutti carried keys that fit into holes in each lock. She kept the tiny keys in a little compartment in her pocket book. My suitcase was smaller than the other two but I still struggled to keep it from dragging on the ground.

I remember a train and lots of walking. In a few days we were at a dock in Belgium. Here people spoke a language that was totally different from German. It seemed that after every train ride one had to learn a new language.

In Antwerp, Mutti, Papa and I crowded into a small cabin on the Pennland. Papa announced with a grin, "We're on our way to the land of milk and honey."

"Hooray," I shouted as Papa lifted me high and danced around the tiny room.

"I'm about to be sick," moaned Mutti.

First, two weeks in Holland, then several days in Belgium and now two weeks on a 600-foot ocean liner. It all seemed like a great adventure to me. This exodus reminded me of the story we tell at the Passover Seder about the flight out of Egypt, crossing the Red Sea and then spending forty years in the desert. Except I saw no desert. We were surrounded by water. Did the captain know how to get to the milk and honey without any landmarks? No streets, no buildings, no parks. Was God guiding the captain like He guided Moses?

The Pennland was not a luxury cruise ship. Everything seemed cramped. But I was happy to be free of the Nazis—although I didn't feel totally comfortable on a rocking boat with water on all sides.

Our cabin had only beds. There may have been a dresser but I remember only beds. Papa lifted me onto the top bunk of a double-decker where I slept quite comfortably. Papa slept on the bottom bed and Mutti had her own little bed. We shared a tiny bathroom down the hall from our cabin with other adults. I didn't see any children.

Pennland steamship

Our little room had one little round window about the size of my face. Huge waves splashed against the window most of the time. Once we left port, I never saw anything but angry water. The slapping of the water against the ship didn't keep me awake but Mutti complained that the noise gave her a headache.

Rough seas during most of the two-week voyage meant that passengers rarely visited the dining room. Nor did they visit the deck, which was often covered with water as the boat tipped from side to side and the fierce wind and rain followed us across the ocean.

I became the crew's mascot, a healthy little boy who was always hungry. When all the other passengers were sick, I ate in the galley with the sailors. The food was much more plentiful than the rationed fare at home in Germany. I tried to eat as much as the crew members did, although they kept warning me that I was not quite tall enough to eat so much. Many of the crew spoke German and translated everything I needed to know. I learned English words like "chicken" and "fried potatoes" and "hamburger." I ate corn and squash for the first time ever. While Mutti and Papa kept to their beds or were sick in our little toilet, I learned to say "please" and "thank you" in at least five languages.

With great fanfare, my new friends presented me with a foot-long toy U.S. army truck which I "drove" everywhere—the conquering military hero. I imagined victorious American soldiers riding under the khaki colored canvas top that covered the back of my truck. Crew members taught me to read the "U.S. Army" logo on each side of the cab. They gave me paper and pencil and had me print "United States of America."

The body of my new truck was made of metal. The crew cautioned me to be careful of the sharp edges at the bottom of the truck. The doors of the cab were sealed shut but the tailgate was on a tiny hinge that allowed the back to open. I wished that I still had the lead soldiers I played with in Germany. They would fit into my truck and I could take them for rides. They surely would prefer riding to all the marching I had them do back in our Hannover apartment.

The halls of the ship were mostly empty because the sick passengers rarely left their rooms. That left great highways for my truck to travel. Together we turned corners, climbed stairs and explored every corner of the ship. Sometimes I couldn't find my way back to our cabin. Then I looked for a member of the crew, knowing he would pick me up and carry me "home"—often finding an extra peppermint in his pocket. I felt loved by as many papas as any boy could ever want.

One day during lunch in the galley crowded with crew members, I reported that I was going to see the land of milk and honey. A few crew members warned me that I would not really find milk and honey on the streets—a huge disappointment because I believed everything my Papa told me. Nevertheless, they assured me that as long as I owned my American truck I would be safe and secure. They were quite correct.

Papa and Mutti had an argument as we entered New York Harbor—the first of many disagreements in our new homeland. We passed the Statue of Liberty at 4 a.m. on the 15th of November, 1939. My truck and I were sound asleep on my upper bunk bed. Papa insisted that he wake me to see the lady that welcomes all refugees. Mama said, "No, no. The boy needs his sleep." Their quarrel woke me and Papa took me on deck.

Papa held me up to see THE STATUE, the symbol of liberty. With tears in his eyes he whispered some words in Hebrew that I recognized from the Passover Seder, "... and God brought you out of the Land of Egypt, out of the house of bondage."

VIII. WHAT'S IN A NAME?

AS WE STEP OFF THE BOAT in New York harbor on that mid-November day in 1939, uniformed shepherds herd us into a cavernous warehouse. Frightened immigrants everywhere, confused and speaking their diverse European languages. A uniformed immigration official calls us to his desk to Americanize our names. We are to become a new breed, my father and I.

"Name?" asks the Gestapo-looking man pointing at me.

"Manfred Amram," I whisper, looking up at Papa for protection.

* * *

We Amrams have traced our ancestors all the way back to the late seventeenth century. But back then we weren't Amrams yet. Most German Jews were not allowed surnames until Napoleon conquered much of Europe in the very early nineteenth century. Until then Jews registered births in the neighborhood synagogue with Hebrew names. For example, my great-great-great-great grandfather Rabbi Judah was born in Abterode, Germany. In 1720, his father registered the new baby in the local *shul*, the neighborhood synagogue, as Judah ben Moshe, Judah son of Moses. Rabbi Judah did not have a secular surname. Rabbi Judah named his son, born in 1745, Moses to honor his father. The rabbi's son then was named Moshe ben Judah. Moshe became a cantor and *shochet*, a ritual slaughterer, in Felsberg, Germany.

My Hebrew name is Moshe ben Menachem, Moses son of Menachem. My daughter's name is Simcha *bat* Moshe, Joy daughter of Moses. Some modern Jewish families now also add the mother's Hebrew name.

In about 1802, Napoleon, having conquered much of Europe, noticed that most German Jews did not have surnames. Jews traditionally were called Rabbi Judah, Butcher Abraham or Uncle Nachum. Napoleon decreed that Jews were to be permitted to select surnames and instructed the bureaucracy to implement that policy.

An official came to Cantor Moses ben Judah, my great-great-great grandfather, and declared, "The time has come for you to select a surname that your family can own forevermore. What shall it be?"

Cantor Moses was a learned man. He knew that in Exodus we read of the famous sister of Moses, Miriam, who, as the story goes, shipped her baby brother off in a basket. We also read of the brother of Moses, Aaron, who became his spokesman and who ultimately led the Jewish people into the Promised Land. We learn that the mother of Moses was Joacheb and no less than six times is it written in the holy book that Amram was the father of the Biblical Moses. All this Cantor Moses knew and decided that he too would be Moses, the son of Amram. Cantor Moses Amram now had an official surname.

Since that day, in every generation, the first born Amram son was given a name that begins with the letter "M" in honor of Cantor Moses Amram and in honor of the biblical Moses, son of Amram, who, it is written, led the Hebrews out of Egypt. And so it came to pass that my grandfather, Moritz Amram, begat a son named Max. Moritz, not wanting to deprive his second son of the "M" tradition, named my father, born in 1901, Meinhardt Amram. And Meinhardt had a son of his own and named him—me—Manfred.

* * *

Perhaps the Gestapo-looking man didn't hear my frightened whisper. He asks again.

"Name?"

"Manfred," I squeak in terror.

"Fred," announces the official. He writes my new name in his record book. Then he prints my American name on my immigration papers.

The officer doesn't seem to know that I need a name beginning with "M." It's my birthright. But I don't complain. My frequent contact with the Gestapo has taught me never to disagree with a uniform.

"Name?" asks the uniformed man looking at Papa.

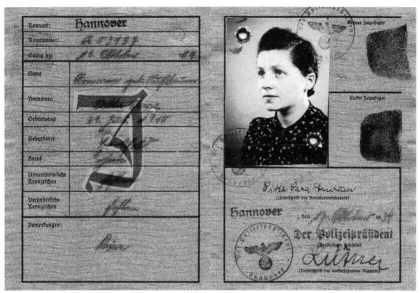

Sitta's (Mutti's) identity card

"Meinhardt," answers my father.

"Milton" says the official and my father becomes an American.

"Name?" asks the uniformed man pointing at Mutti.

"Sitta," answers my mother.

"Sara" says the tall, uniformed immigration official.

Mutti rants and cries. Under the Nazis, each German identity card assigned to Jewish men was stamped "Israel" and each document identifying Jewish women was stamped "Sara." Israel and Sara were middle names assigned to all Jews and used as a pejorative. All German Jewish women were forced to use the same name, Sara. Mutti shouts that she might as well go to the concentration camp if she is to be renamed "Sara." There is no consoling her. The official, a minor bureaucrat with no intent to do harm, writes "Sitta" in his book and on Mutti's immigration papers. And so, Sitta, the most anti-German in the family, the one who argued for years that we should escape, the one who wants most to be American and who already speaks a little English, Sitta, retains her German identity.

IX. THREE TO A BED

LTHOUGH WE'VE BEEN BRANDED with official American names, we're still lost German Jews in a warehouse of other confused immigrants and refugees. Everyone speaks English to us. Mutti, who studied French and English in high school, translates the signs and whatever she overhears. Many of the words are not part of her classroom vocabulary, but she guides us efficiently. We move from table to table until we come to the immigration-paper checker. Mutti shows our papers and answers questions.

The clerk waves us to another desk and we move on. I'm afraid to lose Mutti and Papa in the milling crowd but I can't hold on to either of them. My left hand holds my little suitcase and under my right arm I squeeze my new toy truck. Mutti walks too fast. Even Papa can hardly keep up and people push between my parents. My tired legs leave me trailing behind. "Papa, Papa," I shout. No one waits.

We arrive at yet another desk where we show a certificate and a letter from our sponsor to a uniformed official. The letter is written in English. Mutti translated the letter for us while we were still on the boat. She explained that the Hebrew Immigrant Aid Society, the HIAS, helped find American Jews who would be willing to sponsor European Jews desperate to enter the United States. The HIAS matches the sponsor with a refugee family. Mutti said that our sponsor promised the United States government that if we couldn't support ourselves, he would guarantee our expenses until we could afford to live on our own. Papa added that he must be a very kind man because he trusts us sight unseen.

The official reads the letter quickly. I don't really understand what a sponsor does, but clearly, we can't escape Hitler unless we have an American sponsor who promises that we will not be a burden to the land of milk and honey.

"Yes," says the uniformed man. "Your sponsor's name is right here in the record book. He's a doctor."

Mutti whispers in German, "He must be a rich doctor."

"You're good to go," says the official.

"Go where?" asks Mutti.

The man points to a gate.

"But where will we go?" Mutti whines.

The man points again. "Exit," he says.

The gate sign says "Exit." Mutti can translate that. Mutti explains to Papa in German that she doesn't know where to go in the biggest city in the world. Where will we sleep and eat? But the man at the desk is already talking to another family. We walk through the exit gate, step out of the line of pushing people and stand still. Like most refugees, we did not arrive with riches. In addition to her suitcase, Mutti carries a small briefcase filled with IMPORTANT PAPERS and I'm responsible for my most treasured possession, a toy American army truck.

"*Da, da*," shouts Papa suddenly. "There, There." He rushes to a man with a sign that even I can read: "Amram *Familie*." Papa starts chatting in German with the man. The stranger understands every word. He speaks our language and tells Papa not to worry.

"I'm from the Hebrew Immigrant Aid Society, the HIAS," he says. "I've come to help you settle into New York City." He tells us his name, but I can't remember it. He speaks German perfectly. Papa even uses some Yiddish phrases with our guide. He must be Jewish. Mutti refuses to learn Yiddish. She claims that "only Polacks and boors speak Yiddish." I don't think that Papa is in either of those categories but his Yiddish is pretty good.

We walk a little way to a trolley that doesn't say, "Juden Verboten." The HIAS man pays the fare for all of us. He finds a seat for himself and points to empty benches. We sit. When he stands up, we stand up. We follow him off the trolley, down a busy street. I smell meat. A *Frankfurter* stand. I look up and sound out the words "Hot" and "Dog" but

I don't know what they mean. I move closer to the little cart to smell the sausage and the mustard. Yum. I move on and look into a shop window where dresses are displayed on statues that look like women. One woman is naked and a man is dressing her. Another shop shows men's clothing on statues. I stop when I see a shop that displays oranges and apples and potatoes in large boxes. More food than I've ever seen in one store. I'm a puppy that sniffs at every tree. Suddenly the HIAS man is stroking my hair. He's come back for me.

"Do you want something?"

I'm tongue-tied. I put down my suitcase and point to a green fruit thinking that it's a new kind of misshapen apple—an American apple.

The HIAS man pays. "I'll hold this until we sit down. Then you can eat it."

We walk down steps into an underground train station. I've never been in a tunnel and certainly not one with noisy trains. I'm terrified and need to hold on to someone. The HIAS man sees my predicament and offers to carry my truck. I hand him my suitcase instead and grab Mutti's skirt. The man pays our fare and explains that we will have to learn how to use the subway—but not right now. Mutti remarks that she has once been on an *U Bahn* in Berlin.

When we're seated, the HIAS man hands me the fruit. Mutti says, "Say thank you."

I'm still tongue-tied. I bite into the fruit expecting a tart apple taste. It's sweet. Sweeter than any fruit I've ever tasted. I can almost smell the sugar. America is wonderful. I can't control the tears. The HIAS man rushes over to ask if I don't like my treat. He reaches to take it away. I protect the fruit and continue to cry. Finally I make myself whisper my appreciation, "*Danke schoen.*" I take another bite.

We follow the man off the subway, up the steps to the street. He points to a waste basket and encourages me to throw the core away. I do and Mutti rushes over to wipe my hand and my mouth with her handkerchief. She reaches for the right hand but I refuse to let go of the truck. I stick my lower lip way out and squint. My mean face. She gives up.

We enter a small hotel lobby that smells like very stale food, mostly cabbage. I look at Mutti and see her nose twitching. This room doesn't meet her standards for cleanliness. A desk clerk gives the HIAS man a key and we all squeeze into a closet with lots of shiny brass. The closet— my first elevator—rattles up several flights. I'm nearest to Papa so I hold his hand. He winks. Everything will be fine. He explains that I just ate a *Birne*, a pear. They were once quite popular in Germany but now, in wartime, they're hard to find. He promises more pears if I'm a good boy.

We're shown a small, dark, dusty room with one bed and a dresser. The man explains that this will be our home until we're settled in a better place. The HIAS will pay the rent and give us money for food. He gives each of us a piece of paper money with the number "5" on it. I give mine to Papa.

The next day the man returns to take us to the HIAS office. He wants us to learn how to get there by ourselves. At the HIAS, there are nice men and women who speak any language one could wish. Social workers arrange work papers for Mutti and Papa and English language classes. They help Mutti make contact with former Hannoverians now living in New York.

We eat most of our meals at a cafeteria next to the hotel. Papa holds me up so I can see the foods on the counter and in the little compartments. I point. Mutti uses veto power when I select only meats and desserts. She insists on vegetables and limits me to one inexpensive dessert.

Most significant to me that first week in New York City is our bed. We have one large bed in our hotel room—a double bed. Mutti decides that I must sleep in the middle so that I don't fall out. However, she insists that I sleep in the opposite direction from my parents with my feet near their faces. Papa calls her *meshuga* and says something about the New York moon distorting her brain. Mutti wins the argument on health reasons that I don't understand. So I sleep every night between my parents, looking at their feet which stick out from the covers so that I can breathe. My feet are covered at the other end because I'm still small. After a few nights I become accustomed to the smell of Papa's feet. They smell just like the egg salad Papa selects at the cafeteria. To be sure that my feet don't smell funny, I never select eggs.

A woman from the HIAS helps Mutti contact the Strauss family, comfortably settled refugees from Germany. They have a flat and need someone to share the rent. We move into one bedroom in their three-bedroom apartment in Washington Heights. We have use of the kitchen and living room. It isn't until Papa finds a job and we can afford additional rent that I have my own little "room." I sleep in a little hallway off the living room. A heavy ceiling to floor curtain allows me to pretend that I have a private space. I like that I can overhear all conversations. Yippee. I finally have my own bed! The Strauss's son, Walter, has his own bedroom.

Walter is sixteen and quite independent. I watch him closely so that I can learn how to be an American boy. When he comes home from school, he goes directly to the ice box, takes out a bottle of milk and drinks right from the bottle. He does not need permission to make sandwiches for himself. In America, it seems to me, there are no food shortages, rationing and hunger like in Hannover. One day I go to the kitchen while *Frau* Strauss is washing dishes. I open the ice box and take out a bottle of milk. I remove the cover and drink just a little bit. I cap the bottle and put it back in the ice box. All the while I pretend not to be watching Frau Strauss—although I eye her carefully. She pays no attention to me. I take a cookie and go back to my little space. No food shortage. I can eat to my heart's content—and I do.

X. SCHOOL DAYS

AS SOON AS WE SETTLE IN with the Strausses, a woman from the HIAS comes to visit. She's taller than Mutti and dressed in a black wool suit. Papa has taught me to recognize wool. Her skirt comes almost to her ankles. She has a black coat and a black felt hat just like Papa's hat except that the HIAS lady has a many-colored feather in her hat. And she is carrying a black briefcase. The lady speaks German to Mutti and to me. She says that she has come to visit me. I suspect it's a trick. No grown-up wants to visit a kid. Nevertheless, I play along.

"How would you like to go to an American school?" she asks in German.

"Ya! Ya! Ya! Oh, Ya!"

Mutti interrupts to tell the HIAS lady that I've never been to a school, German or American, and that I can't speak English.

I pipe in that I've learned many words since we moved to New York. I show off a little of my vocabulary: "Cookie, hot, dog, yes, no, school ..."

"Very good," says the HIAS lady before I really get momentum. Everyone seems to be in an interrupting mode so I continue.

"Walter has taught me to say 'encyclopedia.'" I think that it's the name of a book. Mutti thinks I've said a naughty word and apologizes to the HIAS lady. Mutti tells the lady that I'm usually a good boy. She gives me her angry look with tight lips and half closed eyes burning into me.

The visitor is impressed. "Can you spell that?"

I shrug and say a string of letters. "Pretty good," says the lady. "You still have a little bit to learn so I want to take you to the nearby school today to see if we can get you registered." All this in German.

"Yes! Yes! Yes!" I say "Yes!" over and over until Mutti puts her hand over my mouth.

"Of course, you may come along," the lady says to Mutti. I'm disappointed. I see adventures ahead and Mutti often says "No" when Papa and others say "Yes."

We all put on our warm coats and face the winter air. As we walk, I make clouds with my breath.

When we arrive at the school, we follow the HIAS lady to an office and we stand against a wall, trying not to be in the way of traffic. A clerk asks us to sit. Eventually the HIAS lady is ushered into an inner room and we wait. I had never imagined that schools have offices. I pictured going into a classroom with other boys my age. I pictured reading and writing and games. That's how grown-ups described school.

I try to sit quietly, hoping to make a good impression. Mutti often tells me that squirming makes a poor impression. I'm not quite certain what a poor impression does. However, I do know that this is an important day to make a good impression.

When the HIAS lady returns, she has a sad face and she's looking at her feet. "I'm afraid I have bad news," she begins. "The principal won't let you into the first grade until your English has improved, even though you're six years old. You must attend kindergarten until next spring. Then, in the fall, you can attend the next level."

Mutti and the HIAS lady discuss the matter for several minutes. They sound as if the sky has fallen, but I don't understand what they're saying. I'm not disappointed at all. I'm going to school.

The HIAS lady explains that we're to show up here at 8:30 on Monday morning. "Come to this office and someone will take you to the kindergarten classroom." Then she opens her bulging briefcase and takes out a picture book. "This is a story in English and you should look at it over the weekend. Perhaps you already know the story."

I recognize the picture on the cover: A little girl with a red cape and a wicker basket. *Rotkappchen*. A story my Oma Jetchen told me when I sat on her lap in Hannover. The HIAS lady helps me sound out the title, *Little Red Riding Hood*.

"Now let's go for ice cream if the weather isn't too cold for you." Mutti explains to me that it's customary for Jews to associate sweets with learning. Rabbis usually put honey on the fingers of beginning students. When the student learns to read a new letter or word, the child can lick the honey from a finger. Learning should be sweet.

At the ice cream store, the HIAS lady pays after she asks me to pick a flavor. I point to strawberry and say, "Red" to show off the new English word I learned from the cover of my new book.

While I eat my ice cream, trying not to make a mess, Mutti and the HIAS lady have a serious discussion. I listen carefully because they're talking about me. Mutti tells the lady that I seem unable to see with my right eye. It's been like that since birth. Mutti says she noticed it when I was a toddler. A doctor assured her that nothing can be done and that it will probably improve by itself. My eye didn't improve, but when I grew a little older, Jews in Germany were excluded from health care. No more access to doctors. Mutti asks the HIAS lady if she can find an eye doctor for me, adding that we have no money and no jobs. The lady writes some words in a notebook and then she looks at me real funny. I cover my eyes. She tells Mutti that she will do her best to help.

* * *

School is great. I copy the other children all the time. When the teacher says, "Sit in a circle," I sit on the floor with the other children. When she says, "Go to your desks," I watch the other children and imitate. Of course there is much I don't understand. When the teacher reads to us, I recognize only occasional words and when she asks me questions I often shrug. I don't understand many questions or instructions. Some of the children call me "dummy" and poke fun at the slow kid. My pronunciation causes many giggles. Yet I know that I am learning and I'm ecstatic despite the teasing. The teacher praises generously when I succeed at something.

One day our teacher reads a book about jumping frogs. I have no clue what the story is about. Then she has three of us come to the front of the room and stand in a line. She gives some instructions and then says, "One, two, three, jump." "Four," I shout just as the other children jump.

"Can you jump?" asks the teacher.

I shrug.

"Jump," she says and gives a little hop.

"Yump," I say and imitate the teacher's jump. Student giggles.

"Wonderful! Now say 'jump.'"

"Yump." The class is almost out of control with laughter. I try desperately to hold back the tears but a few escape. I quickly wipe them on my sleeve hoping that no one notices.

Our teacher makes some weird sounds, slowly saying all the parts of 'jump.' There is a sort of 'd' sound followed by a sort of 'g' sound. Does she know that the sound she wants from me doesn't exist in German? I have never heard it.

"Now, say, 'jump,'" she encourages.

"Dgump," I try and she claps and all the children follow her cue and applaud. Slowly I am the butt of fewer and fewer jokes.

We sing Christmas songs and I help the students pronounce *O Tannenbaum*. There is a short Christmas vacation during which I try to read books the teacher has lent me. Mutti helps. Her English from high school is so good that she can read almost all the words. With some of the food money from the HIAS, Mutti buys a *Wörterbuch* that has words in English and in German. She teaches me to say Wörterbuch in English: "Dictionary."

XI. THE EYE PATCH

1940 STARTS WITH MUTTI finding a job in a flower factory. She makes flowers out of paper and hates it. But she earns some money.

Then Papa finds a job as a helper in a large commercial bakery. He fills in wherever he's needed. He earns a little money, is delighted to be working and loves the camaraderie of the large bakery. Every night he comes home dirty and has to take a bath. Mutti insists that he walk directly from the front door to the bathroom. Then she makes him leave his clothes in a bag.

One evening, the HIAS lady visits and tells Mutti that she has made an appointment with an eye doctor. Mutti takes a day off from work and we go to a very fancy office with framed pictures on the walls and leather chairs and magazines all around. The doctor insists that there is nothing wrong with my eye. "It's just lazy."

The doctor gives me an eye patch to cover the good eye. "This will strengthen the weak one." With my left eye covered, I'm totally blind. I bump into walls and chairs and into Mutti. I cannot see anything but a tiny bit of light through my right eye. I cry. I scream. I throw the patch on the floor. "I won't wear this. Ever."

The doctor and Mutti persuade me that it's for my own good. I should try. One day my vision will be perfect because I tried. At dinner I spill everything. I can't find the food. Mutti believes that I'm sabotaging the plan for a cure. I eat a piece of bread. Then I'm sent to bed.

The next morning Mutti puts the eye patch on my face as soon as I wake up. I can only eat a piece of bread for breakfast. Our landlady, Mrs. Strauss, suggests an apple. That works.

Mutti and Papa go to work and tell me to be careful when I walk to school. I hold on to the railing as I feel my way down the steps. Somehow, from memory, I get to the first corner without falling. Then I'm stuck. I know there is a traffic light but I can't see it. I don't dare cross against the light. I wait and think. Finally I decide to remove the patch.

Once across I have to make a difficult decision. Shall I cheat by simply keeping the patch off until I get to school—or even until I get home at the end of the day? I can't cheat. I replace the patch after orienting myself carefully. I reach the next corner without any great calamity. I bump into just one person.

I remove the patch to cross the next street and continue to school. After several bumps and falls, I find my way into the school building. A classmate guides me to the correct room. The teacher wants an explanation and half in English, half in German, I try to explain.

I sit quietly at my desk. I can't read. I can't find my own way to the bathroom. I certainly can't jump. During the first few days the children feel sorry for me. "Poor Freddy." "Can I help you with your lunch?" "I'll help you find your coat." After a few days my classmates lose interest in helping me. Then I become bait for teasing. They taunt me by reciting *Three Blind Mice* over and over.

And I'm not learning. I alternate between sulking and crying. One evening I ask our landlady's son, Walter, clearly older, wiser and more experienced, if I should cheat. We sit on his bed with the door closed and I ask if it would be OK to put the patch in my pocket when Mutti isn't watching.

I've never seen happy-go-lucky Walter look sad. However, his response to my question is a sad look. He seems about to cry. His lip quivers. "Manfred," he says, speaking to me in German and using my German name, "We German Jews are different. Our parents have suffered a great deal and they are starting a new life in a strange land. They have left their hopes and dreams, their families and friends, in Hannover. We are the only children they have, the only family they have, and we have to be extra good. It isn't fair to us but we are their future. They've placed all their dreams in our laps. You and I have to be extra good and extra smart and extra successful."

Tears come like a sudden torrent. I don't understand everything Walter said. But I feel the enormous burden he has put on me. The weight makes me feel small—compressed. I sob.

Walter puts his arm around me and holds me close. He's much taller than I am. He's taller than Papa and Mutti. "I know how you feel," he says. "I've tried to cheat, but I couldn't disobey either. We're destined to be good boys. Blame it on the Nazis."

The next day is no different, nor is the next week. I listen as the lessons continue and I hear the other children at their many activities. I refuse to leave my seat and, of course, I can't read or write or draw. The teacher assigns different children to help me with lunch and with my coat. She assigns one boy who lives near me to walk me home.

After a month, I know some tricks to survive. I count steps. I learn to walk along walls to find the end of a hallway. I learn to dress and eat by feel. I learn to recognize voices. But I've pretty much stopped learning language and I'm very unhappy. The teacher tries to cheer me up, but I'm deep-down sullen. I won't talk much and I sit with my head on the desk and I cry. I blame myself for being lazy. The lazy eye must be my fault.

About two months into the torture, Mutti visits with the teacher. The HIAS lady is there to translate. "I've called you in because we can no longer keep Freddy in our school. The principal agrees that Freddy is a disruption to the class and is unable to learn while he cannot see." She explains that before the eye patch I was bright and cheerful and a fun addition to the class. "Freddy was learning to speak English at an amazing pace and his reading skills are—or were—far above the other children." She apologizes over and over that I can't stay in her classroom. I am to be sent to a special school for special children.

When the HIAS lady hears "special children," she reaches over and removes my patch. "Give me a week." She says lots more stuff to the teacher but I only understand that I can't go to this school with my eye patch and the HIAS lady is planning to figure something out. They negotiate lots of mystifying plans that I don't understand in English or in German. The outcome is that I have a one-week grace period in the school—without the patch. Hooray!

The HIAS lady fishes a notebook out of her fat briefcase. She writes really fast. Mutti keeps insisting that not wearing the patch will set my progress back. The teacher insists that there has been no progress and that with the patch I am both blind and unhappy. The HIAS lady ignores my mother and just keeps writing. Then she snaps her notebook shut and walks out, leaving Mutti and the teacher arguing in different languages.

A few days later we're in an eye clinic that has several doctors who are "specialists." I practice saying the word over and over while I sit in the waiting room. I visit with several of the specialists, sometimes one after another and sometimes in pairs. They aim their little flashlights into my eyes until I see pretty dots floating by. Everyone seems amused that the dots only float past my left eye. When the examinations are all over, two tall doctors wearing white coats sit with my mother. The older one speaks German. He tells Mutti that he was raised in Germany and came to the United States as a boy, "Just like your son."

"Oh doctor, I'm so happy we can talk," Mutti bubbles.

Then the doctor who momentarily brought joy to my mother changes the mood. Bluntly he announces that my right eye is blind, that it will always be blind, that I am not lazy nor is my eye lazy and that Mutti is to stop torturing me. My mother tries to argue by reviewing what an earlier doctor said about the need for a patch. The younger doctor explains very slowly and scientifically in English that the earlier doctor was wrong, that my left eye is almost perfect, that I've already made great progress toward living with one eye and that I will continue to adjust.

The HIAS lady is translating like mad. When she catches up, the younger doctor adds, "The boy's right eye will never improve. Blind!" We all watch as he throws the eye patch into a waste basket. With that, he and his colleague stand up and leave the room.

As my mother starts to reach for the patch, the taller, stronger HIAS lady grabs Mutti's arm and guides her out the door. I follow.

When we reach the sidewalk, the HIAS lady points us to the nearest subway station and tells us that she has other business in this neighborhood. On the subway train home, it is Mutti's turn to sulk. I'm overjoyed and I know that tomorrow kindergarten will be wonderful. I start to sound out some words on a red, white and blue advertising placard: U-N-C-L-E S-A-M.

XII. MY FIRST SEDER
IN AMERICA

MUTTI DISLIKES HER JOB making fabric flowers in a factory. One day she describes to us how she twisted green paper around wire to make stems. On another day she reports that she attached yellow petals to green stems for the entire day. Her hands hurt. She hates work—any kind of work. "In the good days, before Hitler," she tells me, "I didn't have to work. Women of my class didn't work." She looks at my face, "Do you remember Grete? That was the maid who took care of you. When you napped, she cleaned the apartment. Then came Hitler and he took all that away."

I do remember Grete, a skinny girl who lived with her parents in a Hannover suburb and had a long bus trip to and from our home in the center of town. One day I overheard a conversation between Grete and Mutti. There was some talk about how Christians could no longer work in Jewish factories, shops and homes. Grete never visited again. Instead we had those scary visits from the Gestapo.

Mutti often explains that she's from a different class and hopes that soon she'll be able to stop working. I'm a bit confused. Am I also different? Different from Papa? Papa loves to work.

Papa finds work in a bakery on the east side of Manhattan. It's a long subway ride to and from the Strauss apartment in Washington Heights. Papa comes home covered with a white powder. He tells us that he breathes flour all day and that the ovens are hot and the bread smells good. Papa is happy to be working. Each Friday he receives an envelope filled with money—his pay for working. Mutti spends some of the money on groceries and Papa gives some to Mr. Strauss for rent. And Papa starts saving. One penny at a time. One day he will be self-employed again. He has a dream. He tells us about it at almost every dinner.

For Papa, the subway ride is a time to read. He picks up newspapers abandoned by other commuters. Papa's fourth-grade education did not prepare him to be a sophisticated reader. And unlike Mutti, he had no courses in English. Like me, he has to sound out the letters and guess at the words. The subway is his classroom. And the newspapers help him keep up with events in Europe. After all, it's the spring of 1940 and the European war is picking up momentum.

At the end of March, Papa is offered a second job. The bakery owns a tenement right next door. The manager has been unable to find a janitor. Would Papa like this opportunity? It would mean free rent and Papa could walk to the bakery.

On the first day of April, we move to the East Side with our few possessions and start buying a few pieces of furniture—used furniture when we can. The bakery manager is so happy to find someone to do this dirty work that he throws in a few dollars to help buy dishes and towels and a couch. The previous janitor left a huge brown icebox and a metal kitchen table with a bright red ring around the entire top surface. We buy four used straight-backed wooden chairs, perfect for our kitchen. They're painted green to go with the paint on the kitchen wall.

Papa's job as janitor is to take the garbage cans out each morning in time for the daily pick-up. Several times each week he mops the hallways and the steps from the third floor all the way down to the cellar. Mutti makes clear that she doesn't mop floors or dust railings or touch other people's garbage. However, with her modest English skills, she's in charge of collecting rent and showing empty apartments to prospective English-speaking tenants. Thanks to the bookkeeping courses she had in high school, she becomes the bookkeeper for the building.

It is April 22, 1940, a warm spring day in New York City. We're sitting in the kitchen of our first American apartment. The table is set for our first Passover Seder in the United States. No more Gestapo. No more hiding. No more fear.

We've lived in this dark, poorly ventilated New York tenement for just a few weeks. The kitchen has no window. However, if we leave the oversized door to the adjoining bathroom open, we can see the outside world from the kitchen table. The bathroom window looks out on a shaft of air surrounded by bricks and more windows. The courtyard, perhaps 30 feet square, allows for minimal light and fresh air. New York City is warm and humid this April. Sounds from many open windows echo in the three-story shaft. Neighbors have few secrets. Fights in the Hennessey household and parties at the Francos became public news. Laundry lines allow soot-gathering underwear to dry. Smells from courtyard trash containers waft into our first-floor apartment window.

I daydream often about our two-week long sea voyage that I spent mostly with crew. Perhaps I'll become a sailor. Right now I'm thinking about the last morning when Papa held me up to see the Statue of Liberty. I remember that Papa talked about the meaning of the statue—about freedom and a new life and about the Promised Land.

We *are* free! An appropriate insight for our first American Passover. The Seder table looks festive with candles lit and almost-new Passover dishes provided by my Uncle Max, who came to the United States a year before we did. The prayer books, the *Haggadah*, the re-telling of the story of the exodus out of Egypt, came with us from the old country, traveling in my little suitcase. Each page is divided into two columns. The right column is printed in Hebrew and the left column shows a German translation. A few black-and-white pictures help stimulate my imagination.

Haggadah brought from Germany

Else Nussbaum (Omi)

Years later, when my maternal grandmother, my Omi, joins us for her first Seder in the States, she cries throughout the evening, mourning the many who will never again experience a holy day. Omi mourns for two of her daughters, their husbands and her granddaughter, all murdered by the Nazis. She mourns three brothers and a sister and their families, all butchered. She grieves for the dead and she is unable to celebrate this moment of life, this holiday of hope.

Tonight Papa feels festive and positive. He talks about our escape, father, mother and son, via Holland and Belgium and two weeks at sea. It had been a long, trying journey, an exodus out of slavery like that of Moses himself. Now we are celebrating freedom at the Seder table.

Mutti lights two candles and recites the appropriate blessings from memory. We all know the blessings for matzo and wine. In my embarrassed, childish voice, chanting in Hebrew, I recite the four questions asked by the youngest participant at every Seder throughout the world, now and in times long past. I begin, "Why is this night different from all other nights?"

"We were once slaves in Egypt." Papa reads from the Haggadah.

In another part Papa reads, "You shall remind your son that he was once a slave in Egypt." He asks me questions about what I remember of Germany and retells stories about our former life, lest I forget.

Every few minutes Mutti jumps up to stir something on the stove. It's an old stove but Mutti has planned a special Passover dinner. She apologizes for what she believes to be a Spartan meal. "That's all we can afford."

Papa assures her that it will be fine. "Much better than any meal we had last year under the Nazis."

I don't recognize any of the smells. I'm very hungry.

Mutti has gathered the Passover symbols on a makeshift Seder plate. There is a lamb bone to remind us of the tenth plague—the killing of the Egyptian firstborn. "And the angel of death passed over the homes of the Hebrews." Somehow Mutti translates that story into, "You, as the firstborn, have a great responsibility." I'm more afraid of this unknown responsibility than of the angel of death.

Mutti has made *charoses*, a mixture of apples, nuts, red wine and spices. The charoses represents the mortar the Hebrew slaves were forced to use when they built structures for the Egyptians. Papa and I like the sweetness of the charoses and take several portions—but we only say the blessing once.

Papa tricks me into taking a large bite of the bitter herb that represents the bitterness of slavery. I chomp on the fresh horseradish root and almost immediately begin to cry. Mutti gives me a handkerchief to blow my runny nose and Papa gives me more charoses to cool my mouth. Mutti scolds Papa.

Papa, a small wiry man with a huge baritone voice, sings the prayers in Hebrew as though he were on stage. He sings with all the energy he can muster. This is, for him, a celebration. Five feet one inch tall. Not a millimeter more. Thin and muscular from slave labor in the *Tiefbau*— enforced road construction. No more than a fourth-grade education. Thirty-nine years old. Papa knows how to celebrate freedom.

Papa sings about Moses and the prophets and about freedom then and now. He sings prayers of gratitude to God in Hebrew and in German. This small man sings with a mighty voice.

"Shhh, shhh," says my mother. "Shhh, the window is open. The neighbors will hear."

My father rises from his chair and stretches to his full height. "I'll sing as loud as I like," he says in German. "Let them hear. WE'RE IN AMERICA NOW!"

XIII. A REFUGEE AT THE 1939-1940 NEW YORK WORLD'S FAIR

MUTTI'S ENGLISH, learned in high school, and the Wörterbuch, the *Langenscheidt Dictionary* she bought at a book store, gets us through life. She does the shopping, translates the signs at subway stations and helps Papa with the janitor's paperwork.

When we move next to the bakery, I transfer to the local school's kindergarten for the few weeks left in the school year. The change is difficult because a whole new group of children have to learn about my poor English skills and my funny accent.

Each morning Papa goes to work at the bakery. Each evening he brings home some rolls and news of the outside world. Only six months in America, we cannot afford a radio or newspapers. Papa's co-workers share what news they know. Everyone is talking about the war in Europe. Each day Papa learns more English words from his co-workers. One evening each week Mutti and Papa go to the HIAS for a class where they learn English.

We sit around the dinner table, relishing our soup thickened with inexpensive vegetables from a pushcart on Second Avenue and supplemented by rolls covered with black dots. We always speak German at dinner. In response to my question about the black dots, Mutti explains, "These are called *Mohnsamen*," using their German name.

"At the bakery," Papa explains, "they are called 'poppy seeds.'" Then he adds his little pun. "Let's call them 'Papa seeds.'"

"That's silly," says Mutti. I don't think much of Papa's puns either, but I like that he's cheerful. Mutti's conversation makes me feel that life is hard.

All through dinner, Papa picks up a few black dots from the oilcloth tablecover and swallows them. "Mmmmm, these 'Papa' seeds are tasty."

One day at dinner Papa announces that he has news. In June he will take me to the World's Fair. "At the bakery everyone is talking about the World's Fair. During our break we looked at some photos in the *Daily News*. It looks spectacular and there are buildings from every country. Hardly anyone at work has been there because they can't afford to go. But my son is going. It will be very educational."

"My teacher has been to the World's Fair," I announce. "She went two times last summer and she tells us about it often. She says they have dangerous rides and food from many countries and people in costumes and ..."

"That's ridiculous," Mutti grumps as she stands up to clear the table. Papa and I each grab an extra 'Papa' seed roll before they are put away. "That's ridiculous," Mutti repeats. "We barely have money for clothes. How can we afford entertainment?"

"It's not entertainment," Papa says quietly. "We won't go on any rides and we'll bring sandwiches from home. It will be educational. My foreman took his children and said they learned about the whole world. Freddy will learn about the whole world too. One day he will even graduate from a university." Mutti has told me about doctors and lawyers who go to a university to learn stuff most people don't know. I hate the responsibility Papa is placing on my shoulders, but a trip to the fair sounds exciting. I won't worry about university just now.

Mutti allows that she had read about the New York World's Fair when we were still in Germany. She says that big corporations have buildings there with science displays. I ask Mutti to explain the word "science." She talks about chemistry and engineering using words I've never heard before like *"Wissenschaft"* and *"Technik."* Mutti has read that many countries have art exhibitions. Mutti loves art and museums. She keeps reminding us that she is a highly cultured person.

"And Freddy will be highly cultured too." And with that Papa closes the discussion.

Papa schedules three paid vacation days in late June of 1940, right after school is out. Weather permitting, we will go on Monday. Mutti has no vacation coming so she will have to work. Papa asks his work-mates how to get to Flushing Meadows, the site of the fair.

It rains on Monday so we go on Tuesday. Mutti packs a lunch. Papa takes enough money for the subway ride, admission and drinks. He tells Mutti that he refuses to carry a thermos all day. Mutti makes him promise to bring home a few postcards with pictures of the fair.

Every day in every way I know that we're poor. The children at school have toys. They have new shoes after Easter. They go to movies with their parents. They take the train to visit grandparents in the countryside. They show off how they break in their new baseball "mitts." We can't afford any of these things. But somehow Papa saved up the money for the World's Fair. On the subway we talk about spending money. He tells me that food is most important. Then education for his son. Then giving to worthy causes. "*Tikkun olam*," says Papa. "That's Hebrew for 'repair the world.'"

"That's the Jewish way," he adds.

When we finally arrive at the fair, we follow a long line of people toward a window. Papa buys our admission tickets. I hold them while Papa carefully puts his change into his pants pocket. "Someday soon I'll buy a wallet," he mumbles to himself. He's wearing a dark gray suit and a white shirt. For Papa's first birthday in America, last December, Uncle Max gave him a tie, the tie he's wearing today. I'm wearing tan slacks and a green, long-sleeved dress shirt open at the collar.

I give our tickets to a uniformed man who directs us through a turnstile. We're at the fair. Buildings tower, paths lead to other buildings and then to still more buildings. Signs are everywhere—in English. The Fair is huge and we are small. We hold hands all day. We hold tight. With the little English I've learned in six months of American schooling, I'm in charge of reading signs. Papa can sound out some words and we translate what we can. I often have to say, "I don't know" when I really don't understand. Pictures and imagination help our translations.

Papa explains that we've been to four countries: Germany, Holland, Belgium (for just a few days) and now we're in the United States. We're about to visit other countries. We step into a building representing Japan. I've never seen Japanese people. I like them. They're short like Papa and me. We sit on the floor and drink tea. Papa explains that the people in Japan drink lots of tea. Mutti likes tea. Papa prefers coffee. I favor milk. A thin woman in a dress that reaches almost to the floor pours a second cup for Papa.

The Holland building shows off lots of paintings by famous Dutch artists. Lots of people in the building wear costumes just like in the paintings. Papa sees the word Palestine on a sign and rushes us to the Jewish Palestine building. We learn that the Jewish people want to build a homeland for the Jews. I worry that I will have to move again and learn still another language. Papa speaks Yiddish with several men. A woman gives me a flag and a map.

We view a typewriter display with machines old and modern. Papa explains what they do. He adds that if I ever want a typewriter of my own, I will have to know how to spell. And then I see a cow named Elsie, almost the same name as one of my grandmothers, Omi, still living in Germany. Mutti has been worried because we haven't heard from her in a very long time.

Many of the buildings give away posters and picture postcards. We collect them all for Mutti. At a souvenir stand, Papa buys a little booklet of pictures to bring home.

We see a radio with pictures; it's called "television." We see a sleek train, several sporty cars, some art on a wall made with magically moving colored lights and a display showing what the future city will look like. I hope that one day I can fly the little airplanes that go straight up and down and sideways. We're invited into a free air conditioned movie theater. I can read the sign that says "cool air" and I feel the chill inside. The movie shows how a car is manufactured in a modern auto plant. I notice that "auto" in English and in German are the same. In the movie, I see lots of jobs that I want when I grow up.

Between us, Papa and I have had four and a half years of schooling. We don't know much geography. Many of the exhibits—art and science—mystify us. And yet we're inspired. Papa keeps saying, "This is what a peaceful world can be like."

Many large businesses have their own buildings where they show off what they manufacture and what they plan to create in the future.

DuPont mural at 1939-1940 World's Fair

One such building has a huge mural two stories high. On the left side of this enormous picture is a scene showing a family from an earlier agricultural time. They struggle under the weight of hard work and poverty. On the right side of the great mural we see a family living in the new, industrial world of comfort and happiness. At the bottom of this mural is a banner with the words, "Better Things For Better Living Through Chemistry." We translate "things" to *"Dinge."* I can translate "Better Living" to *"Besser Leben."* The German and English words sound alike. And from Mutti I learned that "Chemistry" is a science. I translate to "Wissenschaft" and "Technik." I understand.

I promise Papa right then, at that moment, that I will study "Wissenschaft" (whatever that means) so that I can help create "better living." Papa calls it "tikkun olam." Repair the world.

XIV. THE BROWNSHIRTS ARE COMING

WHEN MY PARENTS have a little more income we can sometimes afford a double feature at the neighborhood cinema. The theater provides a few hours of relief from the summer heat. Of course our tenement has no air conditioning in the summer of 1941. Windows at both ends of our flat offer just a little circulation, thanks to a fan at the living room end.

The front door opens into the kitchen. We have a ritual for entering our dark apartment and this Saturday night is no different. Mutti unlocks the door with her key and steps back. Papa takes off his right shoe and holds it as if he would hammer a nail with the heel. The seven-year-old that is me hides behind Papa. We all take a deep breath in anticipation.

Suddenly Papa opens the door, reaches around for the light switch and bam, wham, bam. He is pounding roaches.

Thousands scurry for shelter in the baseboard and the cupboards. They're on the walls and floor and ceiling—everywhere. Roaches flee from the table and the chairs. *Skwoosh, skwoosh, skwoosh* as one after another is crushed by Papa's heavy rubber heel. Sometimes Papa accidentally steps on one or two of the disoriented, frightened beasts with his stockinged foot. Brown, stiff-backed, multi-legged, monster-faced roaches who had been in total control of the darkened apartment are now escaping my father's wrath. Fat bugs, some over two inches long, seem to fly short distances, or are they hopping? I hold on to Papa's belt and hide my face in his back.

When no more live roaches can be seen, Papa cleans up. On a good night Papa kills more than thirty. When each living roach has found shelter from Papa's shoe and each dead roach has been dropped into the garbage can, Mutti enters the room as if nothing has happened. My heart races. I am terrified. Surely these roaches reproduce faster than Papa can kill them.

The cockroach chase fills my mind, even replacing the memory of the movie. Before undressing, I check under the sheets and inside the pillowcase. I know that once the lights are turned off for the night, our creepy tenants will reappear. I fear I will dream about the roaches—and I do. Do I dream that they walk on me during the night or do they really?

In the morning I check my body and inside my pajamas. I turn my slippers upside down and bang them, individually and carefully, against the bed frame. Too often a roach falls to the floor and scampers away.

Concern about roach droppings becomes an obsession and prompts careful daily washing and inspection of my body. I welcome my weekly bath and I wipe each dish before I allow it to cradle my food.

There are cockroaches everywhere. I don't mean just everywhere in the apartment. I mean all over the city. New York is a city of roaches. We have been living in the United States about sixteen months, escaping from Germany via Holland and Belgium, a step ahead of the Nazis. The next-door commercial bakery, where Papa works, provides food for much of the big city and for the roaches. Poison around the baseboard does not have a big impact. There are way too many millions of them to control. Surely, I imagine, there are at least 1,000 roaches for each of New York's seven million residents.

My dreams become ever more frightening and, as the weeks pass, the roaches seem to grow larger. And they feel heavier when they walk on me. In one dream they have hot feet and burn my skin as they wander aimlessly on my chest and arms. When I awake, Mutti is holding me. I've been screaming and I ripped the buttons from my pajama top.

Anna lives at the other end of our block in an apartment house slightly more upscale than our tenement. Hers is a larger apartment with a separate entrance to her father's medical office. Anna is a special friend, almost a girlfriend, and I visit her apartment often. Anna's family escaped Nazi Germany quite early and learned to speak English while living in Manchester, England. They moved to New York when the European war seemed imminent. The family speaks German and a British version of English at home. They help with my developing command of the new language.

One evening, when Anna's mom has invited me to dinner, I regale the family with one of my dreams. Mrs. Wertheimner's response—horror and disgust—encourages me to elaborate in great detail, even identifying the number of legs each roach has and describing the fuzz on the legs. Doctor Wertheimer outdoes me. He tells about another Jew who wrote stories in German. "Franz Kafka," he says, "wrote a story called *Die Verwandlung*, *The Metamorphosis*, in which a young man wakes up one morning to discover that he has been turned into a monstrous bug, perhaps a cockroach." Anna's father then proceeds to tell Kafka's horrible story, simplified so that the two youngsters in his audience can understand. In dismay, Mrs. Wertheimer leaves the room. Anna cries a little and I try hard not to. I skip dessert.

That evening in bed, I think about Dr. Wertheimer's story. Will I dream about being turned into a roach? What if I were really changed? What if my family became disgusted by me and disowned me? Could I live with the Wertheimers? Could Dr. W. cure me?

I am *not* changed into a giant cockroach. I remain a small boy. However, giant roaches come to my bed. Giant roaches wearing shiny boots and brown uniforms. Hundreds march in parade formation past my house. They wear pistols and carry large clubs like the SS officers I saw in Germany. They march four abreast and as they pass my house, the last row peels off and walks swiftly toward our front door. I hear the outside door slam and the boots in the hallway. They stop at our apartment door and one of them knocks. No, he pounds. *Bang, bang, bang!* Pause. *Bang, bang, bang!* Loud, determined knocks. A third series of three bangs. Another pause. The apartment door bursts open and crashes to the floor. The four roach brownshirts are in the room. Their armbands seem familiar but I can't quite place where I've seen them before.

"*Aufstehen*," commands one of the soldiers. "Stand up." The brownshirts are larger than Papa and Mutti. The shiny boots on their many legs confuse and frighten me. In one motion the lead soldier tears the blanket from my bed. Four large roaches and my bed are now squeezed into my tiny room. "Aufstehen!" Louder than before. Where should I stand? Sitting on the edge of the bed, I move my bare feet to the floor. It now occurs to me that Papa and Mutti have not come to the rescue. Where are they? Still sleeping?

I look down. Usually, when I step out of bed I'm careful not to crush a roach with my bare foot. Now, out of respect, no, out of fear of the roach soldiers, I certainly don't want to crush a bug of any kind. I picture the small roaches that dominate our tenement. Are they all now larger than me? But there is no time for speculation. The four soldier roaches now move apart, making a narrow path for me to walk out of the room. They march me out of the cramped bedroom into the kitchen, past the broken front door and into the dark hallway. "*Raus. Raus aus dem Haus,*" they order. "Out. Out of the house."

They guide me outdoors and into a waiting truck. I climb up and they lock the doors behind me. I stand in total darkness. Something touches me and I let out a huge scream. Scream after uncontrolled scream. I can't stop myself. Anna's voice reassures me, "I'm here." But I can't stop screaming. "*Ich bin hier* Freddy. *Ich bin dein Freund* Anna," Anna keeps saying. "I'm here. I'm your friend Anna." She touches me again and we both allow ourselves to cry.

When we stop crying, Anna says, "When the truck door opened to let you in, I noticed that the roaches have boots on all their feet. They have no hands, only feet. That's why they push with their bodies." That is all we know except that we are locked in a large black box.

We sit in silence. Suddenly I remember that the roaches at our house scramble about feeding in the dark. "Are there roaches with us?" I ask.

Anna assures, "I saw none when you were pushed aboard. And no humans either."

Anna had been first into the box. Apparently the parade had passed Anna's building before it reached my end of the block. Four soldiers had peeled off the back of the parade to arrest her. I was second.

"Will there be others?" Anna wonders. Almost immediately the truck door pops open and another girl is pushed into the truck. Anna rushes toward the door and starts talking very loud so that the girl will immediately know that we are also in the truck. No more fearful screaming. The girl quickly crawls to Anna who is ready with a hug. The frightened little girl cries for quite some time. Then between sobs she announces, "My name is Lisa and I'm six years old." Her heavy accent hints that she, like Anna and me, is not American.

After Anna calms Lisa, we learn that she is Jewish and from Austria. Her father had been hauled away after the *Anschluss*, the Nazi annexation of Austria. Lisa and her mother hid in the woods and secretly made their way across the Alps into Switzerland. She arrived in the United States only a few weeks ago.

I blurt out the obvious, "They're rounding up the children." Something makes me uncomfortable. The phrase "rounding up" troubles me. I heard my parents use that phrase. Dr. Wertheimer used it. Why are the words so disturbing?

The three of us wait. We agree that Anna will again talk to any newcomer while Lisa will use the opportunity of light to study the inside of the truck. I will see what I can learn from the outside world.

It is a long wait for the next child. Pincus yells at the roaches as they kick and prod him. He fights back. Several especially large roaches pick him up by biting his clothes. Others crawl beneath him and a few butt him with their heads. Without hands the roaches have difficulty placing Pincus into the truck. The roaches create a ladder by standing on one another and eventually are able to push and kick their victim into our box. Pincus's resistance gives each of us ample time to accomplish our tasks.

Anna introduces herself, Lisa and me. Pincus tells us that he is twelve years old, a Polish Jew who, with his older brother, escaped from a concentration camp. An uncle arranged Pincus's trip to the United States and he has arrived just a week ago. That explains his bitter fight with the ... but who are the roach soldiers?

"They're rounding up Jewish refugee children!" Anna observes.

There's that phrase again: "rounding up." The image is horrible. Millions of giant roaches are rounding up Jewish children. Who are these monsters?

None of us know the time although we can tell it is still night. Pincus suggests that we set aside one corner of the truck box as a toilet. He

WE'RE IN AMERICA NOW: A SURVIVOR'S STORIES

has had some experience with boxcars. We look to Pincus for leadership. Anna takes on the role of mother, providing comfort.

Yitzak, Rachel, Sarah, Manny—we are soon thirteen children clustered in our dark box. Not yet crowded. Pincus warns, "When we are too many for our space we will start fighting for territory. Then they will either move us in this truck or they will kill us all right here. Perhaps this truck is a mobile gas chamber."

"Will the roaches scatter when daylight appears?" I ask naïvely. I remember how they scatter when Papa turns on the apartment lights. The very first rays of light were noticeable when the most recent child had been pushed into the truck.

Of course, no one could know the answer.

"Who are these monsters?" asks Anna. "What are those marks on their armbands? They look so familiar."

"Don't you children know anything?" We can't see his face but we can hear Pincus's frustration. "Those are the Brownshirts."

"What are Brownshirts?" asks Lisa.

"The Brownshirts came to get my father when we still lived in Germany," Sarah announces. "Those marks on their armbands are swastikas." The picture was becoming clear for me. I had heard Mutti and Papa talking about "rounding up the Jews" on Kristallnacht, the night of broken glass, in 1938. The roach Brownshirts were rounding up the Jewish children.

Anna, realizing that we have to take action, asks, "Pincus, what shall we do?"

"If Freddy's question about light makes sense, we will have to wait all day for them to come back at night," suggests Pincus. Rachel, who is beginning to get the gist of the conversation about light, announces that she always sleeps with a flashlight and that it is still in the pocket of her pajamas. With that she provides a strong beam of light that reaches the top of the truck.

"It's almost light outside," Pincus says. "If the roaches bring one more child before full daybreak, we can use the flashlight to frighten them and we can fight until the sun rescues us. If God helps us with the sun, we may be saved. I cannot see you. However, I'm guessing that I am the oldest and perhaps the strongest. If you like, I'll use the flashlight to frighten them and all of you will have to fight for your lives. Beware. They bite."

"What if they don't come before daybreak?" asks Anna. Just as she finishes her sentence the door opens. Rachel hands the light to Pincus who pounces out like an angry tiger. We follow our leader, a huge gust of children leaping on the roaches. We children outnumber the Brownshirts guarding the truck, although they are much larger than we are.

I awake to find myself pummeling my Papa who is holding me on the bed with all his strength. I am wild! Fists swinging! Kicking! Papa is shouting for me to calm down.

That evening Mutti takes me to meet with Dr. Wertheimer. She and the doctor speak in German. He explains that dreams help us cope with terror—real and imagined. The Holocaust has done that to many children—and to millions of adults. Dr. Wertheimer tells my mother that Anna, too, has fearful dreams. "As do I," he adds. Mutti allows that she has nightmares quite regularly.

"Those who have died and will die in the Holocaust pay the ultimate price," says Dr. Wertheimer in his most reassuring voice. "We survivors also pay a price—a price we are willing to pay to be alive and to have our children alive and not in the gas chambers. We can live with our nightmares"

"But the cockroaches in our apartment are real," I say. Or am I asking a question?

"They are," assures Dr. Wertheimer "They disappear when you turn on the light. I hope that you and Anna will enjoy the security of light and that one day you will no longer have to fear the darkness."

When we arrive home, Papa promises to buy me a flashlight of my own.

XV. UNJUST DESSERTS

BY THE MIDDLE OF 1941 we're almost American. My parents have jobs and I attend school. We're learning to speak English although we speak only German at home.

Papa tends ovens in a commercial bakery. He is also the janitor of the adjoining three-story Manhattan tenement that is owned by the bakery. His official title is "caretaker," but in New York City the janitor is always called the "super," never superintendent. If something goes wrong, a tenant calls the "super." Sometimes, when I feel mistreated, I threaten to call the super which causes everyone to laugh and I'm off the hook.

Cleaning hallways and moving garbage cans means free rent. Papa often helps tenants carry groceries to their apartments and then carries their garbage down on the return trip. The occasional tip means extra money for our groceries.

Sometimes Papa has to move a belligerent drunk from the building's entryway. He is not an imposing figure. Yet, a year of slave labor on one of Hitler's construction crews has left him fit, even muscular. And, of course, the drunks have a disadvantage: They're drunk.

Mutti works in an artificial flower factory by day and is co-janitor after hours—although she prefers to be called "caretaker." Her high school English studies give her some ability to take care of business matters like showing empty apartments and collecting the monthly rent. When needed, she might help with some cleaning duties—but never with the garbage.

I attend the neighborhood school where I am older than the other children in my class because I started school late. Now I have to learn a new language while trying to make friends—not an easy task for a kid with limited English and a foreign accent.

Our building is a dirty, soot-covered brown on the outside. The hallway walls leading to our apartment are made of chipped plaster painted a dirty yellow and penciled with hostile messages. I translate these messages for Papa and Mutti as best I can although my limited mastery of English and my childish German do not yet include the many obscenities on the wall.

Walking home after school is a treat because of the smell of bread that emanates from the bakery, permeating the entire block. Each day I stop a moment before entering our building to savor the delicious odor and anticipate the roll that I will enjoy when I reach the kitchen. Between the sweet smelling street and the safety of our kitchen is the hallway which always stinks of pee, even after Papa mops with disinfectant. I hold my breath to avoid gagging.

The front door of our apartment opens directly into the kitchen so I didn't have far to go before I reach the painted tin bread box that holds my afternoon treat. The body of the box is red except for the door which has a white background with pink flowers. They are the only flowers in my life. There are no gardens on our cement and tar street. Folks in our neighborhood cannot afford window boxes. I sometimes think of the trees and flowers and parks in our Hannover neighborhood.

The largest piece of furniture in the kitchen is a huge, brown, oak icebox. Once each week an ice man comes to our door. He wears a leather sheet over his left shoulder on which he balances a block of ice secured with a special pair of tongs apparently only owned by the ice man. With his right hand he opens the top compartment of the ice box and slips his ice into the box. Once he picked me up with his icy hands so that I could look inside to see the gray metal lining on the inner walls of the box. On another occasion he let me try to lift a block of ice with his tongs. I lacked both talent and strength.

Although I am not allowed to open the top door of the ice box, I have permission to open the bottom door so long as I only remove milk, and do that quickly lest the ice melt before the ice man returns. I have free reign over the milk bottles—a luxury that didn't exist for us in Nazi Germany. Papa only drinks milk in his coffee and Mutti claims that she is allergic to milk although she seems to have no problem with foods prepared with milk—especially desserts.

Before opening the bread box I might turn right from the apartment entrance to visit the bathroom, the only room in the house that has a door. The bathroom is my favorite room. It is bright with a large window that looks out on another building and other people's windows. White walls reflect the light from the window—so different from the darkness elsewhere in the apartment. A chipped white bathtub stands on four tall legs which meet the linoleum floor on animal claw feet. I need to climb onto a chair to enter the tub. A white sink sits on a sculptured pedestal and the toilet base is decorated with similar abstract sculpting.

We live in a typical shotgun flat. There is no hallway. One room runs into another. As I enter the kitchen, I can turn right and walk into the bathroom or I can turn left and walk into a closet-like space that holds my bed and a dresser, one piece of furniture on each side of a path that leads to the next room. Continuing on through my bedroom space, one enters a small living room that is home to one upholstered chair, a side-table and a convertible couch that doubles as my parents' bed. The living room has two windows that overlook the street.

* * *

American shores are off limits to "enemy aliens" even if those "enemies" are refugees fleeing Hitler's death camps. Each year a few thousand lucky Jews fill the quota and are welcomed by the Hebrew Immigrant Aid Society—just as we were only 21 months ago. New arrivals are put up in cheap hotels and provided with transition care.

Early one evening, just before supper, a HIAS man in a mismatched suit, brown tweed pants and a double-breasted black jacket, perhaps a social worker or a volunteer, arrives at our door. He introduces himself in German. Mutti stands in the doorway while I keep a polite distance— but close enough to hear. Brown fedora in hand, the man explains that the Goldfarbs, acquaintances from Hannover, have arrived via Portugal a few days earlier and would like to say hello to the only people they know in America. Mutti explains that Papa isn't home, but that he might telephone the HIAS office if he has time. Politely but coolly she asks, "Could you give our regards to Mr. and Mrs. Goldfarb?"

With a large white handkerchief the HIAS man wipes August heat from his face. I wonder if I should offer a glass of water. Mutti, however, is already trying to close the door. Our visitor has his foot on the threshold and begins to describe the Goldfarbs' situation. "Their children have been taken away along with most of their relatives. They have no other contacts in the States."

Mutti sighs and repeats, "Please give them our regards." After a small pause she adds, "And our sympathy."

The HIAS man wipes more perspiration and talks a bit more. I want him to sit a while and to drink a little water. Before I develop a strategy for inviting the man into our apartment, I hear the door click shut. He is gone.

That evening Mutti and Papa discuss the matter while Papa sits at the kitchen table and Mutti fusses near the stove preparing dinner. The kitchen table has a white metallic top with white wooden legs. The top is surrounded by a red stripe on all four edges. I liked to listen for the sound of Papa's wedding ring when he touches the table. Sometimes, at meals, I am scolded because I try to tap out songs on the metal table top. It seems to me that I'm displaying great musical potential. My parents think that my behavior is *"sehr ärgerlich."* Very annoying.

As usual, Papa and Mutti show their respective colors as they discuss the HIAS man's visit. I become an invisible listener. After hearing Mutti's report, Papa, in his quiet manner, says, "You should have immediately invited the Goldfarbs for dinner."

"We can't afford to feed them," Mutti argues.

Besides, she adds they are in some way inferior. She doesn't explain what is inferior about them. Everyone is "inferior" to Mutti. She imagines herself a princess. Even the people who generously sponsored our trip to America, a Jewish physician and his wife who selected our name from a list of the needy, did not, according to Mutti, do enough. Not even the Gentiles, the righteous Christians who hid my father under their bed when the Gestapo came for him, were good enough to join her for tea. After all, they were only a bricklayer family.

Papa promises, "I'll only eat a small portion to save money."

He ignores the "they are inferior" argument but counters. "These people were our friends; they are fellow Jews; they are refugees in need of a *landsman*, a compatriot."

I had already learned that Mutti did not always argue consistently. When the "princess" argument doesn't work she tries a complete turn-about, "The Goldfarbs were wealthy jewelers in Hannover. They wouldn't be comfortable in our tenement hovel."

Papa rejoins, "*Most* Hannovarian Jews were well off. Now we're all happy to be poor in America rather than in Dachau, Auschwitz or Buchenwald."

Mutti wins most arguments in our household. Papa likes to joke, "I make all the big decisions like when we should go to war. Your mother makes all the other decisions." This day, however, Papa prevails. With a big sigh (she sighs often), Mutti agrees that Papa can invite the Gold-farbs for dinner. When Papa asks for the HIAS man's name, Mutti says that she can't remember.

"Herr Rubinstein," I pipe in. I was going to add that he looked ex-hausted and hot and that I wanted to give him water and that I wanted him to sit down for a while and that Mutti didn't open the door all the way. But I only say, "Herr Rubinstein."

The next day, during his lunch hour, Papa walks to the phone booth on Second Avenue and 75th Street. He carries four nickels. Each nickel allows three minutes of conversation after which a female voice cuts in with, "Your three minutes are up. Please deposit five cents." Papa calls the HIAS, tells the receptionist that he cannot speak English very well and asks for Mr. Rubinstein. After a few minutes, a German-speaking woman comes to the phone. Papa explains that he wants to invite the Goldfarbs for Sabbath dinner on a Friday evening ten days away. He sug-gests six o'clock. The friendly voice agrees to arrange the reunion. Papa hangs up and pockets his last nickel.

* * *

The guests arrive—all three of them. Only two were expected. Mutti had already learned from the HIAS man that the Goldfarbs' adult chil-dren had been taken to concentration camps or deported to mysterious places. In her haste to chase the HIAS man away, she had not learned, or had misunderstood that Mr. Goldfarb's elderly father had escaped with his son and daughter-in-law. The two men are wearing ill-fitting suits with ties. The elder Mr. Goldfarb is bald and stooped over. He seems to be looking at his shoes. His son is tall and thin. His jacket looks as if one day he will grow into it—a line I learned from Papa when he and I took the subway to Delancey Street to buy clothes for me at wholesale prices from Yiddish-speaking merchants. The younger Mr. Goldfarb shakes my hand with long bony fingers. Had I been that sickly when I arrived? Had Papa and Mutti?

Like the others, Mrs. Goldfarb is thin. Yet she has a beautiful bright face highlighted with a touch of lipstick. Her sad eyes look at me with a friendly smile. I feel close to her at once and would have accepted a hug but she only offers her hand.

Papa hugs everyone and leads them into the living room. Mutti removes her apron and joins the guests. "We hope we're not too much trouble," says Mrs. Goldfarb.

"Not at all. We're delighted to see you again after all this time," proclaims Mutti as if she's been rehearsing this line for a week.

Our living room has seating for four, five in a pinch. I sit on the floor and Mutti stands, occasionally stirring something on the stove. The pink walls are bare except for some cracks which, to me, act as decoration. When I'm at home alone after school, having finished my afternoon roll from the next-door bakery, I occasionally tap on the living room wall to see if I can make the cracks grow or change direction. Once I tapped hard enough to cause a paint chip to fall from the wall. I threw the pink chip out of the window and have felt guilty ever after.

When our guests are settled and chatting, Mutti calls me into the kitchen. She explains that she has prepared for two guests. Three visitors means that there will not be enough food. "When the chicken is passed, say that you don't want any." *Kein Huhn,*" she repeats. "No chicken!" For an always-hungry, growing eight-year-old, this is a painful command. I try to understand the context. The space in my stomach is in conflict with the empathy I've learned from Papa.

After nostalgia about the "good old days" in Hannover, Mutti invites everyone into our kitchen. We crowd around the small metal kitchen table protected with an oil-cloth covering. I associate the smell of oil-cloth with special meals like the Sabbath dinner. In addition to our four straight-backed wooden chairs, Papa borrowed a folding chair from the bakery office. I am sent next door to hurriedly borrow an additional chair. The table sits four comfortably. Six requires some people sitting shoulder to shoulder. Plates touch one another. Bowls are passed and have to be returned to the stove.

Dinner begins with the customary Sabbath prayers and the blessing for food. We are rich in bread from the bakery where Papa works, so the blessing over bread, "the fruit of the earth," is a big deal. Although Mutti doesn't serve the traditional Sabbath *challah*, the bread twist, we have more than enough of the bakery's free leftover rolls. We skip the traditional blessing for "the fruit of the vine" because we cannot yet afford Sabbath wine. Instead Papa substitutes the *shehecheyanu*, a blessing in which he thanks God "for giving us life, for sustaining us and for enabling us to reach this season."

Finally the food. Mutti serves me a small piece of potato and some string beans. When the chicken is passed to me I lie that I don't like chicken. "*Nein, Danke,*" I say even though the chicken has my favorite gravy. The space in my stomach is winning over my humanity. To help me out of this dilemma, I picture the starving children in Europe who I read about in the *Aufbau*, the German-Jewish newspaper available in New York City once each week. The starving children are described as skeletons. According to the stories they often receive only one meal of thin soup each day. I remember that not long ago my own diet had been limited—but now there is food on the table and I am hungry.

The table conversation includes statements of gratitude that we are all alive and progresses, with many tears, to prayers for the many who were not with us (and, as it turned out, never will be).

"*Wo sind die Kinder?*" asks Mrs. Goldfarb. "Where are the children?" Gestapo had taken them away from their lovely Hannover apartment. Along with cousins, uncles and aunts, they were "missing."

"Wo sind die Kinder?" The question repeats in my head as if in an echo chamber. "Wo sind die Kinder?"

"Here I am," I want to shout. "Here I am." But the Goldfarb children are not here at the table. Nor is my cousin Aaltje, six years my junior. Nor are all the other children about whom I read in the *Aufbau*. But I am at the table.

In Hebrew one says to God, "*Hineni*," Here I am. I have recently learned at the synagogue that when God asked Abraham, "Where art thou?" Abraham shouted "Hineni." And so I mumble to myself, "Hineni."

Mutti wonders about her sisters and her mother. Where were they? I silently wonder about Papa's mother. Mutti never worries about her although she, too, is missing. Papa's mother had lived with us for a while in Hannover. I used to sit on her warm lap and cuddle close. She told me that Papa was the youngest of her three children and he, too, used to sit on her lap. I wonder if I'll ever see my Oma again.

I have trouble handling all the tears. However, I guess that it would be rude to leave the table. And I'm hoping for more food.

The Goldfarbs express fear about surviving in this new country. "Can one find work as a fifty-year-old man? Who wants an old jeweler with no English skills?"

Papa tells hopeful stories about our first year in America. He boasts that Freddy, looking at me with pride, is a good student and exaggerates that I can already speak "almost perfect English." He adds, "Jewish children are allowed all the privileges of a free education, just like everyone else."

Papa boasts that at the bakery he has already been given two pay raises and that the boss is grooming him to be foreman just as soon as his English skills improve. "All it takes is hard work," he says. "*Arbeit*!" Work! "The bakery next door owns this building and they trust me to be the superintendent. In Germany they took everything away. In America they trust the Jews." And then, after a pause, Papa adds, "Only in America."

I look at the sad faces and hear Papa, like the rabbi, preach about hope. I sip my water and watch Papa. Surely he will find the right words to bring cheer to the table.

Suddenly Papa stands up. He raises his water glass as if to offer a toast. In his big baritone voice he proclaims, "The streets are not paved with gold. However, there is work. Above all, there is freedom."

At the moment I have little interest in the future. Having missed out on the chicken, my concern is with food in the here and now. I keep eyeing the teaspoons on the table. Papa has taught me that if there is no coffee or tea on the table, teaspoons mean dessert. Sure enough, in a glass bowl, a plain, smooth, round bowl with no decoration, a bowl which I had helped Mutti select at Woolworth's 5 and 10 cent store, the same bowl which had earlier held canned string beans, Mutti brings out canned peaches, the only dessert that I ever remember her serving—other than the occasional canned fruit cocktail with its bright red maraschino cherries. I like playing with the peach slices because they're slippery and hard to capture on a teaspoon. I liked the bright yellow color and the thick, sweet juice in which they float.

I ready my teaspoon. The guests are served first, then Papa. As I reach for the bowl Mutti snatches it away. "No, no," she says. "No chicken, no dessert."

XVI. BOMBS BURSTING IN AIR — AGAIN

WHAM! BANG! My head hits the school desk and then the chair to which the desk is attached. I'm the first to hide, the only kid in Mrs. Brower's 1942 second-grade class who knows how to respond to a New York City air raid drill. How am I to know it's just a drill? I'm a real air raid expert.

The other children seem puzzled. They look around to find the source of the shrill, whining cry. Mrs. Brower has been trained for this moment. Calmly she explains the routine to her students. "That sound is called an air raid siren. Whenever you hear this siren I want you to quickly and *carefully* hide under your desks." The "carefully" was surely added as a special caution after my painful and noisy escape into my cocoon. She explains air raids to the bewildered children. "You know that we're at war with the Japanese and the Germans. They probably won't come here. But, just in case ..."

I don't need instruction. I remember hiding under a table with Papa when the RAF flew over Hannover. None of my classmates understand about hostile airplanes flying over our school. Airplanes loaded with bombs that could blow us all to smithereens. This is a class of innocent babes without a clue about war. One of the girls starts to cry. From under my desk I hear Mrs. Brower's words, warm, encouraging, protective. "I'll be right here with you." Her training manual has anticipated the children's naïve fear.

Despite her preparation for this moment, our teacher's voice quivers just a bit. Perhaps, for the first time, she has an image of an airplane with an open bomb bay. Perhaps she imagines the piercing whistle of a bomb dropping onto *her* school, *her* children. Even *herself!* She has seen pictures of burned and dismembered European bodies in the daily newspapers. Until this moment those pictures were just images of a far-away place. Perhaps now, as she tenderly guides each of her charges under a desk, she imagines them as corpses.

As I peek out, I see my teacher's head move from side to side, then up and down. The manual did not tell Mrs. Brower where to hide. A momentary distraction. She remembers her job. Her reassuring voice returns. Her warm hugs around the frightened children come easily. She lightens the moment by joking about me, suggesting again that my classmates have entered the mini-spaces under their desks more gently than little Freddy who has now been in his shelter for several minutes—before the instructions began.

We survive the drill. After the "all clear" signal, we go to recess. We run in the school yard like little maniacs releasing stress. We play war with the "ack, ack ack" sound of machine guns, the "boom" of bomb explosions and we moan "argh" as we fall dead on the playground tar. The realistic sounds, learned from war movies, suggest that perhaps these American children aren't as innocent as I had first thought. Acting out scenes from movies allows them to act out their fears and mock bravery.

Mrs. Brower calls me aside to ask how I knew about air raid sirens. She wonders why my response was faster and more frightened than the others. She knows something of my story from my school record and from my accent. I tell the teacher about the British airplanes and the leaflets and the air raid shelter. I tell her about "Juden Verboten" and watching the planes from my window. I tell her about the buildings on fire and about hiding under our dining room table with Papa. With the limited English language skills of a newcomer, I tell my story as seen through the eyes of an eight-year-old. I teach the teacher.

XVII. TODAY I AM A CITIZEN

LARGE POSTERS PLEAD WITH THE PUBLIC to conserve on food, clothing, metal products, everything. "There's a war on, you know," shout the posters. Everything for the troops. World War II is everyone's war. Many housewives leave their kitchens to join Rosie the Riveter on production lines to support the war effort. Able-bodied men volunteer to serve "our" country and the elderly come out of retirement to take jobs.

We carefully hoard our rationing stamps and tokens. No one complains because the cause is good. Gasoline is rationed and, because our troops need the rubber, so are tires. Our troops need leather so shoes are rationed too. Sugar, coffee, meat, cheese, everything for the troops. Radio broadcasts encourage us to use less than our allotted food. Every bite we save will feed our soldiers, sailors and airmen. We're discouraged from buying any manufactured goods. After all, manpower is needed to manufacture guns and planes.

School children—and I am one of them—compete to find used tobacco wrappers. We undo the packaging, clean off the aluminum foil and create a ball. Every week each of us brings a shiny ball to school. Some are bigger than our teacher's fist. We too are doing our bit.

Homemakers are asked to save unwanted grease in metal cans. Butcher shops become collecting stations where parents send us kids to deliver fat in cans. We're told that both fat and cans will help us win the war. We giggle when the radio announcer shouts an unintended pun, "Ladies, remember to bring your fat cans to your local butcher."

Papa becomes a Gallon Club member at the Red Cross. He donates blood so often that sometimes the nurses turn him away because he hasn't allowed enough time to elapse between donations. He receives several medals for being a champion donor.

Papa's most important task is as block air raid warden. This diminutive man with poor English skills has volunteered to jump out of bed at any hour of the night to patrol our neighborhood when the sirens scream. New York City hasn't experienced real bombings like we saw in Hannover. Nevertheless, the air raid drills seem real and it is Papa's job to see that everyone takes the exercises seriously. The bombs may come on any night. Who knows? Papa's main task is to ensure that all lights are out during a drill. No one is allowed on the street except police officers, firefighters and Papa.

I'm enormously proud when he shows off his government-issued helmet, armband and flashlight. This is not the armband with the yellow Star of David that we—all Jews—were required to wear in Germany. This is an official American armband which, he points out, gives him special responsibilities even though he is a Jew. "Only in America," he proclaims with grave sincerity. He often returns late in the evening from training sessions with stories of what he has learned and what he must do in the event of a real air raid. Papa tells his stories in German and always ends with, *"Wir sind jetzt in Amerika."* We're in America now.

In January of 1945 the war news is positive. The Allied Forces are winning the war in Europe and the war in Asia has also turned in our favor. In our household, every available minute is dedicated to following the international news on the radio.

By February, a new interest enters our household: passing the test for citizenship. We arrived in the United States at the very end of 1939—that important moment when Papa held me high to see the Statue of Liberty. Early in 1940, Papa and Mutti applied for American citizenship. They also applied on behalf of their six-year-old son. Now, five years later, we will become naturalized citizens if we can pass the test. We will be required to show that we know enough about our new country and its government to be allowed to stay and vote and to enjoy all the privileges of being an American. And the test has to be completed in English. A booklet helps us prepare and prepare we do through the remainder of the winter and into the spring.

I have learned much of the information in school and that gives me a head start. My English language skills are much better than my parents'. These advantages put me in charge—and my parents, proud of their clever son, are pleased to follow my lead. I ask questions from a set of perhaps one hundred samples in our study guide. I explain each answer and its importance.

Which president freed the slaves?

Which amendment freed the slaves?

Why do we have three branches of government?

How many stars are on the American flag? Why?

How many stripes? Why?

What does the cabinet do?

I create flash cards with questions on one side and answers on the back. Sometimes I show the side with the answers and ask Papa and Mutti to tell me the questions. We take the challenge seriously and study almost every evening. Sometimes Omi, who arrived in the United States two years after we did, joins us. One day, she too will be eligible for American citizenship. For us, family time is educational.

In April, a few concentration camps are liberated by Allied Forces. Photos of skeletons and piles of dead began to appear in the daily newspapers. Bergen Belsen, located close to my home town, was liberated by the British army. The camp has been devastated with a huge typhus epidemic and *The New York Times* reports that on the day of liberation, April 15, 1945, 13,000 unburied corpses lay around the camp. Photos show living skeletons, sitting near barbed wire fences with outstretched hands begging for the soldiers' rations.

The world is shocked. Finally Americans believe what survivors have been describing for the past several years. Omi, sitting on her chair in the kitchen, cries quietly. Mutti, hysterical, chest heaving with loud sobs, rushes aimlessly from room to room. She imagines that, among these skeletal survivors and heaps of corpses, she sees her sisters and cousins and circle of friends. Papa is too busy planning for the future to have energy for looking back. Papa calmly talks about earning extra money so that he can send it to the starving Jews in Europe. He starts to work longer hours.

I study the pictures searching for my only cousin, Aaltje, who, if alive, would be almost six years old. I see no children. I look for myself in the pictures but I'm not there. I'm here in America. I'm studying to be an American citizen. I have lots of food and lots of books. I have to be extra good, extra smart, to deserve these riches. I must earn my freedom and my right to life.

* * *

On May 7, 1945, we dress in our best Sabbath clothes as though we are going to the synagogue. It is, however, a Monday and we're headed to lower Manhattan. Miss Levy has excused me from school and Papa has taken a day off from work.

We emerge from the subway station, walk a few blocks filled with crowds of busy people, admire the tall office buildings, climb several steps and enter an enormous Federal building. A shiny copper-looking elevator operated by a uniformed police officer carries us to a large open space where we sit at long tables, fill in forms, bring them to a clerk wearing a business suit and a badge. She's smothered in a strong perfume that makes me gag. Perhaps it's my nervousness. We wait. This is Citizenship Day for us.

Papa is called first. He is directed through an ornate doorway to ... we don't know. In the old country there were many government doors from which people never returned. Papa reminds us, "We're in America now."

When he emerges through the same doorway he is smiling. "*Alles ist gut*," he whispers. All is well.

Mutti is called next. "Wish me luck," she sighs. I'm certain that no luck is needed. Her English skills are much better than Papa's. After all, she studied a little English in high school when she was still a girl. Nevertheless, she is unusually pale. She straightens her hat, the one with the long black feather. She places a lace hankie over her nose, blows quietly and tucks the hankie back into her left sleeve.

Mutti also returns with an "Alles ist gut." She has passed her test. A few moments later my name is called and I, a young almost-man, 11½ years old, open the beautifully carved door and enter a large, carpeted room. Behind the desk sits a gray-haired gentleman in suit and tie. The room smells of sweet pipe tobacco and I can see a large pipe sitting in an ashtray. I climb into an oversize wood and leather chair—certainly oversize for my frame. A name plate spells the gentleman's name: "Mr. Jensen." I immediately have a life goal. I want a job with a name plate that spells "Mr. Amram."

The man asks my name and checks to see if I filled in the forms correctly. He addresses me as Mr. Amram and treats me like the grown-up I pretend to be.

"Does the constitution give women the right to vote?"

"No," I squeak in my most manly voice.

"How did women achieve the right to vote in the United States?"

"An amendment to the constitution." I pray silently: *Please don't ask which amendment.*

We discuss Abraham Lincoln and the Civil War. Our interview ends with, "Good work young man. You passed. Congratulations."

I'm instructed to stand and to raise my right hand and, before two witnesses (are they paid clerks?), I swear allegiance to my adopted country. Then the official wishes me luck and promises, "Your papers will be mailed to you in a few months."

By way of celebration, Papa treats us to lunch at a downtown deli. We celebrate our success and good fortune. Papa promises a great future for our family—especially his son who coached the family toward passing the citizenship test. Mutti talks about the past. I enjoy *latkes* one-half year before Chanukah when Omi will make the traditional potato pancakes.

On Tuesday morning, May 8, Miss Levy tells the class that I am now a United States citizen. She uses the opportunity to teach a lesson about what it means to be an American. She asks the class to stand and has us recite the Pledge of Allegiance.

I pledge allegiance to the Flag of the United States of America, and to the republic for which it stands:

I remember one of Mr. Jensen's questions on the citizenship test, "What's the difference between a monarchy and a republic."

one nation indivisible, with liberty and justice for all.

Certificate of Citizenship

That last line has special meaning. Boys at school have been saying bad things about Germans and about Jews. They sometimes call me nasty names. Secretly I hope that the "dirty Jew boy" name calling will now stop. Now that I'm a citizen of the U.S.A., a land that promises liberty and justice for all, I'd like to leave the German hatred of Jews behind me.

Right after lunch everyone in the school is hustled into the assembly hall. The principal waits until the room is quiet. Then he says something about this being a joyous day. I hope that he is not about to make a big to-do about my new status as a citizen. I like being a star, but this is too much. Miss Levy has already made a fuss.

Mr. Principal continues to talk about patriotism and the war and our brave soldiers and sailors and airmen. "Please don't talk about citizenship," I think. Finally he comes to the point. "Today is VE Day, Victory in Europe. The Axis Forces surrendered just hours ago and, even though there is still war in Asia, we are near the end."

Then he turns to a news program on the radio and we listen to great jubilation in many European countries. The principal has determined that this is an occasion we all must share—a history-making occasion. None of us knows how to behave so we sit silently. Should we cheer? Should be sing songs? We wiggle quietly in our seats.

I think about the coincidence of victory over the Nazis just a day after I officially join the winning side. Am I no longer German? Am I truly an American like the other kids in my class?

I look over at Miss Levy and see tears on her cheeks. She dabs her eyes with a lace hanky just like the one Mutti carries in her sleeve.

Finally the principal sends us back to our classrooms just in time to hear the three o'clock bell. We fumble for our jackets and sweaters. As we file out of the classroom, Miss Levy touches my face, just a light touch, perhaps an accident. What is she thinking? Does she understand how it feels to be a Jewish refugee?

On the dash home, as I pass a newsstand, I see another picture of a liberated concentration camp. More sick people who look like skeletons. I'm not in the picture. Not one child. Are all the Jewish children in Europe dead? I realize that, American citizen or not, I will always be a Jewish refugee—a survivor.

XVIII. PAKN TREGER

WHILE I ATTEND SCHOOL, Papa changes jobs, Mutti quits her job and our financial situation improves dramatically. Papa's career changes impact the entire family.

The proud, modern Jewish-American parent tells of "my son the doctor," "my son the lawyer," perhaps even "my son the rabbi"—although some say a rabbi's pay isn't good enough for a Jewish boy. Instead of telling about my son the poet, let me tell you about my Papa the peddler.

In German, a merchant is a *Kaufman* and that is the job listing on my father's German marriage certificate. In Yiddish, a peddler is a *pakn treger*, a package carrier. In the old country, Papa left school after the fourth grade to apprentice in the textile trade. When he became a journeyman he was authorized to sell what we now call yard goods—fabric sold by the yard, except in the old country it was sold by the meter. Papa and his brother, Uncle Max, went into business together. In Hannover, Papa lived in a fairly large apartment with my mother, Mutti, and his little son. One room was dedicated to the business. I remember shelves upon shelves holding large bolts of fabric. Papa, expert in all types of fabric, weaves, quality and color, travelled to the towns and villages around Hannover to peddle his wares home-to-home, door-to-door. He brought his charm to the ladies and sold them yards of fabric to be used when they sewed their clothes. Uncle Max, the bachelor, had the more distant Hamburg route. A century earlier, each of them would have traveled in a covered wagon. Instead, in the 1920s, they were early adopters of the automobile.

Meinhardt (Milton) Amram
as a youth

Papa liked to tell this story about his first automobile. He was on a date, driving with one hand holding his girl and one hand on the steering wheel. A police officer pulled him over and, so Papa reports, said, "You should use two hands." Papa responded, "You're right, officer. But I need one hand for driving."

The peddling business was a huge success. We lived well—until the Nazis determined that Jews could not own businesses.

After we arrive in the states, Papa, with no education and no facility in the new language, has difficulty finding work. When in early 1940 he takes the jobs in a bakery and as a janitor, he has a start. Now he has income and a place for his wife and son to live.

In 1942, he learns about a job as a cutter in a shoe factory—a skilled job cutting leather samples to be assembled and sewn into new shoe designs. Pattern makers are fairly well paid as factory work goes. Papa doesn't have the skills. He lies. He guesses that with the knowledge he has about fabrics and clothing manufacture he can fake the skill. He learns quickly and becomes a star pattern maker, the person who cuts the individual parts of leather shoes in different sizes, pieces that become prototypes for machine dies. He likes to show off his special little knife—a small curved blade, like a scimitar, held by a small green wooden handle—so tiny that it fits into the palm of Papa's hand. No one but Papa is allowed to touch the little knife. He warns about its super sharpness—which he proves one day when he accidentally cuts his thumb so deep that it almost falls off. Surgeons re-attach the thumb and he is back on the job in a week.

Papa joins the union and after a while becomes a shop steward representing the workers on labor issues. He is proud that, broken English notwithstanding, he is nominated and elected to his union position by his peers—a *ganser macher*, a big deal. Mutti is aghast, certain that Papa will lose his "high status" job. Papa claims he is too good a sample cutter to be fired. Apparently he is correct.

Of course, leaving the bakery job means leaving the janitor job. We move again and Papa has to pay rent. However, he's a risk taker. He has goals, ambition—*chutzpa*. The shoe factory is just a way to save up for something bigger. Something better. Papa has "peddler" in his blood. He is determined to become self-employed and to hit the road.

We move only two blocks from the bakery, two blocks north to 77th Street between First and Second Avenues. We don't move far, but we move up. Literally. We now live on the fifth floor of a six-story apartment building. The building even has a slow, rickety elevator—although I rarely take the time to wait for it.

With the December 1941 arrival of Omi, my maternal grandmother, Papa has four mouths to feed. He saves and saves and saves and when the moment is right, the summer of 1944, Papa quits the shoe industry and becomes a Fuller Brush man. He is assigned a route in New Jersey, visiting women on the farms and in the villages. Home-to-home and door-to-door. He buys a car, his first in the new country. He can't or won't drive in the big city. Where would he park? How would he deal with the morning and evening traffic?   And gasoline is in short supply.

He wants to move to New Jersey, close to his Fuller Brush route, but Mutti refuses to leave New York City. New Jersey, she claims, is too rural. So Papa awakes every day at 4 a.m. and takes the subway to the train. He takes the train to where he had left his car the day before and begins his Fuller Brush route. As he becomes more successful on the route, he starts adding pots, pans, house dresses. He takes orders for whatever folks want. Working for the Fuller Company is part of a plot, a ruse, to become an authentic peddler. In Arthur Miller's *Death of a Salesman*, Willy Loman hits the road and acts as a salesman for a large company. That isn't the same as being a peddler. Papa wanted to be *self-employed*. To take the risks. To work twice as hard so that he can be free of employers. He has a plan.

I don't understand why Papa isn't more forceful about his wish to move to New Jersey. Why does he put up with the long subway and train rides? Does he have arguments with Mutti when I'm not looking? Is he just so good natured? He hates confrontations and so do I.

In the evening I'm allowed to help with the business. I use a stamp and stamp pad to press my father's name and address on Fuller brochures. I stamp dozens, hundreds, surely thousands of brochures. And I count the combs and letter openers, the freebies left at the doors of Fuller customers. Meanwhile my father keeps the books.

One day each week—usually on Sunday—Papa goes to the Delancey Street neighborhood to buy from the Jewish wholesalers. He bargains hard and the "dealers" make deals. Occasionally, if I'm free from homework, I join Papa on the subway to the Lower East Side. Perhaps it's time to buy a new suit—wholesale, of course. Just like in the joke, the salesman really does say, "Good gabardine, two pair pents," with a Yiddish accent. And the suit really does have two pairs of pants. And it really cost only half as much as it would cost in a retail store. I remember one suit that had two pairs of scratchy woolen knickers. The second pair was put away for the time the knees wear out on the first. However, by the time I wear out the knees on the first pair, knickers have gone out of style and, fortunately, I've outgrown them. They're given to charity because they are "as good as new."

Saturday is delivery day. Subway to train to car to customers. On rare Saturdays I'm allowed to carry packages which are distributed to all the good folks on "the route." Those occasional trips with Papa are the only times I ever see his car—except on those even rarer occasions when he brings his car to the city on a long weekend so that we can all go for a Sunday drive in the country. Because Mutti refuses to go to New Jersey, she *never* sees some of Papa's cars. Each car is bought in New Jersey, lasts a few years and is traded for a new one. It "lives" at New Jersey train stations. And it has a name. Papa calls all his cars "Anton"—even those he had owned in Germany. Papa treats his cars like pet puppies. He checks the oil daily. And he praises them aloud when they successfully climb a hill: "*Guter* Anton." Good Anton. Each morning he greets his pal cheerfully and each evening he wishes it a good night—always in German.

For Papa, buying gasoline for his car is like buying a treat. He reasons that the more gasoline he buys, the more miles the car has carried him and that means more customers. Papa also likes to pay taxes. He reasons that the taxes reflect his income. The more taxes, the more income.

Saturdays in New Jersey we stop for a bite, usually a sandwich, at a diner. Papa has coffee and I have milk or hot chocolate, depending on the season. Papa explains the mathematics of buying and selling and charging interest. But mostly he talks about his customers. They are his life. He empathizes with the farmers' hardships and advises the housewives in towns how to make ends meet. He takes incredible personal pride as his customers' children grow up, often sending graduation cards or bringing a small gift. His pockets are always filled with hard candies and chewing gum for the children who flock to his car as he drives up.

As 1946 begins, Papa concludes he is paying more attention to his private sales than to his Fuller Brush business. He drops the pretense of being a Fuller salesman and simply becomes a freelance peddler. Many customers are poor farmers who can only pay in milk or eggs or chickens. Why not? Papa is a one-man central New Jersey social welfare agency.

Papa speaks English poorly with a heavy accent and I marvel how he charms his customers so well. The hard candies in his pockets probably help.

He does magic with numbers. I watch amazed as he multiplies a three digit number by another three digit number. In his head! He makes lists of numbers, perhaps income or expenses, and then draws a line under the last number. He stares at the columns for a few moments and then he writes the sum at the bottom of the list. Pure magic. He can calculate the value of eggs or chickens in comparison to an apron or a pan or three yards of cotton fabric—and turn a profit.

A homemade loaf of bread baked by a farmwife has worth beyond cash. It shows Papa that *he* is valued.

XIX. THE OUTSIDER

TODAY I SIT in Miss Christie's sixth grade class. It's September of 1945, the end of the first week of the new school year. Miss Christie stands in the front of the room: tall, muscular arms, large breasts, black hair, black dress, stern expression. She's teaching ten new spelling words to be memorized in alphabetical order by Monday.

I recall Miss Levy, my fifth grade teacher. I felt her warmth when she patted my shoulders for a job well done and when she scolded with an almost inaudible whisper. She stood at the side of the room when she talked to the class, her back to the window, surrounded by light.

Spelling lessons in Miss Levy's class were full of helpful hints. "Bicycle: B-I-C-Y-C-L-E. On the test some of you confused the 'I' and the 'Y.' Remember this sentence: 'I see why you want a bicycle.' Can you hear how the 'I' comes before the 'WHY?'" A smile. "Isn't that fun?"

"English spelling can be confusing," Miss Levy warned. "For example, there is P-R-I-N-C-I-P-L-E and P-R-I-N-C-I-P-A-L." Miss Levy walked to the blackboard clicking her one-inch heels as she talked. "Remember that the principal of our school is your P-A-L," underlining the last three letters.

During another spelling review, Miss Levy coached us in spelling P-A-R-A-L-L-E-L. "One R and three Ls. Do you see the parallel lines in the Ls?"

I still love Miss Levy. I still love spelling. I still love words.

Will I like this new teacher's spelling lesson? Miss Christie begins. "The first word is 'austere.'" My English language skills have now surpassed most of my classmates and my German accent is almost gone.

I can almost hide that I'm a refugee from Holocaust Europe. However, here is a word I've never used before.

A-U-S-T-E-R-E. I can learn to spell that. I whisper the word as Miss Christie explains, "Severely simple. If we take down all the decorations in this room it would look quite austere. Imagine a prison cell with no furniture except a bed. That would be an austere room."

She lets that sink in. Then she continues, "Poor people have an austere diet—a very simple diet." I conjure up memories of our last years in Germany and our first year in the United States. I understand "austere." She calls on a few students to put our new spelling word in context. Judging from the confusion, I'm not the only sixth grader for whom the word is new.

Miss Christie then explains how some words have more than one meaning. We nod. Most of us already know that. "Austere can also mean having a stern or strict expression. Can you make an austere face? Yes. Now, everyone make a face like your mother makes when she's angry. Yes. That was a stern or strict expression.

A-U-S-T-E-R-E."

I'm way ahead of Miss Christie. She is austere in both senses. Never smiling, always standing tall, Miss Christie looks stern. I was frightened the moment I saw her. She also looks austere, simple, plain in the first sense. She's worn a black dress every day this week—perhaps the same black dress—unadorned; although today she's wearing a simple silver pin near her left shoulder. Miss Christie's desk looks austere. Not a book, not a blotter, not a paper weight. Nothing. A-U-S-T-E-R-E.

* * *

Every Friday the bell rings promptly at 1:45 p.m. All the children gather up their books and sweaters and quietly head to the door. Quietly because the fear of Jesus is already in their veins. All the children from my public school on the east side of Manhattan, P.S. 70, are going to church. The Catholic kids line up in silence and a few teachers walk them to nearby Saint Somebody's church. I can't remember which saint inhabits the church. I don't let myself think about saints. Sometimes teachers have asked me to behave more like a saint. How can there be a Jewish saint? But I don't argue with teachers.

The Protestant kids also line up quietly and go to their neighborhood church. It's named after some mountain. Certainly not Mount Sinai. I've never been inside.

Every Friday all the students from our school are dismissed early for religious instruction. Miss Christie stays behind. Each year, the teacher of my class has to stay behind with the only Jewish kid in the school.

Last year Miss Levy gave me a special book to read each week and then, on Friday afternoon, instead of religious instruction, she and I would talk about the book. *The Secret Garden* was fun to read and Miss Levy confessed that when she was a little girl in the city, she loved to imagine a life in the country with flowers and trees and animals. She told me that she still likes to visit the Central Park Zoo and the Botanical Garden in the Bronx. My favorite religious-instruction-substitute book was the *Just So Stories* by Rudyard Kipling. I loved "How the Camel Got His Hump" and "How the Elephant Got his Trunk." Each new story was more magical than the one I had just finished. Miss Levy asked if I like to make up stories. I told her that I like to make up words combining English and German like *rhinocerwurst*. We had just finished talking about Kipling's "How the Rhinoceros Got His Skin." Miss Levy smiled.

Today I'm sitting in my chair waiting to see how Miss Christie will handle religious instruction day. I take out a book pretending to be busy. Miss Christie, large Miss Christie, rolls her chair next to mine. "*Gott im Himmel*, God in heaven" I think. "What will happen to me now?" There, leaning close, is Miss Christie with that C-H-R-I-S-T in her name. I spell it out in my head. Perhaps we can have a spelling bee. I always win the school spelling bee.

"Fred," Miss Christie begins. Miss Levy called me Freddy.

"Fred," she repeats. "How does it feel being left behind when the other boys and girls leave the school?"

"I'm Jewish," I explain. Of course she knows that. It's written on my forehead just as plainly as the numbers on Auschwitz survivors' left arms.

"But how do you feel?"

I start to cry in my head but I don't show it. Never show weakness!

"Have you ever talked about your feelings with anyone?"

"No."

"Can you tell me how you feel?"

"Lonely. No, I feel different. Maybe both." I'm still crying inside.

Large Miss Christie touches my arm with a steady hand. She wraps her large fingers around my skinny wrist. My terror increases.

"How does it feel to be different?"

The war has just ended. Every day we see pictures in newspapers and magazines. I'm one of the people in the pictures and yet I'm not. I'm not one of the six million. I survived. I'm different from the Jews who were butchered and I'm different from my classmates. How can I explain all that to Miss Christie? And what will she do with whatever I confess?

In my turmoil I blurt, "Once I tried counting to six million but I quit when I realized how long it would take."

She still holds my wrist.

"I've read your records. You're different in another way. You're the smartest student in our school. Let's not call it 'different.' Let's call it 'special.'"

Miss Levy had treated me as if I were special. Now Miss Christie was saying it. "Different." "Special." Then another word comes to mind. "Outsider."

"I feel like an outsider," I say.

Miss Christie captures the moment. "How does it feel to be an outsider?"

I look at the floor. That's more than I can handle.

"Well, we've got many more Friday afternoons to talk about it," whispers Miss Christie. She walks over to her desk, removes some papers from the drawer and asks, "Would you please take these reports to the principal's office for me? Here's a hall pass."

* * *

After school I rush home for milk and a cookie. I change clothes. Sometimes, rain and snow keep me inside reading books or playing records. However, on this perfect September day, I join the other kids on my block for outdoor play. First we play stick ball, a game like baseball but played with a broomstick and a pink rubber ball marked "Spalding." We call the ball a "spaldeen." My poor vision assures that I am not a favorite at bat. True to form, I'm picked last when we choose up sides. Again, true to form, the police come and tell us that we can't play stickball because we hit too many parked cars. The officers are gentle and invite us to join the Police Athletic League—a program to help the cops keep an eye on low-income kids with the potential for getting into trouble. I'm wearing my PAL pin to show that I'm already a member.

Three of us then walk over to a tenement two buildings west of where I live, a building that has a really wide entrance with six steps leading to the front door. We all have spaldeens and we bounce them against the stoop again and again, honing our catching skills. After a while the building owner chases us away. He often chases us even though we believe that the stoop is public property. It's our playground. We're angry and plot revenge. Ralph, Tony and I decide to let the air out of our enemy's tires. Tony points out the car. He has seen the guy get in and out of that car. Ralph's and Tony's families, like most New Yorkers, don't own a car. My family does, so I have to show them how air goes into and out of tires. I open the valve on the first one while my buddies watch for pedestrians. Then Tony and Ralph each empty a tire. We leave the fourth tire full so that the car now sits at an eerie angle.

After supper I, the tire hero, get to pick the evening activity. I've already brought my roller skates with me. I'm a star on wheels. I strap the skates to my shoes, tighten the clamps over the toes with a skate key and off I go, skinned knees and all. I can outrace almost anyone except Bobby Schneider who is way taller than the rest of the kids on our block and goes to a private school. Bobby, already wearing his skates, joins Ralph, Tony and me as we roll up and down the block. We four plan a race from Second Avenue to First. Our intent, as always, is to avoid the sidewalk. We race in the gutter. Ready, set and off we skate. Halfway down the block a car drives toward us down our narrow street. Bobby dashes between two parked cars and jumps onto the right sidewalk. I do the same on the left side. We re-enter the gutter just as soon as the slow-moving Chevy has passed—almost at the same time. Bobby reaches the end of the block a second before I do. We look back and see that Tony has bashed into the moving car and Ralph fell trying to jump the curb.

In the schoolyard, kids sometimes tease me with "smarty pants" and "teacher's pet." However, I have friends on our block from other schools who appreciate my love of learning.

Albert is one of the few children on our block with whom I have on-going conflict. Albert lives in a tenement directly across the street from my house. I once overheard Bobby Schneider's mother, while boasting about the superiority of Episcopalians, refer to that building is an "enclave" of Italian Catholics. I looked up "enclave" as soon as I arrived home.

Albert likes to get kids excited by calling me names like "dirty Jew" or "dirty Hun." That hurts and sometimes other kids join in. To them Germany is still part of the evil Axis, the enemy of the United States and the other allied nations. Consequently I sometimes become the German enemy. At the same time, I'm still a "dirty Jew." Luckily I didn't have to contend with Albert today. Tony, who goes to a Catholic boys' school with Albert, tells me that Albert got in some kind of trouble and his mother had to go to school after hours.

Because I run and skate faster than almost anyone, I avoid most confrontations with Albert and his pals. When I do have to fight, I usually lose because my heart isn't into hurting people and I'm neither big nor strong.

Albert's cousin, Josephine, who lives in the building we call "Little Italy," is one of my friends, although we sixth-grade boys don't play much with girls. Josephine, two years my senior, sometimes invites me to turn one end of the clothesline the girls use when they jump rope. She claims I have natural rhythm. Do all Jews have natural rhythm? She and I occasionally play jacks when no one else is around.

* * *

Today is Tuesday. I wear the required white shirt and red tie to school. Most of the boys wear dark blue pants and we look quite patriotic. The girls, just as patriotic, wear white blouses, small red scarves around their necks and blue skirts. At ten o'clock, just like every Tuesday morning, we file in straight lines to the auditorium for an assembly. Sometimes the principal introduces a boring speaker and some of us fall asleep. Occasionally we have musical guests and I love their concerts on piano or violin. The rare church choir keeps everyone awake. I learn all the Christmas songs by heart—even the *Ave Maria* which becomes one of my favorites. My mother teaches me the same songs in German and a few in French.

I like Tuesdays because, dressed up as we are, we all behave better and the classroom is less chaotic. Austere Miss Christie is less tolerant of classroom chaos than other teachers. Yet even in her class everyone seems more calm on assembly day.

On Tuesdays we're all dressed alike. I feel less different.

The assembly guest today is an inspirational speaker who tells us that God wants us to do our best. Jesus should be our guide and we should all behave like good Christians. Somewhere during his presentation he tells us to not let the Devil into our lives. "Don't tolerate the enemies of Christ." World War II Jews, even those who are only in sixth grade, have special antennae when it comes to hearing about the enemies of Christ.

Sure enough, during recess I hear a lot of "dirty Jew" remarks and several kids try to pick fights. Apparently, after today's speaker, they feel obliged to protect Jesus from his enemies. Miss Christie monitors the playground with an iron fist. No nonsense. She comes to my aid when fights are brewing. As we file back into class, Miss Christie whispers, "Special is worth defending."

The three o'clock bell rings and we file out of class in an orderly line. As soon as our shiny Tuesday leather shoes touch the sidewalk we run toward home. Pent up energy needs an outlet and the run home helps. As the fastest runner, I'm first to arrive on our block.

Josephine and some of the other kids who attend a Catholic girls' school are home early today. Instead of bounding up the five flights for my milk and cookie, I linger with Josephine and her friends. My mother will be angry if I dirty my white shirt but I'm invited to turn rope so that the girl I replace can jump. I show off my natural rhythm and chat with the girls. We're turning two ropes in opposite directions and some of the more talented girls can create a double jump between the two ropes. They call it "Double Dutch."

Soon other P.S. 70 children arrive. One boy taunts me with "sissy." Others join in. Albert arrives and embellishes the name-calling with "sissy Jew boy." The girls stop jumping. Albert punches me in the stomach. I drop the rope. He punches me in the chest. I haven't moved. "Sissy Jew boy," he repeats. He tackles me and I push him away. I grab his left arm with my left arm and twist him around so that his arm is between my chest and his back.

"You're breaking my arm," Albert whimpers. I barely hear him. Instead I hear Miss Christie, "Special is worth defending."

I place my right arm under Albert's chin and reach for my left shoulder. I squeeze. Albert isn't in my head anymore. Miss Christie is asking, "How does it feel to be an outsider?"

"Anger," my brain says. "Rage," I hear myself telling her. I squeeze Albert's throat harder. "Fury." I spell all the words correctly as if I were in a spelling bee.

FURY. F-U-R-Y. FURY.

I'm no longer on our block across from "Little Italy." I'm in Miss Christie's room and Albert isn't here. I squeeze. Once, in a comic book, I read about a stranglehold.

STRANGLEHOLD. S-T-R-A-N-G-L-E-H-O-L-D. STRANGLEHOLD.

Slowly I return to our street. Some of the older boys are pulling on me and shouting my name.

"Fred." "Fred." "You're killing him." "Stop." "Let go." "Fred." Each boy gives a different instruction and I remember that my right arm is locked around Albert's neck. My left arm is still bending Albert's arm. At least four boys are pulling at me but I'm all powerful. I will kill.

An adult passing by slaps my face and I come back to reality. I don't want to kill anyone. I loosen my grip. Albert slumps to the ground. The right sleeve of my white shirt is covered with blood from Albert's nose and mouth. I look at my bleeding victim writhing on the cement and immediately I regret. Regret what? Regret everything. I don't want to be a killer. They killed six million. I'm not like them. I don't want to be like them.

I help Albert to a standing position. I ask Josephine to take her cousin home. I go upstairs to our apartment. I remove my shirt, wash my face and hands and arms and wish that I could wash my soul. I leave my white shirt in the bathtub.

On Saturday, Papa brings home a new white shirt. My parents never mention the blood.

* * *

Another Friday. I'm still a "Jew boy" and a "Dirty Jew" in the school yard. However, no one on my block makes fun of me again.

I tell Miss Christie what happened. She holds my arm with her firm grasp. I tell her that I'm sorry. She points out that several people learned lessons last Tuesday. "It isn't over," she warns me. She repeats, "Special is worth defending."

Then she sends me to the principal's office with a pile of papers. "Here's the hall pass."

XX. TWO OUTSIDERS

"Anton was the only Jewish child in his classroom, but he was not afraid...
That is why we came to America."

From a HIAS brochure

AFTER LUNCH on a rainy November Friday in 1945, we open our arithmetic workbooks. The heavy rain keeps us from outdoor recess. We're all a bit antsy. Lunch was especially noisy and I feel a bit edgy about the last hour of the school day—religious instruction time.

Miss Christie goes on as usual. "Open your arithmetic workbook to page 19 now." She often adds "now" to her sentences with emphasis in her voice and with a forefinger pointing out of her large fist. Antsy students or not, Miss Christie demands respect.

Silently we read one of those awkward word puzzles that require us to use problem-solving skills. "Farmer Brown has planted 27 acres of corn. He expects to harvest 120 bushels per acre. He buys another ten acres from his neighbor just in time to plant more corn ..." I solve the problem in my head the way Papa does his business calculations. I have time to daydream. I wonder what an acre looks like, where farmer Brown got the money to buy more land and how I might grow corn. I wonder why we are working on such an obscure problem. We all live in Manhattan, the concrete jungle, and most of us have never seen a farm. The building in which I live holds 61 families. Our block alone must have a population of about 5,000.

Mary Jane, the girl who sits in front of me, leans over to her neighbor and asks in a whisper, "What's a bushel?" Silently I imagine a bushel basket. Papa, who sells "stuff" on farms around Freehold, Matawan and other towns in central New Jersey, once brought home a bushel basket full of vegetables that he accepted as payment from a farmer. The basket was heaped with fresh vegetables, a dead chicken and some eggs in a carton designed to protect them. Does the arithmetic puzzle refer to bushel baskets? I don't know. Miss Christie gives Mary Jane a stern look and notices that I'm not holding my pencil. She walks over to my desk. "Why aren't you working?" she asks in a whisper. The other kids are writing and erasing and calculating madly. "I know the answer," I whisper back.

Our whispering continues: "How do you know the answer?"

"I figured it out."

"Let me see your work"

"I figured it out in my head," I tell her as I write the answer on the top of the workbook page. Then I write the answer to tomorrow's problem on the next page.

* * *

The bell rings. It's 1:45 and all the children stand up ready for religious instruction. I keep my seat. As they pass my chair, several boys punch my arm. I'm still a "Jew boy" and a "Dirty Jew" at school.

When I told Miss Christie about the Albert event she warned me, "It isn't over." Then she added, "Special is worth defending."

She was right. The tension isn't over. I still absorb "the slings and arrows of outrageous fortune." I had read *Hamlet* and, despite lots of words that I didn't understand, I understood that, like me, the Danish prince resisted fighting when he might have confronted his opponent. Should I or shouldn't I?

When the boys punch me as they leave the classroom, the girl who sits behind me stands up and stops next to my chair. Wendy is the tallest kid in the class and the boys have to squeeze by her to pass. She blocks their punches. Now I feel embarrassed that a girl protects me. And why does Wendy decide to stand at my side?

After everyone has left the room, I take a book out of my desk and begin my homework. Miss Christie interrupts. "The principal has asked that we come to his office during this hour." At first I panic. What did I do wrong? Then I remember Miss Levy's lesson, "The principal of our school is our P-A-L." I hope she's right. Mentally I cross myself just as some of the kids have done before their turn at bat—just in case. It couldn't hurt.

The principal's office is well lit with windows facing north and east. Plants line a shelf under the windows. I can't remember his name and I search for a sign. Miss Christie shows me to a comfy tan seat. The chair has more cushions than anything we have in our living room. She walks into the inner sanctum. I stand up and walk to the rain spattered windows. Outside I see gloom and doom. I look at the door. Should I escape now?

I touch some of the plants and admire some yellow flowers. Their petals seem sticky and the leaves are silky smooth. I wish I knew more about plants but I don't even know the name—except in one corner is a small cactus. I know its name because we have one on a windowsill in our living room. I don't like our cactus because it's not friendly to the touch. I really like touching.

I see a magazine called *The Teacher*. Still standing, I start reading an article advising that grandparents should be invited to schools to tutor "reluctant readers." I write "reluctant" in my notebook. "What are you writing?" Miss Christie is standing behind me and I jump at the sound of her voice. "Oh, I'm sorry to startle you." I show her "reluctant" and explain that I need a dictionary. "I don't know enough English words yet," I tell her.

Miss Christie puts her arm around my shoulders and says, "Your ability with languages is why we're here today." She guides me to the principal's inner office and points to a straight chair near his desk. She sits in another chair, just like mine. We're facing the principal. Papa taught me to stand up when someone enters a room. The principal remains seated. He looks directly at me and begins talking, "I understand that English is not the language you grew up with."

"That's true."

"And Miss Christie tells me that you now speak as well as any student in your class."

I shrug.

The principal stands up from his cluttered desk. His office is not as A-U-S-T-E-R-E as Miss Christie's classroom. "I understand that you're a very good student and that you're sometimes bored in the classroom."

Did Miss Christie snitch on me? I was just beginning to trust her.

Mr. Principal continues, "I have a challenge for you. Do you like challenges?"

Uh oh. What kind of punishment is this challenge?

"On Monday a new student will join your class. He's from Palestine and he doesn't speak English. Miss Christie and I would like you to translate everything for him until he learns to speak English. That would be helpful to us and to the school."

"What language does he speak?" I ask.

"We don't know for sure. His mother speaks Russian and Hebrew and a little English that she learned in school. Unfortunately, Miss Christie and I only know English."

"I'll do my best." I want to call the principal by name, but I still don't know what it is. I'm puzzled by the challenge, but I think that I've figured out something they haven't mentioned. Maybe it hasn't occurred to them yet. If someone in his family speaks Hebrew, he's probably Jewish.

"Did you say he comes from Palestine?" I ask to be sure I heard correctly.

"Yes, Palestine," says Miss Christie, her first words since I came into Mr. Principal's private office.

"OK. I'll try." I may like this challenge.

"Thank you," says the principal. "I'll appreciate whatever you can do to help."

"I'll do my best," I say earnestly. And I mean it.

Miss Christie guides me out of the office and we walk silently to our classroom. Just as we enter, the bell rings. I put my coat over my shoulders and collect my books. I can see that the rain has stopped.

"*Yom tov*," I say as I open the classroom door.

Miss Christie looks at me quizzically. "What did you say?"

"I said 'good day' in Hebrew."

"I'm glad you're here," she sighs. "I want our new boy to have a good experience."

"I'll do my best."

* * *

I run home for my milk and cookie. I'm really excited. Omi, my grandmother, is home. I ask her about Palestine. She knows very little except that European Jews have been trying to go to Palestine in large numbers because they have not felt welcome in Germany and Poland.

The sun has come out. I put on a sweater and run to our nearby Carnegie library. The librarian knows me and gives me free rein of the entire building. However, today I need her help. First I need a map that will show me where Palestine is located. Then I need a book to tell me about that country. At the librarian's direction, I study an atlas and several encyclopedias. Just before five she walks over to the table where I'm reading and reminds me that on Friday the library closes at five. She has collected three books for me to check out. She invites me to her desk.

I'm in love with the librarian. She's clearly younger than my mother and she has long brown braids. The sign on her desk reads, "Miss Hannah Orlofsky." She once told me that her parents came from Russia. She expressed interest in my accent and wondered if I, too, came from Russia. When she's not busy we have good talks about books and she asks questions about what interests me. I feel as if I'm her favorite customer.

I must admit that I'm in love with several women including Edith Piaf and Rita Hayworth. I'd marry any of them in a minute if one of them would have me. Of my many loves, Miss Orlofsky is the only one I've met in person.

I show my library card and Miss Orlofsky gives me the books about Palestine. I also check out a medical book. She asks if I plan to be a physician. "Yes, yes," I say and I can feel my face blush. I really study the medical books so that I can learn about sex which, I assume, will be useful when I marry one or more of my true loves.

I arrive home just in time for supper. On Fridays we eat early so that Omi can go to synagogue—an eleven-block walk from our apartment. Omi begins by lighting the Sabbath candles. Then Papa leads us in saying the Friday evening prayers thanking God for bread and wine and work and just about everything Papa can think of. He thanks God for letting us live in America and for having a good student in the family and for our food. Papa is the most thankful person I know.

At this supper, I'm the star. My news is more dramatic than anyone else's accomplishments this day. I tell about the new boy whose mother speaks Russian and Hebrew. I summarize what I've learned about

Palestine, which is in the Middle East and populated mostly by Muslim Arabs. A few Christians live in and around Jerusalem and Bethlehem to be near the Christian holy sites. Jews have been going there in dribs and drabs during the early 20th century but began to seriously settle in communities during the 1930s as they were escaping the Holocaust. Since the war ended, they have been flocking to Palestine when they can get in. I report that apparently the British govern Palestine because of a mandate, although I haven't yet learned what a mandate does. It seems bad because the British are keeping Jews out as best they can. The Haganah and the Irgun, Jewish underground resistance forces, are organizing illegal immigration opportunities and violently resisting the British—even blowing up bridges. When I was reading about the Haganah at the library, I slowed down to think about Jewish resistance. Should I become a resistance fighter at P.S. 70?

I can't stop talking. I feel like a sermonizing rabbi. Jews live in *kibbutzim*, collectives, where they farm. Several books say that Jews are turning the desert into a garden and one book says that they are recreating the beauty of the Garden of Eden, which Arabs had turned into a desert. I don't know the accuracy of my information but I say it as though it is God's word. My mother keeps interrupting to remind me to eat but I'm much too excited. Halfway through my lecture, Mutti volunteers to do dishes and sends Omi off to synagogue. I know that Papa is interested because he asks for a second cup of coffee.

After dinner, I read more about Palestine and then I read *The Human Body*. When Omi comes home from synagogue, Mutti serves dessert. Papa has brought home a fresh apple pie that he received from one of the farm wives on his route. Papa calls them *his* farm wives. Finally it's his turn to tell about his day in New Jersey. He loves to tell about the people he meets all day—especially the children who are not yet of school age with whom he plays and to whom he gives candy. Candy may be as big a business expense as gasoline. He describes what people bought that day and why they needed it. Today he sold three housedresses, many yards of fabric to women who still make their own clothes, several pots and other kitchen utensils and a razor which will become a Christmas gift for one of the farmers. Papa loves his work. He loves talking to people.

He really understands their poverty and is happy to let them wait a week or two with their payment. In turn, of course, they love him and give him fresh apple pie.

Omi doesn't eat the pie. It isn't kosher. She only eats pie that she made or that she bought at the "right" store. We've probably contaminated the dishes but no one mentions that.

On Saturday morning, Omi persuades me to go to synagogue with her. I go reluctantly, but I can tell how urgently she wants to save my soul. I dress in my Sabbath finest and off we go.

Men and women sit separately at our synagogue so I sit downstairs with the men while Omi goes to the balcony. I don't like sitting with the men when Papa isn't there. Mostly I need him there so that I can ask permission to go outside and play with the other restless boys. When I'm on my own I can't give myself permission so I stay through the whole service. Omi and I walk home and Mutti has lunch ready.

After lunch, I go out to play with my friends. Mostly we roller skate. I see Josephine and skate a few rings around her and do some tricks. Why do I show off for Josephine? Is it her smile?

Tony wants to play marbles so I run upstairs to get my bag—a little white bag with a drawstring filled with wonderful pieces of glass. I don't understand how anyone can create such beauty. My favorite outdoor pastime after skating is "mibs." We play with marbles on a manhole cover. I lay the marble in the middle of my right forefinger and shoot it with my thumbnail. Mutti doesn't like me to play "mibs" because I kneel in the street and get my pants dirty. She also doesn't like me to touch the street because I'll pick up germs and bring them into the house. I never tell Mutti that I use my finger to trace the design on the manhole cover. I trace the pattern and the letters that spell "New York City." As soon as I come home she drags me into the bathroom to wash my hands with a brush.

At dinner, Omi leads us in the *Havdalah*, a mini-service ending the Sabbath. The Havdalah service transports us from the sacred world to the secular—the weekday world of work and school. Then Papa tells about his plans for tomorrow when he'll shop on Delancey Street where he buys wholesale. He will purchase several housedresses, some pots and cutlery and many bolts of yard goods for his customers. He'll also buy several pounds of hard candy for the children on his route. He pulls a fistful from a pocket. I'm allowed to select three pieces. I pick a green candy, a yellow one and a red one.

Then I read.

By Sunday morning I'm eager for Monday to arrive. I want to meet the new boy from Palestine. I'm a little afraid. What if he and I don't have enough language in common?

I always do homework on Sunday mornings while the other kids are at church. After lunch we play stickball. I'm assigned outfield—far out. That means I have to chase the ball when it rolls down the street toward First Avenue. When I'm at bat, the pitcher accidentally hits my stick. I run to first base—a black Chevy, and everyone cheers.

* * *

Monday morning arrives and there is no new boy. Miss Christie tests us in spelling and then we take turns reading from a book about knights in shining armor and princesses who are in grave danger. At about 10 o'clock, just before recess, the principal brings in Morris Pearlstein and tells us to welcome Morris to our school, to our neighborhood and to our country. Morris has light brown hair, freckles, blue eyes and thin lips. He doesn't look Semitic—Arabic or Jewish. Morris is assigned to the seat next to me and Anika is moved to the back of the room. I'm a little disappointed because I like Anika with her dark eyes and her name that rhymes with Chanukah. But I'm happy to make friends with the new boy. Mr. Principal leads the other kids out for recess leaving Miss Christie, Morris and me alone. Miss Christie busies herself at her desk. I realize this timing has all been staged. I turn to Morris and start talking in English. He knows a few words, but not enough to do a Farmer Brown arithmetic problem. He tries Hebrew and I have to slow him down. My religious school Hebrew is not good enough to keep up with Morris's speedy communication. However, we now have a little Hebrew and a little English. Morris tries Arabic. He's fluent in Arabic, but that's not useful to me at all. Next he tries German. Bingo! His German, while not as good as his primary languages of Hebrew and Arabic, is very good and we have a common language.

He tells me that he's been in this country a few weeks and that his parents are starting a business here. They plan to be in the U.S. permanently. He loves soccer and was an outstanding player in Palestine. I explain that the teacher has assigned me to be his interpreter, like Aaron was for Moses. He understands and we immediately know that we're both Jewish. I explain that we are the only two Jewish students in the school. He's shocked. How can that be? He grew up in a Jewish community and he describes how on his kibbutz the men took turns guarding against Arab raiders.

The other students return to our classroom. Miss Christie walks over to my chair. "Apparently you were able to converse. How did it go?"

I explain that Morris speaks more languages than I do and that we have at least one common language. At that moment I witness a miracle. Miss Christie smiles. She smiles a big full-faced smile. She's truly happy. Mr. Principal has been listening to the conversation between Miss Christie and me. He points a thumb toward the ceiling. I have no idea what that means. I hope that it doesn't mean the same as when Americans point their middle finger into the air. I'll have to ask Bobby Schneider about this new gesture. Bobby never makes fun of me for being foreign.

* * *

Our afternoon at school goes quickly. Morris and I whisper as much as we like. We catch up on each other's lives and when Miss Christie wonders what we are saying I lie that I'm translating. School is fun.

Morris and I walk home together and discover that he lives one building to the east of where I live. We're neighbors. It's Monday afternoon and I have to go to Hebrew school so I invite Morris to go with me. I want to show off my new friend who speaks Hebrew as well as the rabbi. But first we stop at his apartment.

Morris introduces me to his mother whose English is fair and whose German is as good as Morris's. She explains that they spoke German at home in Palestine because that's Mr. Pearlstein's first language. It seems that Morris's dad also speaks a little English, fluent Hebrew and a little Russian. No one but Morris speaks Arabic, a language he learned from Arab friends on the street.

Mrs. Pearlstein has milk and cake waiting for Morris and invites me to join in. I ask them to start without me while I go home to tell Mutti where I am. I don't want her to worry about me and I have to collect my Hebrew text book and my Bible studies text. I run out the door and leap down five flights of stairs taking three steps at a time. I have a new friend and an interesting adoptive family.

Back at the Pearlsteins', I gobble down milk and cake and become acquainted with Morris's mom. She has brown curly hair and is a little chubbier than slim Mutti. She's wearing an apron over a brown dress.

We run to Hebrew school because I'm now very late. The rabbi scolds me and then forgives when I introduce my friend who speaks to the rabbi politely in fluent Hebrew. They talk fast and I have no idea what they're talking about. I go to another corner with the other Hebrew school students to tell them about the new Jewish kid.

On the way home, I learn that the Pearlsteins are secular Jews. They don't believe in God but they are loyal to Jewish traditions. Morris invites me for dinner. We check with his mom. Then the two of us go to my apartment so Morris can meet Mutti and Omi. Papa comes home and joins the conversation. Everyone is very pleased that I have a Jewish friend in the neighborhood and "he's such a nice boy." When we finally arrive back at Morris's apartment, Mr. Pearlstein has returned home from his job. He greets me in English and German. Mr. Pearlstein is about the same height as Morris and me but he's got broad shoulders and is built like a box. He looks strong, like my Papa.

During dinner we talk about the Holocaust, Palestinian politics, life under Russian Communism and the Pearlsteins' plans for the future. I'm delighted to learn that all plan to take English lessons. I'd hate to be a translator for life.

On Tuesday, we take school seriously. I involve Morris in the lessons, introduce him to classmates, warn him about which kids don't like Jews and I remind Miss Christie to give Morris the reading assignments and workbooks so that he can keep up with the others. After only one day I'm certain that Morris will be the second smartest student in the school—and I'll have to work hard to keep my number one ranking.

We walk home together and discover that we both know some Yiddish. We have another common language. We rush home to tell Mrs. Pearlstein and to have milk and cake. Mrs. Pearlstein then has some chores for Morris and explains that they will have an early dinner. They have signed up for English classes and the first session is tonight.

At our dinner, my family wants to know all about the "nice boy" and his family. I tell as many details as I can remember. After dinner I do a little homework, study *The Human Body* and listen to the news on our radio with Papa.

On Wednesday at recess, Herbie calls Morris a dirty Jew. Morris doesn't understand. "*Schmutziger Jude.*" I translate the words literally and explain that it's an expression and that I don't know if Herbie actually means "dirty" or "dusty." Morris wants to hear the expression again so that he can learn to recognize it. I tell Herbie that Morris wants to hear him say it again. "Dirty Jew," says Herbie looking straight at Morris. A crowd has gathered. Morris calmly looks at me and then at Herbie. Suddenly, before Miss Christie can intercede, Morris starts pummeling Herbie so hard that within seconds he has blood running from his nose and mouth. He has cuts and bruises all over his face and his clothes are torn. He's lying on the ground screaming and his eyes are already swelling before Miss Christie can grab Morris. Morris hasn't broken a sweat and his clothes are as neat as ever. It turns out that Morris is a fighter and likes it. He explains that he had so many Arab friends because they "respected" him.

When both mothers come to the principal's office on Friday morning, I'm Morris's "attorney." I tell the "dirty Jew" story as dramatically as possible. I add that Herbie has called me even worse names. "A fine welcome to our country," I add innocently. I emphasize "our" country as though I weren't also a foreigner. Mr. Principal makes Morris and Herbie shake hands. Morris, with his innocent face, blue eyes and freckles reaches his hand out quickly. Herbie is slow to agree, demonstrating to all that "poor Morris" is the innocent victim in this dispute.

On our way to the classroom, I tell Morris in German how happy I am that Herbie has two swollen eyes and band-aids on his face. I report that I overheard that Herbie might have a broken nose. I add that

I feel guilty that I'm so happy. Miss Christie asks what we're talking about. I lie that I've told Morris that he should avoid fighting. I translate my lie for Morris and he smirks.

After my episode with Alfred there were no more dirty Jews on my block. After Wednesday's recess, dirty Jews vanish from the school yard.

XXI. GOOD-BYE TO P.S. 70

O N FRIDAY AFTERNOON I explain early release for Christian religious school to Morris. Then he and Miss Christie have a nice conversation with me translating like mad. They talk about schools in Palestine and Morris's grades and how teachers behave in the Palestinian classroom. Miss Christie is trying to figure out how much arithmetic, history and geography Morris has learned. Recalling Wednesday's pummeling of Herbie, she is also concerned about Morris becoming a street fighter. I'm not at all concerned. I love my bodyguard and I'm no longer afraid to fight. Between us we can lick everyone. But we rarely have to fight. We've been accepted, more or less.

Morris and I become brothers. Like brothers, we compete for our parents' affection. Of course we each have our own parents but Morris' parents love me and my parents love Morris. We help each other succeed at school and at sports and we protect one another on the playground. I'm not very good at my Hebrew lessons and Morris tutors me. I, in turn, help him with English. Like brothers, we argue about everything. If Morris wants to go to a movie, I want to ride my bike. If I want to see a movie, Morris wants to visit a museum. It's good to have a brother. We didn't know it before, but as solo children, we each have dreamed about brotherhood.

Most of all we argue world politics. Morris's parents are avid Zionists. They want a Jewish state that includes Jerusalem. While they don't believe in God, they believe that the Jewish people have a history in and around Jerusalem. They believe that Europe's history of pogroms and the recent Holocaust provide evidence that the Jewish people need a state of their own. I, the escapee from the Holocaust, argue that a Jewish state would become a theocracy with Orthodox Jews running the show. I point to Saudi Arabia, Yemen and the Vatican. Mrs. Pearlstein points out that the Vatican is not really a country in the same sense. An unfair example. I love having dinner with the Pearlsteins because, unlike my parents, they're so well read and argue so well.

Morris and I continue to bicker about Palestine as we walk home from school. We read newspapers voraciously to buttress our points of view. That leads to other arguments. Was Truman right in dropping an atom bomb? Morris says no. I say yes. Should the British help Jews settle in Palestine? We both say yes. Is Palestine the "promised land?" Morris says "yes." I insist that he has to tell me who promised it—a dilemma for Morris because he's a secular Jew who doesn't believe in God.

Morris is intrigued by my Orthodox home with kosher meals and blessings for everything. In turn, his parents reflect my secret desire to have a world without God. Morris and I struggle to develop an understanding of creation. As sixth graders, our scientific learning is not well developed. But we don't know that.

* * *

By the end of April, Morris rarely needs a translator. Some parts of American culture are still foreign to both of us and we rely on Bobby Schneider for explanations. But Bobby can't explain why Americans don't play soccer and why most have so little respect for learning. Morris tells Bobby that most Palestinian Arabs don't care about schooling either and that they don't read books. Morris says Arabs are lazy. Neither Bobby nor I have ever met an Arab so we can't judge.

One Friday afternoon Miss Christie asks me if I've told Morris how clever I am at school work. I blush, look at my shoes, and say, "No."

"Tell him now," commands Miss Christie. I shake my head indicating another "No."

"If you don't blow your own horn, no one will blow it for you." While I struggle with this piece of philosophy, Morris has captured the sense of the conversation. He tells Miss Christie that he already knows.

"Fred is almost as smart as I am," jokes Morris. We all laugh and Miss Christie acknowledges that Morris is indeed a prize student.

One week later, Miss Christie tells me that the P.S. 70 teachers have picked me to give a speech at the June graduation. "You'll receive an award from the Daughters of the American Revolution for being our best student and for being a good citizen."

On the walk home from school, Morris and I laugh at the idea of a Daughter of the American Revolution. How many such daughters are still alive? They must be very old. We each describe our vision of such an old woman. Would one of these old women actually totter to P.S. 70 to give me the award? Would she have a cane? A wheelchair? Would she be wearing an 18th-century dress? Our fantasies continue until we arrive at our street.

After milk and cookies, I run to the library. I usually visit Miss Orlofsky without Morris. I guess I want to keep her for myself. Do brothers have to share everything?

I tell the librarian about the Daughters of the American Revolution. She explains that they aren't really daughters. They may be many generations removed from the Revolution, but they are related to someone who lived in the American colonies at the time of the Revolution. Miss Orlofsky adds that they are generally a right-wing organization not very fond of foreigners and Jews. She remembers that they opposed Jewish immigration during the war. I wonder if Miss Christie didn't tell them everything about me.

* * *

It's early June and we're at graduation. Papa bought me a new blue blazer for the occasion. I wear it with light gray pants and the black shoes that Mutti shines before every special occasion. I love the gold buttons on the jacket.

Miss Christie helped me write my graduation speech. Morris and my mother took turns listening as I rehearsed. I've memorized all the words.

The time has come to say good-bye to good old 70 and separate to other schools to continue our education. We have learned much but we still have a great deal left to learn.

My speech goes on for several paragraphs. I'm not listening. It's all rote memory now and my lips move without my brain paying attention.

Instead I look around the assembly hall from my place on the stage. All the sixth-grade students are watching me. The students from each class are sitting with their teacher. I can see Miss Christie sitting with my classmates. Behind the graduating students sit many of the students' mothers. It's a Tuesday afternoon and the fathers are probably at work. I look for Mutti, but I can't pick her out from the many women in the back rows.

I'm finished talking and I walk back toward my chair at the back of the stage while I listen to applause. The principal catches my arm and guides me back to the lectern. He lies about the joys of the past six years and about his wonderful students at P.S. 70. I see Morris in the front row. He's holding his hand over his nose to make me laugh. Morris is always teasing me about my big nose. He has a cute little nose and freckles—not very Jewish.

I'm becoming impatient standing next to the principal all this time. I still don't know his name. Finally Mr. Principal looks directly at me and says some words that surely will make Mutti proud. Then he talks about our wonderful country and goes on with patriotic words that will make the old Daughters proud. Finally he holds a fancy little box in the air and shows the audience the medal and ribbon inside. He closes the box, hands it to me and then gives me a framed certificate. I don't know how to hold all the goodies. Finally he guides me back to my seat.

A man dressed in black with a funny collar steps forward and says some words about Jesus. We all sing "America the Beautiful."

America! America!
God shed His grace on thee,
And crown thy good with brotherhood
From sea to shining sea!

Mr. Principal wishes us a happy summer and dismisses us and we're no longer in sixth grade.

XXII. LESSONS FROM PAPA

I T'S THE SUMMER of 1946, one year after the end of World War II, and, I am almost 13 years old. A few months shy of being a bar mitzvah boy. Surprised teachers praise my improved English language skills although I still feel foreign, an outsider. A few years earlier we were indigent refugees from Nazi Germany. We're still relatively poor, but Papa insists that he will take "the boy" on a week-long vacation as a pre-bar mitzvah present—a bonding experience that he never had with his father.

Papa has steady income. He worked hard and climbed the occupational ladder. He no longer has to haul garbage as a janitor in a New York tenement. He no longer sweats in a hot bakery. He no longer works under a foreman in a shoe factory. Papa has earned this holiday.

Papa and I are going on a trip. That was decided. But where should we go? The family gathers at dinner to explore vacation options. For the past two weeks we've studied advertisements in the fat Sunday newspaper. Papa can't afford the time and money to travel very far—no farther than a few hours from New York City. Because of the exciting conversation, dinner lasts long enough for Papa to drink a second cup of coffee.

Mutti's idea is to visit the Catskill Mountains where wealthy American Jews, booked into a hotel for two or three weeks, are pampered and enjoy entertainment by Jewish "Borsht Circuit" comedians. However, we can't afford such a luxurious holiday. A few years later, as a high school student, I worked in the Catskills first as a busboy and later as a waiter. Mutti hoped that I'd earn some money toward college and, "God willing," meet some nice, *rich* Jewish girls.

Friends at the synagogue recommend the chicken farms in New Jersey, which are becoming fashionable destinations among moderate income German Jewish refugee families like us. The farms are close enough to New York City and are owned by other German Jews trying to generate new careers in a new country. Mutti worries that combining a working farm with hospitality might mean that guests will have to share the dirty work. She was right. Years later, when I was working in the Catskills, my parents tried a chicken farm vacation. Mutti thought that feeding chickens and retrieving eggs was "icky." Papa appreciated the opportunity to get close to the earth. The experience reminded him of his rural youth.

Papa learned from a work colleague that the Pocono Mountains in Pennsylvania are an inexpensive vacation destination, easily accessible by train from Penn Station and with healthy mountain air and lots of hiking trails. Papa loves long walks. We pass around some of his friend's colorful brochures with pictures of beautifully appointed hotels, being careful to not get food stains on them. We discuss each photo and finally agree that the Poconos would be a good choice.

The following Thursday, before dinner, Papa and I walk to a neighborhood travel agency. On Thursdays the shop stays open late to accommodate people like Papa who work during normal business hours. As we stroll, Papa tells me how much he looks forward to this adventure with his boy, his only son, his only child. I'm surprised. Papa hardly ever discusses his feelings so directly.

At the travel agency, an attractive young woman helps us select a hotel from the many options. Papa asks if I would like to ride on a horse. "Oh yes," slips out with great enthusiasm. I picture riding with the Lone Ranger and Tonto. My uncharacteristic passion makes the decision. Papa points to the picture of the hotel that offers horseback riding. When I hear the price, I almost faint, but Papa calmly writes a check that will serve as a deposit on our room. The young travel agent gives us each a peppermint candy and assures us that she will take care of all the details. The candy makes her seem all the more wise and trustworthy.

We're almost ready for our trip to the Poconos—just father and son. Mutti packs carefully and completely. She packs warm clothes—long sleeved shirts, sweaters, hats—for this summer trip into the mountains. Mutti is certain that cold breezes or wet weather causes the dreaded "grippe," if not pneumonia.

I await the train ride eagerly. Our local Carnegie library has books about trains and the Pennsylvania Railroad. I study photos of the New York City train station and the engines that will pull our train.

Being with Papa is a big deal. I am 12 and idolize my Papa. Bombs and guns and Gestapo made me a little fearful of life. Papa represents stability and goodness. He is old-fashioned and often naïve. I am already better educated than he. However, to me he represents virtue. He models the value of hard work. This vacation, so soon after starting life over in a new country, is evidence of his belief in building our future on the back of work.

Papa demonstrates kindness every day. Each holiday is celebrated with checks to different charities and every success, however small— a good grade, a raise in pay, recovery from an illness—is worthy of a contribution to an appropriate cause. Last week on the Fourth of July, Papa donated money to a veterans' organization. "Tikun olam," he tells me often. Repair the world.

While he warns that I might become a "bowery bum" if I don't apply myself to the fullest, he never passes a homeless person without sharing a coin or two. Papa teaches me the art of generosity to friend and stranger alike. Some of my school friends aren't close to their fathers. Some even talk about hate. I don't understand. Papa is my model.

We take the subway to Penn Station. Two beggars sit at the subway entrance with hats out. Papa looks at me, "See, you better work hard at school or you'll sit on cold cement in dirty clothes." Then he reaches into his pocket, retrieves some coins and divides them between the two men.

I am dressed in brown slacks, a tan, short-sleeved shirt, open at the collar, and a new checkered sport coat. Papa wears a brown suit and a white shirt. He sports the crimson and gold tie I gave him for his birthday. The salesman assured me that it was the kind of tie worn by Harvard men. I assumed that was good. Papa wears a brown felt hat while I'm bare-headed. Each of us carries a small suitcase.

On the subway, Papa reads a newspaper he finds lying on a seat. I watch every station, not wanting to miss our stop. I had memorized the stations and alert Papa two stops in advance of Penn Station—just in case.

We follow signs from the subway up an escalator to a long passageway lined with enormous advertising signs, up another escalator to the train station, a huge marble hall with hundreds, perhaps thousands, of people milling about. I find a large, magical sign with constantly changing information. Near the top is the information the travel lady has written on a piece of paper for us. I have memorized the note. I have memorized the travel brochure. I have every detail locked in my head.

"Papa, look there," I point. "There is the train number and the track number and it says the train will leave promptly in 27 minutes." Papa buys some Chiclets chewing gum at a candy stand and leads us to track number 8.

The train ride goes just as planned. Above our seats is a rack where Papa places our suitcases and his hat. Papa calls it a "hat rack." We talk about earlier train rides that were more frightening than this one. A few years back, on our escape route from the Nazis, we traveled on trains from Holland to Belgium. Our documents were always suspect and even after crossing the German border, we were certain that every uniformed official was hunting Jews. At every station we expected Gestapo to board the train and when they didn't, we still had to deal with customs agents and train attendants who spoke languages new to us. On this trip to the Poconos, we feel safe. No Nazis pursue us and my English is good enough to translate almost any American situation.

I look out the window and watch city slums turn to countryside. I enjoy the abundant trees and occasional cows and horses. Rows and rows of tall plants stand in the fields. Papa calls them "maize." After a while, Papa falls asleep. He seems to be starting his vacation early. I'm much too excited to close my eyes.

Just as the brochure promised, a bus from the hotel picks us up at the station. The olive green Mountain Transit Company bus takes visitors to and from several hotels. The burgundy seats are clean but the windows are so dirty that I can hardly admire the scenery. I can make out mountains and trees, tractors and wagons. After a 15-minute ride, the bus driver drops us off in front of a grand building. A young man immediately picks up our suitcases and hustles inside before we have an opportunity to study the vast expanse of green, the many trees in the distance and the well-groomed flower garden at our feet. I'm already disappointed because I see no horses and no cowboys.

The young man with our suitcases directs us to the hotel check-in counter. I've never been to a resort and hold tight to Papa's sleeve. Sure, I am almost a man. My pending bar mitzvah proves that. And yet Papa's sleeve provides some extra assurance.

The lobby feels like a large musty living room out of the 19th century. An ornate carpet, mostly green with large pink and red flowers, looks as if it had once been expensive and elegant before its wool was tattered by too many shoes. Floor lamps stand at attention next to enormous overstuffed chairs enveloping a few elderly men reading newspapers. The counter, also elegant and worn, made of a dark hardwood, consists of three check-in stations, each staffed by a man in a blue uniform with lots of gold braid, designed for an admiral demoted to hotel clerk.

My father walks up to one of the clerks and in his best broken English, announces, "We have a reservation for a whole week."

"Sir, we don't accept dogs or Jews," says the clerk.

Without missing a beat Papa looks to the right and to the left. "Jews," he shouts in a frightened tone. "Jews. Where are Jews?"

I recognize the trick. The clerk doesn't. Apparently Papa's act convinces the clerk that we're not Jewish. He apologetically explains that the resort has never allowed Jewish clientele. "Of course!" says Papa. "I understand."

Encouraged by Papa's sympathy, the clerk begins to babble assurances about cleanliness and racial purity. "Had it not been for the Jews," he whines, "we wouldn't have had this terrible war with the Germans."

Papa's occasional, "Yes, yes," loosens the clerk's tongue even more. He leans close to Papa and looks straight into his eyes.

"The Jews control the banks in New York and they're greedy to the core. I went to one of their clothing stores to buy a shirt, but I left. I could tell that the Jew was getting ready to cheat me." A momentary pause for air and the clerk wanders in a new direction. "Everyone knows that they rarely bathe and I can smell a Jew two blocks away."

A line is growing behind us. I dare not look around and silently pray that no one can hear the conversation at the desk. Papa says nothing but an occasional "Yes." His nod at appropriate moments works like a windup key on the clerk.

"And they're anti-religion, anti-Christ. Surely I'll not meet them in heaven." Ever more energized, the clerk rambles on, but by now I'm hoping the clerk will throw us out. I don't want to leave Papa's hard-earned money at a resort where there is no room for "our kind." Papa, too, has heard enough. Apparently he's satisfied that he has created a fine joke. Papa grasps the clerk's forearm holding him close and in a loud whisper says, "My boy and I really are Jewish. It seems you can't smell us after all."

Quietly Papa tells the clerk that we'll not be staying at his resort. This time Papa is looking directly into the clerk's eyes. Papa firmly demands an immediate return of his deposit, payment to cover the cost of our wasted train tickets, a free taxi ride back to the train depot and compensation for our trouble. Papa tells the clerk that if he has not made himself clear, he can make his demands much more loudly. While Papa says this, he looks at the men reading newspapers and then at the line behind us.

I'm disappointed with Papa. I want him to make more of a scene. I imagine a free-for-all fight like I've seen in cowboy movies. I would like to see the elegant furniture smashed. At least a few mirrors should have been cracked. Mutti would have made a drama involving managers and bystanders and maybe police. But Papa is always a gentle man.

When Papa releases his grip, the clerk confers with an older man who invites us into a tiny private office. The man writes a check, gives some orders and a bellboy comes to pick up our suitcases. Within five minutes we are in a taxi on our way back to the railroad station.

While traveling to the Poconos, I had told Papa about the Lone Ranger and Tonto. Now, as we wait for the next train, Papa explains that Tonto would not have been welcome at this hotel either.

On the train back to the city, I struggle with my distress that America does not quite live up to its promise. Our experience in the hotel underlines the many times bullies on the streets of New York have threatened to pummel me because they saw the Hebrew books that I carried.

XXII. LESSONS FROM PAPA

I learned to outrun the bullies. The occasional swastika chalked on New York sidewalks frightens me. And now this confrontation with the hotel clerk reminds me of the sign on our air raid shelter in Hannover: "Juden verboten."

I suggest that we spend the vacation week planning to blow up the hotel where Jews are not admitted. I've already devised a few improbable scenarios including World War II hand grenades and land mines. Papa, not partial to explosives, proposes an alternative. "Each day this next week we'll have a different adventure in the city—just the two of us. We'll explore New York and you can select some of the places we visit."

"Shouldn't we teach those hotel people a lesson?"

"No," Papa says. "We'll report them to a Jewish agency and let some sophisticated lawyers deal with the problem. We're not killers."

* * *

We adopt Papa's plan. One day we go hiking in Van Cortland Park— a one-hour subway ride from our apartment. Another day we go to a movie and a stage show at Radio City Music Hall. We let Mutti join us for that.

The highlight of this non-Pocono vacation is the day we walk to the Metropolitan Museum of Art. I love museums and especially the Metropolitan, less than two miles from our apartment. I usually walk there alone. I try to understand how the Impressionists made their paintings with short, thick strokes of color. I marvel at huge tapestries that tell dramatic stories with colored yarn. I never leave without stopping to see one or two naked women with their bosoms exposed—sex education for a twelve-year-old.

On this trip I am not alone. Papa lets me do the planning. We walk west to Central Park and then turn north toward 92nd Street. It is a warm, sunny summer day and we walk slowly, talking all the way—commenting on the many images that meet our eyes. Papa needs help translating some signs into German. He misses their meaning. More important, he sometimes misses the cultural significance. Not all these products were available in Germany.

"Why are they showing that?" asks Papa when he sees a display of corn on the cob at an expensive Lexington Avenue food shop.

"Because they want to sell it," I respond foolishly.

"In the city? Food for pigs in the city?"

And then I understand that in Germany corn is food for pigs while in the U.S. it can be fed to animals and eaten by sophisticated consumers on Lexington Avenue as a delicacy. We both learn a lesson.

A record store poster promises "jazzy" music with images of black musicians.

"What means 'Jazzy?'" Papa asks.

"Jazz" needs more than a literal translation. It needs an introduction to "Satchmo" and to a new sound. Papa helps by transforming a New York jazz club into a Berlin cabaret.

"Jazz" suggests musical improvisation, a new concept to Papa. I don't even know how to translate "improvisation" into German. With lots of effort, we finally agree that Papa is improvising a new life in the United States.

A few blocks away from our shabby tenement neighborhood, Park Avenue comes into view: THE Park Avenue. Only in America can tenements and elegant buildings protected by doormen dressed in what appear to be spiffy band uniforms, sit only three blocks apart. The fancy doormen are constantly alert so that they can spy residents coming from inside their buildings and those approaching from the street, ready to enter. "Good afternoon, Mrs. Laslo. Nice to see you, Mr. Swenson."

Will we, from cobblestoned Second Avenue, need a visa and passport to cross this street? We can't even imagine the inside of these buildings. When we try to peek into the entryway of a fancy building with an elegant awning, the doorman looks at us suspiciously and straightens himself to appear more menacing. Our glimpse into high society is abruptly shut off. Two years later, when I become a delivery boy at a local pharmacy, I'll have opportunities to use the service entrance into these buildings and to peek into spotlessly clean kitchens with freshly painted green walls where deliveries are made only at back doors. I will meet maids wearing black dresses. Their white frilly aprons will remind me of my mother's doilies. Tips will be fabulous.

Madison Avenue features elegant apartment buildings mixed with stylish shops. An occasional high-end gourmet grocery with an Italian name seduces us with delicious smells of cheeses whose names are quite foreign to us. Delicately spiced sauces are tempting, but the price is not. Nearby, a pharmacy, calling itself "Apotheke," displays antique vials and bottles, fine perfumes and hand-made greeting cards.

Along our meandering route, Papa asks questions. What did I learn at P.S. 70? Am I eager to attend junior high school in the fall? Do I want to be a doctor? What books am I reading? Do I still talk to Anna who had been my "girlfriend" when I was eight? Perhaps he wants to guess if I might ever live in this neighborhood and buy the available fineries.

I complain about the afternoon Hebrew school where a few boys sit around a long table with the rabbi in an inadequately lit room. Dark wood and heavy maroon carpeting give the room a warm but depressing feeling. The rabbi never praises and often scolds. Unlike Jewish tradition which encourages argument (didn't Jacob wrestle with God's angel?), our elderly, heavily bearded Orthodox rabbi doesn't like us to question or disagree. Memorization is the watchword and creativity is not permitted in the shul. Papa doesn't care much about my need to rebel against the rabbi. His main concern is that I do a wonderful job at my bar mitzvah ceremony.

Public School 70, on the other hand, was grand. I learned a great deal and the teachers gave me out-of-class responsibilities such as using the ditto machine and running errands to the principal's office. Papa is interested in the details. He wants to be sure that I work hard so that I can become a professional, preferably a doctor, one of the few professionals poor folks encounter on a regular basis.

Papa never had much experience with schools. He tells me that he went to a one-room country school for a few years. Each afternoon he had to help on his parents' small farm. He learned more about horses and cows than about reading and writing. When he was ten, he was sent to be apprenticed to the owner of a dry goods shop in a big city. There he learned numbers by figuring dimensions of textiles and calculating costs and profits. He learned about colors and thread counts. No geography lessons beyond his customer base. No philosophy beyond his prayer books. No collections of short stories by Kafka or novels by Hemingway. Only Bible stories.

We arrive at Fifth Avenue with its grand mansions and museums. We watch strangers strolling by, dressed in tasteful summer outfits. Chic dresses in reds, pinks and yellows, embellished with ribbon to show off hips and thighs, are topped off with large straw hats decorated with silk flowers of every variety. Many men wear Palm Beach suits, white with blue stripes. Although men's hats are in fashion, on this summer day, most of the men, dressed, for warm weather, are hatless.

We find an entrance to Central Park, turn north and wander on, chatting sporadically. Papa isn't much of an intellectual conversationalist. No deep philosophy. No commentary about great books. Sometimes he ventures an opinion about world politics. He likes to listen to news programs on the radio and occasionally he argues with Walter Winchell who speaks to us from inside the wooden device with two knobs that sits on top of the ice box. Winchell wants to punish the Germans and the Italians for the harm they did. Papa speaks quietly to the radio— and in German: "The horrible war is over," he insists. "Let's not prolong the horror. Perhaps, if Americans demonstrate goodness and justice, the rest of the world will follow."

Mutti sides with Walter Winchell. "Let them suffer," she snorts.

What I like best about our walks are Papa's tidbits about manliness. He teaches me, for example, that a gentleman should always walk on the outside, the curbside of the street.

"Why should I walk on the outside?" I really want to know why it is good to be a gentleman, but I start with an easier question.

"A gentleman," I learn as we meander in the park, "walks on the outside because occasionally horses run wild and the man must protect his lady."

That made sense when horses were more common on city streets. In 1946, one sees horses only on Second Avenue, old weary horses pulling vegetable and fruit wagons. Papa agrees and speculates that perhaps now it might be better for a gentleman to walk on the building side to protect his lady from drunks and robbers. This is, after all, New York, city of crime.

I learn that a gentleman should always precede a woman when walking up stairs to avoid the temptation to look up her skirt.

"Therefore," I counter, "a woman should always be first when descending." I am glad that Papa doesn't ask if I ever look up skirts when climbing steps.

Papa suggests that we find a bench in the sunshine—never in the shade. Sun is healthy. I hope we will discover an ice cream vendor before we sit.

A voice from the side calls, "Freddy." I turn to see Miss Levy, my fifth-grade teacher, sitting on a bench. I introduce my father who looks quite uncomfortable. He speaks English poorly and with quite an accent. Papa always feels inadequate in situations where he has to converse with a "learned" person. He clasps his hands, fingers interwoven tightly, and nods a great deal to assure the speaker (or himself) that he understands. He had hoped for an anonymous walk in the park without the embarrassment of meeting an American teacher.

Miss Levy, partial to dark blue dresses with stripes or large dots, wears no hat, allowing us to see her graying hair pushed up into a bun. In class I admire her trim figure for what, at my age, seems to be an "old" woman of fifty. She looks more like a Park Avenue lady than most of the dowdy-looking teachers at P.S. 70. Miss Levy invites us to sit with her and so we do. Papa sits in the middle. Miss Levy begins by praising me. "Freddy is a remarkably good student." Papa says that he hopes that is true. "One of the best I've ever met," she adds. Papa beams. In Yiddish one would say he kvells.

Having put Papa at ease, she proceeds to ask him about his early years. She wants him to talk about the years before we came to this country. Is Miss Levy Jewish? Certainly she has a Jewish name. She never lets on and, of course, we never ask. However, after our Pocono experience, it would be reassuring to meet a fellow Jew. There are very few in our neighborhood.

Miss Levy praises my father's ability with the English language after only a few years in the States. Papa, always humble, has trouble accepting the compliment. No, his English is not good, he claims quite accurately. "Freddy's English is good, mine not good."

Then Miss Levy raises a question. "Do you think in English or in German?" she asks Papa. I had completed sixth grade but I had not yet explored such a profound linguistic problem. Thank you Miss Levy.

The question remains unanswered while Papa thinks about its meaning. He looks down as if hoping to find the answer written on his shiny leather shoes. He frowns. He bites a finger nail. "Do you think in English or in German?" We wait.

Finally Papa allows that he thinks in German.

"Then, do you have to translate your thoughts while we're conversing?" inquires Miss Levy. Again Papa does not find the answer written on his shoes. More nail chewing.

Clearly these ideas are as new to Papa as they are to me. He has to think. "Yes, yes, yes," he finally blurts out. Papa is now certain, and he explains that when Miss Levy speaks in English he translates into German, "inside my head." He formulates an answer and translates that into his broken English. Now I understood why he likes to speak German with me. He doesn't have to translate.

Miss Levy is impressed. "Continue to speak German to Freddy," she encourages, "so that he doesn't forget his mother tongue. Then he can be an excellent student in two languages."

"Bilingual" and "bicultural" are concepts that I will learn much later. Right now I am happy with the new insight.

Papa is still kvelling.

Miss Levy, the perfect lady, finds a way to bring closure to our little talk. Papa and I continue on our walk toward the Museum. He links his arm in mine and I sense that he is proud. Papa is not one to express his pleasure directly. Instead he suggests, "Let's find ice cream." I understand.

* * *

We arrive at the Metropolitan Museum of Art content with our walk, our conversation, our visit with Miss Levy and our ice cream. Could a vacation in the Poconos have been so satisfying? Father and son bonding.

This is my father's first ever trip to a museum. He had a rural history. Papa certainly had little of the "culture" that comes with museums and concerts and big city life. Having left school after finishing fourth grade, he hadn't been provided with much opportunity for developing familiarity with the fine arts. Yet, for me, my father is willing to venture into a new world.

First Papa and I enter the Egypt wing and I explain the time frame and the culture of the pharaohs, a theme Papa translates to the exodus out of Egypt and the evil pharaoh mentioned at our Passover Seder. This Jewish context helps him understand the notion of a different culture in a different time. He is obviously proud of his knowledgeable almost-a-man son.

We view some abstract art that neither of us likes or understands. Then we visit a room displaying early Italian Renaissance art. I love the massive paintings with rich colors. I love the stories from Greek literature. Can I run as fast as Mercury? Does Zeus look like the God of Abraham? And I am fascinated by the biblical paintings, albeit they often tell stories from the New Testament, not a part of *our* Bible. I've studied our Bible in Hebrew school and wonder why some painters depict the stories differently from the pictures in my head.

My father relates well to the agricultural settings. He knows a great deal about horses and cattle—new information to this kid born in a large city and raised in an even bigger one. I learn more about Papa's rural upbringing as he puts himself into the scenes. We both marvel at the skill of the artists.

In a room dedicated to Flemish art, we come upon a pair of Rubens paintings. Large, buxom, naked women! I've visited them often with the curiosity of an adolescent. I've dreamed of touching these big bosomed thrushes with their ample bottoms. However, on this visit I'm a bit embarrassed. What is Papa thinking? We focus on one of the paintings in which we view a fleshy woman from behind. I wait.

I'm guessing that Papa, too, is in an awkward position. First, he is with a young son looking at a nude. Second, having no experience with museums, especially with paintings, he struggles to comment about the art. Fortunately, we speak in German. I have no worry that others around us will be shocked by our conversation.

"Now there," my father announces, "is a woman who is built to put in a good day's work on the farm."

XXIII. ...AND GOD CREATED BEGINNINGS

The first three words of the Torah are *"Bereshit bara Elohim."*
Traditional translations read, *"In the beginning God created..."*
Modern language scholars with a more sophisticated appreciation of ancient
Hebrew grammar suggest another translation: *"God created beginnings."*

ALWAYS FULL OF HOPE, Papa celebrates beginnings. Although he
was forced to leave his German homeland at the age of 38, arriving to poverty, a new culture, a new language, a new career—still
Papa loves beginnings. Every tomorrow is full of possibilities. Every day
is New Year's Day.

Papa feels doubly blessed that we Jews have two opportunities to
celebrate a New Year: Rosh Hashanah and the secular New Year. Rosh
Hashanah, the Jewish New Year, comes in the fall, ten days before Yom
Kippur, the day when our name is written in the book of life. Or not. The
days between Rosh Hashanah and Yom Kippur are the days of atonement when Jews reflect on their sins and ask God's forgiveness.

Rosh Hashanah 1946 comes one year after the end of World War II
and just three weeks before my bar mitzvah, the day when, according
to Jewish law, I become a man. The days of atonement are difficult for
me. Rabbi Reuben, my Hebrew school teacher, has convinced me that
we are all judged by a punishing God. That's how he keeps his hyperactive students' noses in their books. I am convinced that my sins are too
many and too great to be forgiven no matter how much I atone and beg
forgiveness of parents, teachers and God. Each year I am convinced that
I will not be written in the Book of Life and that the ten days after Rosh

Hashanah will be my last days on earth. I secretly write a will: marbles to Morris, roller skates to Ralph, books to Anna ...

My fear is abstract and irrational. Surely I sinned and I am sorry. My real concern, however, is that I cannot atone for all the sins I had unknowingly committed. Six million Jews had been killed by the Nazis—many burned in the crematoria of Auschwitz and Dachau. Millions more suffered torture and slave labor. Was God punishing all these people for their sins? Was the book of life mostly empty of Jews during those war years?

In 1946, Papa spends the first day of Rosh Hashanah in our east Manhattan synagogue, Kehilath Jeshurun, just as he spent every Rosh Hashanah in synagogue except when he served in Nazi slave labor. He prays from dawn 'til dusk. My mother and grandmother also go to pray. They sit in the balcony reserved for women and girls. I am at Papa's side most of the day.

On this 1946 Rosh Hashanah I sit next to Papa all day and try to pray like a man. In earlier years when I was still a boy, Papa occasionally let me go outside to run with other fidgety boys who, like me, were sure their sins were unforgivable and therefore had no reason to attract God's attention. I had eaten unkosher food. I had teased my grandmother. I had fights at school and sometimes—this, according to our rabbi, was a major sin—I boasted.

We boys did not discuss our fear of God's wrath. Instead we ran foot races around the block and when we were tired, but not too sweaty, we went back to sit with our fathers.

During the scary parts of the service, the parts that tell about death and an angry God, I hold Papa's arm. I can't hold his hand because he needs it to turn the pages of his black, leather-bound prayer book. He bows and chants and whispers. As he comes to the end of each page, he licks his finger, pushes the page aside and is already reading several lines down the next page.

A full day of worship bores me. The sermon always begins with an exciting Bible story and ends with the synagogue building fund. I play with the fringes of Papa's *tallis*, his prayer shawl, white wool with black stripes near the ends. The fringes at each corner, the *tsitsis*, have eight strings twisted in a complex, prescribed sequence and tied with five ritually spaced double knots. In Hebrew school, the small, bearded, unsmiling rabbi teaches his boys that God requires fringes on the prayer shawl "that you may look upon them, and remember *all* God's commandments, and do them." All 613 commandments!

I count and recount the knots. I tie a few extra knots—very loose so that I can remove them quickly. I don't need yet another transgression, the sin of despoiling a tallis, to add to my unending list of unforgivables.

Mutti and Omi leave before the service ends. Their goal is to have dinner ready when the men, Papa and I, arrive home. And dinner is ready! A great feast with chicken when we were poor, pot roast now that we can afford it. Boiled potatoes decorated with parsley or dill, carrots, green beans—but first the blessing over the wine. Papa never has more than one glass. Omi might have a second.

We four squeeze around our wooden kitchen table with its metallic cover. Instead of the usual oilcloth, the table boasts a cotton tablecloth. Dishes donated by my bachelor uncle, who arrived in the U.S. a year before us, have been supplemented with glasses collected as a premium for being loyal customers at a store I cannot now recall.

We clink glasses, I with my grape juice. Papa's toast is always the same. "To another year." Unlike me, he is convinced we will all be written into the Book of Life, all sins forgiven. He is happy. Although he will again pray all day on Yom Kippur, the holiest of all the holy days, he is now convinced that all will be well. He offers many toasts as he nurses his one glass of wine.

Omi, not certain she will be listed among the blessed, toasts in Hebrew "*L'Chaim.*" To life. Papa responds with "To health" and Mutti follows with "To prosperity." Life, health, prosperity are the priorities in that order. Papa never reminisces on Rosh Hashanah. He always looks to the future. During the war he spoke of peace. He spoke not of Holocaust victims but of survivors.

There is always dessert on Rosh Hashanah. Papa loves dessert even more than I do. "To a sweet year," he toasts over the apples and honey.

After the food and the prayers, Papa adds a last toast with the few drops of wine still in his glass. Just like at the end of the Passover Seder, he announces in his booming baritone, "Next year in Jerusalem."

Does Papa really want to leave this new country? Does he really want to learn yet another new language? Is he sincerely hoping to spend the next year in Jerusalem? Well, Papa liked beginnings.

* * *

Rosh Hashanah is not the only new year we recognize. In our home we have two calendars, a Hebrew one for prayer and ritual and another for work and school. That second calendar also lists a new year.

The secular New Year's Eve is totally different from Rosh Hashanah. Omi gives the first toast. "*Prosit,*" she says, holding her glass high. We clink our glasses to that. Prosit, like New Year's Eve itself, is not Jewish, but rather a German toast which literally means "may it benefit." More than health, more than prosperity, prosit is a generic toast hoping that those who join in will experience everything good.

On New Year's Eve our family brings back the German customs. *Silvester Abend*, as Germans call it, is named after Pope Silvester who died on December 31 in the secular year 335. He had been pope for more than twenty years and had ushered in a time of peace. For some in Germany, Silvester is a time of prayer. For most, it is a time of revelry.

In our little New York City kitchen on this last evening of 1946, we have traditional German food. Herring is a required appetizer. Indeed, it is the only time during the year, other than the Passover Seder, that we have *any* appetizer.

After the herring, Omi serves her homemade lentil soup, cooked in the German, not Jewish, tradition. Beef bratwursts are rolling in the boiling soup. We fish them out and eat these sausages with sauerkraut, a frequent addition for special occasions, a substitute for the less expensive and more bland cooked cabbage which we eat on ordinary week nights.

Even Mutti is happy for a change; she has survived another year. Unlike the Rosh Hashanah dinner where Papa talks only about the future, at this feast Papa reminisces about all the successes of the past year: promotions, pay raises, good grades for Freddy...

After New Year's Eve dinner, we all go to a movie. Mutti makes a selection from films playing in the neighborhood. Usually she picks a sad, slow-moving romance. I remember a 1942 release called *Mrs. Miniver*.

I think Mutti's favorite novel is Somerset Maugham's *The Razor's Edge*, which becomes our 1946 movie. She never chooses *The Lone Ranger*.

Afterwards we go to a cafeteria, usually the neighborhood Horn and Hardart Automat, where we eat pie and ice cream. Omi doesn't eat because the food isn't kosher. Papa and I always have apple pie. The automat is special. Food is behind little windows. We slip a coin into a slot and a window pops open. We remove our selection and slam the little window shut. If all the apple pie cubicles are empty Papa taps on the window with a key or a coin. Eventually a man in white, working in the kitchen, notices and fills the little box behind the window. On New Year's Eve, Papa lets me slip his coins into the slot he selected for apple pie. Mutti, too, lets me insert her coins for a dish of pudding.

Then comes New Year's Day. Everyone sleeps late. Omi creates a huge breakfast with soft boiled eggs for Papa and scrambled eggs for everyone else, sweet rolls, hot coffee (hot chocolate for me) and pumpernickel bread which we smear with *schmaltz*, leftover chicken fat. Cholesterol is not a cause for concern in the 1940s.

On New Year's Day, Papa writes out checks to various charities. The Hebrew Immigrant Aid Society, the Red Cross, our synagogue. There is no hesitation. Clearly he has been thinking about the year's recipients. Papa celebrates success by giving to charity. During the whole year, if something good happens—Freddy recovered from appendicitis—Papa selects a charity and donates generously. There is no reason to stint on the first day of the new year. The coming year will be even better.

Papa and I usually go for a walk on New Year's Day, one of our "walk and talk" adventures where we become better acquainted. Not a long walk because it's winter. This year is special. Now that I've completed the bar mitzvah ritual, Papa and I talk man to man.

One tenement is much like another and neighbors, Hungarian, Italian, Polish, German, are all equally poor. Papa and I cross cobblestoned Second Avenue, quiet on New Year's Day. The locals never say, "Avenue." We simply cross First or Second or Lexington.

Papa links his arm in mine, a common European gesture of friendship. He doesn't hurry. This is, after all, a day off from work, a day set aside for our leisure time together. Sometimes we pass street-level apartments with open or broken windows. We try to guess what is cooking when the smells are sweet and we rush on when the garbage smells cause us to gag. We admire the cars parked, bumper to bumper at the curb. Papa likes useful cars. I like the sleek, sporty ones—pretend racing cars with room only for two.

I imagine that those who live on Third Avenue are particularly poor. Third has both trolley tracks and an elevated train. The trolleys spark overhead as their electric contacts skip imperfect wires or jump city dirt or pigeon droppings. The overhead train rumbles at third story level, shaking buildings and rattling windows.

Next comes Lexington with its elegant shops, closed today but still available for leaning one's forehead against the glass to imagine owning the fancy luggage and elegant art deco radios. Each store front is an adventure.

On this New Year's Day walk, I ask Papa to select the favorite moment in his life. We exclude the moment I arrived because, after all, I am his first born, favorite and only child. He thinks for a long time, makes a few false starts and then his face brightens. "When we first saw the Statue of Liberty." Apparently that symbol closed one chapter and opened another.

Papa has an afternoon nap on New Year's Day and in the evening we sit around the radio to hear the news and enjoy a program. Mutti selects movies; Papa selects radio programs. *Duffy's Tavern* is a favorite. I pay close attention to the Shick razor blade commercials. Someday I will need those blades. Papa also likes Groucho Marx who, like us, is Jewish and, then, late in the '40s, *Abie's Irish Rose* makes its debut and Papa becomes a loyal fan.

Before bed, at the end of New Year's Day, Papa has a shot of schnapps. Authentic German schnapps can be likened to an 80-proof, fruit-flavored vodka. Papa drinks his shot in one gulp, lets out a sound that combines a gasp with a satisfied sigh.

"To the new year" says the man of hope.

XXIV. TODAY I AM A MAN

MUTTI AND I WALK to P.S. 30 on a Thursday morning in late August of 1946. As we enter, a young, skinny woman hands my mother a packet of papers. A badge identifies her: "English Teacher." Mutti passes the papers to me so that I can read the cover: "Welcome to Yorkville Junior High School Orientation." We head to a table under the "A—D" sign. When our turn comes, I print my name on a pad as instructed by a smiling woman. Her badge is affixed just above a very large breast: "Mathematics." Why do I keep looking at breasts? Now I'm embarrassed. Am I blushing?

Miss Mathematics finds my name on a list. She writes quickly on a slip of paper and hands the note to Mutti. "Mr. Halvorson/room 127/10:45 a.m." We easily find room 127 and see that, according to a hall clock, we have 20 minutes to kill. We return to a bench we saw near the building entrance. We study our orientation booklet. One page identifies the school address, phone number and office personnel. Another page lists the courses offered along with the names of faculty members that teach those subjects. A note about required attendance is followed by school hours and legal holidays. I'm puzzled by an explanation of "required physical education" and reasons for being excused. Why would one want to be excused from physical education? A list of "clubs, student government and other extra-curricula activities" is of interest to me but I don't have a chance to study it. By the time I explain "extra-curricula" to my mother, it's time to see Mr. Halvorson.

As we enter room 127, I notice a sign on the door: "Mr. Halvorson." Just below is the word "counselor" and below that "assistant principal."

I came for a schedule of classes. Why do I need a counselor and a principal? Now what did I do? Mutti apparently doesn't notice.

Mr. Halvorson stands up and walks around his desk to shake my hand and then introduces himself to my mother. He's even taller than Miss Christie and looks as if he could be a tough police officer.

He picks up a folder. "I see here that Fred started school a year late. Why is that?" he asks my mother. He has the file in his hand. Surely he knows the answer to his question. Why is he pretending that he's reading the file for the first time? Mutti explains that we came from Germany and I was not permitted to enter first grade in midyear because I knew no English.

"I see here that Fred did extremely well at P.S. 70. Is that correct?" Again I'm suspicious. He's got the file. He knows the answer. Mutti proudly tells him about the Daughters of the American Revolution award and my graduation speech.

"I've talked to the principal at P.S. 70. We believe that we should try to help your son catch up to his age group. If you agree, we can squeeze the three years of junior high school into two. Then Fred would start high school at the appropriate age. He's a good student and we believe he can manage the catch-up." This little speech proves that he knew the answers to his questions all along. Why was he fishing?

Mutti doesn't quite understand Mr. Halvorson's little presentation. Speaking German, she asks me to explain. I tell Mr. Halvorson that I will translate his words for my mother. I've learned to warn people when I'm about to switch languages. Some Americans can be real touchy about "foreigners" and "foreign" languages. Perhaps they think we're talking about them.

Mutti asks for details. Before I turn back to Mr. Halvorson, I explain to Mutti that he is no ordinary teacher. I tell her about "counselor" and "assistant principal" on his office door. I believe that Mutti should have all the available information. Clearly we're talking about a life-changing decision. Then I turn to Mr. Halvorson and explain that my mother wants details.

Mr. Halvorson is ready for the question. He produces a list of classes that a typical student might take in three years. He explains that I would have to forego all minor courses. He deletes music, art, shop and foreign language from his list. Further, based on my record in elementary school, I could surely test out of certain English and math courses. He puts a star by those. Finally, he tells us that I would have to attend summer school to make up some work. I request time to discuss the matter with my mother. He suggests that Mutti and I can leave and then return in two hours to give him our decision. I request only five minutes to see if my mother has questions. Mr. Halvorson offers to leave the room but I ask that he stay. Privacy is no problem. We'll speak in German.

I explain the offer with some difficulty. I don't know the German words for "minor courses." I create a category of "must take" courses and another group of "choice" courses. Mutti understands summer school but needs to explore "testing out" of some subjects. She points out that there is some risk because I might not pass the tests or, if I do pass, I might not learn something important. I ask Mr. Halvorson about this issue and he says that the more tests I pass, the fewer summer classes I would take. He assures me that my previous teachers have confidence in my ability. Mutti understands the English and she asks in German what I want to do. I explain that I would be afraid of failing, but that I would like to try. Skipping a whole year of school strikes me as a practical opportunity. Mutti gives her blessing.

Mr. Halvorson, despite all his inane questions, has anticipated our decision. He hands me a schedule of classes for the first semester. He assures me that we will work out future schedules and tests after school starts. "I'll be here to help make this plan work," he promises.

* * *

School starts right after Labor Day. Moving between classes is fun. I like meeting new kids and greeting old friends from P.S. 70. Teachers hand out text books and workbooks. I'm energized. I listen for bells because I don't want to miss any clues that will help me move from room to room.

After the last bell of the school day, I linger on the sidewalk with some new friends before I have to walk the three blocks to Hebrew school. I'm in the last throes of preparing for my bar mitzvah—my passage to manhood. Now that I'm a student at Yorkville, I feel much older. I feel responsible for attending all my classes and for not disappointing Mr. Halvorson.

Die Barmitzwoh uns. Sohnes
Freddy
findet am 19. Okt. 1946, vorm.
9 Uhr, in der Synagoge Kehilath Jeshurun, 117–25 East
85th St. (zw. Lexington und
Park Ave.) statt.

Milton und Sitta Amram
geb. Nussbaum
315 E. 77th St., N. Y. C.
(fr. Hannover)

Bar Mitzvah notice in Aufbau, a German language newspaper for Jewish-American readers

Rabbi Ruben coaches me on chanting from the Torah and reading my portion of the *Haftarah*, a selection from the Bible's Book of Prophets that is linked to the Torah reading. I hate chanting in Hebrew. The words in the Torah are written without vowels. And I'm supposed to learn little squiggles that the rabbi calls "trope marks." I continue to confuse these little scratches that tell me how to pitch my voice and how long I should hold the note. My voice is changing and I can't predict what sound will come out. I want to run away.

Several weeks after the first day of classes at J.H.S. 30, I awake to my big day. I say aloud, "Today I am a man." I dress in a new white shirt and a new suit with a vest. It's my first vest and it makes me feel very manly and elegant. I also have a new striped tie. Yesterday I practiced dressing in my new finery to make sure that everything fit perfectly. I timed how long it would take to be ready. It took seven tries until I got the tie right. It either hung over my fly or didn't reach my belt. Finally I achieved the perfect length and memorized just how to place the tie before I make the knot.

Three weeks ago, Papa took me down to Delancey Street to buy my bar mitzvah outfit. All the salesmen knew him because that's where he shops for his New Jersey customers. The men treated me as if I were an important person and congratulated me on my bar mitzvah. They heaped blessings on me and my new suit. "You should wear it in good health." The tailor pinned the length of my pants and the sleeves of the jacket. "Nice shoulders," he mumbled. "Stand straight." When he was finished pinning, he grasped my hand, "*Mazel tov*." Much to my disappointment we had to leave the store without the suit because the tailor still had to make the alterations. As we said our goodbyes, the store owner said, "You should live a long life." A very old wrinkled man with a long white beard, who was sitting in a corner reading a book as he rocked, added, "And you should become a scholar."

After breakfast, dressed in my new suit, I walk with my family to the synagogue. Papa is wearing the tie I had given him for his birthday. I remember him saying, "Oh, a new tie. Now all I need is a new suit to go with it." I knew he was joking. He's wearing his gray Sabbath suit, the one he always wears to synagogue.

Mutti has a new hat. It's the color of the ink I use in my pen—royal blue. I think it's made of felt and it has a dark ribbon all around, just

Kehilath Jeshurun sanctuary circa 2008

above the rim. A few large blue and black feathers stick out. I wonder if they're from real birds—perhaps large tropical birds that preen for *National Geographic* photographers. Her hat matches the blue silk dress that Papa bought wholesale on Delancey Street. A belt, like the ribbon on her hat, is cinched at the waist. Mutti likes to show off her hourglass figure.

Omi wears a black dress. She always wears a black dress with long sleeves. On the Sabbath she also wears a lace handkerchief pinned to the sleeve of her dress. It is forbidden to work on the Sabbath. That includes all forms of carrying. However, wearing is permitted so Omi wears her hanky. No purse.

I'm rehearsing in my head, humming the chants. As the synagogue comes into view, I panic. I stand still and start to turn around. Papa grabs my arm and guides me forward. I wonder how he felt at his bar mitzvah, but I don't ask. I'm too frightened to speak.

We enter the building. Papa and I take our seats in the main sanctuary. Women sit in the balcony so Mutti and Omi climb the stairs and find seats where they can watch me. In the Sephardic style, a stage, the *tebáh*, is in the center of the synagogue, a large, slightly raised platform, probably eight-by-ten feet, with a beautiful railing all around broken by an opening on one side to allow readers to ascend via a step. Hand rails on both sides of the step imitate the design of the railing that encircles the tebáh. A padded carpet allows old bearded men to stand comfortably before a built-in reading stand which faces Jerusalem. A bench fills the back of the platform, also facing Jerusalem; a bench always waiting for the rabbi, the cantor and honored worshippers. Long wooden pews surround the central platform. Many hours spent daydreaming in the temple helped me memorize the architectural details.

The service is no different from any other Saturday. Yet I keep breaking out in sweats and I feel dizzy. The rabbi drones on and on. The cantor sings and chants and I know that I can't ever become a cantor. Will I fail this important test?

With great ceremony, several old men take a Torah out of the ark that stands at the front of the sanctuary. They parade the Torah to the tebáh. The rabbi calls me up to the platform using my Hebrew name, Moshe ben Menachem, Moses son of Menachem. I ascend the four steps, a trembling boy. I stand next to the rabbi. Papa is called up to bless the reading of the Torah. Next, Uncle Max is called up to say a blessing. Uncle Max, Papa's brother, is here from New Jersey. I'm told that Tante Beda and Uncle Ernst are in the synagogue, but I haven't seen them. The rabbi shakes Papa's hand and then whispers in Uncle Max's ear. They both return to their seats. The rabbi sits in one of the lion chairs and the cantor stands next to me.

I read from the Torah. The cantor is mouthing some of the words, encouraging the new initiate. Papa beams as I chant in my ever changing, ever cracking voice. I stop reading and work from memory. I look up at the women's section, searching for my mother and Omi. I pretend that I am a star in a theater-in-the-round with thousands of seats. I make a few mistakes, but I catch them and make corrections.

When I'm done, the rabbi ushers me to the bench. I'm trembling. Literally shaking. I hold the railing with one hand and squeeze. While I gather my thoughts, the rabbi and the cantor roll up the Torah and place it in a stand. Then I'm called forward to read from a book—the Haftarah—that has been opened to the correct page. I haven't memorized this portion so I can't look around. I stay focused on the book. I try to read with feeling just as the rabbi has coached me. However, I hear myself going faster and faster. How many pages to go? How many paragraphs? I'm finished.

The rabbi puts an arm around my shoulder and says the appropriate blessings. He recites the responsibilities of a Jewish male who has made the covenant. I ignore him. When I descend the step, I am a man. Papa shakes my hand. "Mazel tov," he whispers. I notice that I am taller than my father.

* * *

As we leave the synagogue, I realize that lots of friends and relatives were there to watch the show. I receive congratulations and begin to look forward to the party waiting at our apartment. I was so focused on the chanting that I forgot about the party. Morris witnessed my chanting and, on the way home, he teases that my Hebrew is almost as good as his English.

We arrive at our apartment to find that a caterer has put up a Happy Birthday sign and there are lots of kosher sandwiches and sweets. My bed has been designated as the repository for presents. There are lots of gifts. I eat and try to be polite and grateful. In the privacy of the bathroom I practice the speech I'm about to give. It's in English, but I'm no longer concerned with languages. I'm a man.

Mutti squeezes everyone into the living room and instructs me to open the presents. She hands them to me as they're passed from the bedroom. I hold up a sweater from someone who thinks I'm a giant. A fountain pen and then another. Several Parker pens, one with a gold looking cap. Lots of checks. An older boy at the synagogue warned me to say, "and a generous check from Al Sherman" instead of, "Here's a measly $1 from some cheapskate." Two more fountain pens and three dictionaries. New roller skates from Uncle Max. No wonder he's my favorite human being in the whole world.

I give my "spontaneous" speech. I begin with the traditional cliché sentence, "Today I am a man." Some boys tell the joke that they were so overwhelmed with fountain pens that they began, "Today I am a fountain pen." I recite the responsibilities of being a Jewish adult trying to be as vague and noncommittal as possible. I thank my parents and cite my grandmother for being my model of a good Jew. When I'm all done, there is some applause and I give Uncle Max an extra hug for the skates.

When everyone is gone, I count the loot. Over $400 dollars. Papa suggests I save $400 for medical school and "enjoy the rest." I plan to buy a fancy Gilbert Erector Set.

* * *

On Sunday, I do my homework so that I'm ready for my new courses at Yorkville Junior High. I'm now committed to Mr. Halvorson's plan. I want to graduate in two years. Now that I'm a man, I should be a high school student or, better yet, in college.

The reality of my "manhood" can be found in the old Jewish joke sometimes stated as a haiku:

Today I am a man.
Tomorrow I will return
to the seventh grade.

XXV. MORE RITES OF PASSAGE

SEVENTH GRADE requires more homework than elementary school. Two hours every evening keeps me in the good graces of my teachers. Weekends are mostly for play and to spend time with my "brother" Morris and his family. Mr. Pearlstein, now in the business of manufacturing tents and sleeping bags, is doing well. Business success hasn't diminished his socialist spirit and we talk often about the working class and about all the injustice in the world. While he highlights Jewish persecution, he also tells stories about American Negroes. He lends me pamphlets about Jim Crow and shows photos of "whites only" drinking fountains and public restrooms.

I have a flashback to the park in Hannover. I remember the bench with a sign reading, "Nur für Juden!" Only for Jews! At first I thought the sign identified privileged citizens. A few months later, Jews were dying in concentration camps.

Morris is less enthralled with our social justice conversations than I am. I'm quite upset about racism—perhaps because of my Holocaust memories. "Never again" should mean never again for more than Jews. Someday soon I'll work to end these problems. But right now Yorkville Junior High is my main focus.

Morris and I have no classes together. We don't even share the 12-block walk to school. Morris leaves home early and kicks his soccer ball all the way. I leave late and race to beat the school bell.

I make new friends who don't worry about my religion and we no longer have Friday afternoon religious hour. My new friends, dark haired boys—like me—are mostly Italian. They call each other Dago and Wop, slap each other on the back and generally enjoy each other's company. During lunch hour we walk a half block to Third Avenue and put pennies on the trolley tracks. After the trolley passes, we rush in to retrieve our penny which has now been flattened and feels smooth. I suggest putting a flattened penny on the track to see what happens. Chuck and I try it. Clickety clacking and sending off sparks, the next trolley passes and we rush into the street to be the first to show off our double flattened penny. It's even shinier than before and thinner. The edge is sharp enough for cutting paper and, we guess, skin. We talk about gangs and a few of the older boys show their switchblades. Push a button and the blade pops out of the handle. I ask to try one. Wow! I want one of my own.

Chuck and I try our pennies a third time. They don't become smoother or shinier or sharper. Tomorrow we'll try nickels. We finish our sandwiches, throw the paper bags in a basket on the corner and return to class.

When the afternoon bell releases us from school, we rush out and the boys play kick ball. I chat a while but then I'm off to Hebrew school. Monday through Thursday, one hour every day plus homework. I hate it. I hate God and my parents for making me spend my afternoons with the rabbi. I want to play with my new friends. I bought into the bar mitzvah ritual. What more do they want?

Hebrew school is like a one-room school house. The students range in age from the eight-year-olds planning to be rabbis or cantors and hoping that their beards will appear soon to those who are two years older than I am. The boys who've completed their bar mitzvah are, like me, ready to escape and practice their manhood. Like me, they've lost interest in further Jewish learning.

On Fridays I bring my roller skates to school. When school lets out, I roll with some of my new friends. Rich, whose torn pants and scuffed shoes make him look the opposite of rich, teaches me to hold on to the rear of busses and hitch a free ride. I know this is dangerous and love the adventure. We ride uptown into a new neighborhood and then roll back south holding on to the back of another bus. Rich falls occasionally and we examine his skates. They're really rusty and the wheels stick sometimes. I suggest oiling them. Rich says he only has a dime.

"Let's see what oil costs," I suggest. He agrees and we go to the store right near school. It's a five and dime store that also has lots of stuff costing way more; $1.98 seems to be a popular number. We walk over to Second Avenue and enter the store. I was there once with Mutti. I'm impressed with the great variety of goods—even some products that I've never seen before. We wander about looking for the oil. I find the paperback books and stop there to look at the covers. I focus on some romance novels showing pictures of shirtless muscular men with women looking helpless and parts of their clothing torn off. I open some of the books to see what they're about. I'd like to read one but I don't have a quarter.

After a few minutes, Rich pulls me away from the books. "C'mon, Fred. Let's get out of here."

"Did you find the oil?"

"Yup. Too expensive."

We skate over to First Avenue, then York and then to the East River. We sit on a playground bench and Rich removes a can of oil from his pocket. "How do I use this?" he wonders.

"I thought you didn't have enough money."

"The can fell into my pocket. I couldn't stop it."

We figure out how to open the oil. We pour the stuff into every opening and crevice on his skates until the wheels and our fingers are dripping. We rinse our hands at a drinking fountain. When Rich tries out his skates they leave a trail of oil on the ground and roll more smoothly. It's time to go home for supper. We live in opposite directions. "See ya at school on Monday."

"Yup. Monday."

When I arrive on my block, some of my friends are playing stick ball. Josephine is playing jacks with a few other girls. I wave to everyone and go upstairs. It takes lots of soap to clean all the oil from my hands and fingernails. Omi asks where I've been.

"Roller skating." And then I start my homework. Papa will be home soon and we'll have supper.

* * *

One morning my homeroom teacher tells me to see Mr. Halvorson right away. She gives me a hall pass. Mr. Halvorson is waiting. We talk about some exams I could take to test out of some classes. I'm eager to skip eighth grade and catch up to my age level.

The English examination requires no prep work. Mr. Halvorson is eager to set dates. We agree on the week after next. Monday, Tuesday and Wednesday after school. I pick those days so that I have to miss Hebrew School.

On Friday after school, several boys go to Central Park. Ferguson invites me to come along. Lots of the boys call each other by last names. Ferguson is a tall kid who can be tough and yet the girls seem to really like him. They walk with him after school when he lets them. In the hall-way I hear conversations like, "Isn't he cute?"

"Yeah. But I saw him first."

"So what. That doesn't give you lifetime ownership."

"Finders keepers."

These conversations don't always make sense to me, but I do know that the girls like Ferguson and compete over his attention.

At the park, the boys take out their switchblade knives and play a game they call Land or Territory. Someone draws a box about one foot in each direction. The first person throws a knife into the ground. The blade has to stand on its point inside the square. Wherever the knife lands you draw a line and the smaller area becomes the target. The second player throws a knife which must stick in the new target territory and so on. Whoever misses the target is out of the game. Similarly, if the knife doesn't stick, that player is out. I can't play because I don't have a knife. Sal lets me try his and after a few tries I can make it stick in the ground—although I need to practice hitting the right spot.

On the way home I ask where I can get a switchblade. Frank wants one too because his broke when it hit a rock. He agrees to take me to a place where they're available. We're to meet tomorrow, Saturday, at 10 on the southbound platform at the 76th Street subway station.

I have a dollar in my pocket and change for the subway. Frank and I make our way downtown. Frank takes us to the basement of a dress fac-tory. We ring a bell and a burly man lets us in. It's a gun shop. There are rifles hanging on all four walls and pistols in glass-covered display cases. Frank asks to see knives. There is a table of hunting knives and another, smaller table of pocket knives. We're allowed to rummage through the pocket knives by ourselves. Some are ordinary folding knives and some have the little buttons that makes them switchblades.

For a few minutes I'm overwhelmed. We're in a wonderland such as I've never experienced. I'm a little frightened by all the guns and sharp knives and the burly man at the front door. But I'm also exhilarated. I start to sweat and then I feel dizzy. I'm a good boy. Should I be in a place like this?

Frank is focused on the knives. He separates out the switchblades until he has three that he likes. While he's deciding, he encourages me to make a decision. I find one that has a handle that looks like marble embedded with jewels. Its tag reads, "75 cents." I happen to look at Frank just as he slips a knife into his pocket. Then he selects a regular knife with a loose blade and announces real loud, "I guess I can afford this one." He shows me the tag that reads, "20 cents."

"Are you ready to leave?" I'm reluctant to admit that I've never been to a store like this and that I'm overwhelmed and that I'm scared and that I really want this 75-cent knife. I suddenly realize that this is a test. Will Chuck and Rich and Frank and Ferguson like me if I wimp out now? Surely Frank will tell.

I find my bejeweled knife and a 30-cent knife and announce for all to hear, "You didn't tell me to bring this much money." Just as the burly guy goes to the door to let more customers into the shop, my fancy knife finds my pocket. I hold the less expensive one in my hand following Frank's example. We walk to the cash register and Mr. Burly takes our money without a "thank you." We walk toward the door, but Frank can't turn the handle. I stop breathing. Burly Man saunters over, presses a button and lets us out.

The street is busy with boys and men pushing wheeled racks filled with dresses, coats—all kinds of clothing. This is the garment district. I have trouble not bumping into people. I'm trembling. I suddenly remember what the rabbi said at my bar mitzvah. I remember, even though I wasn't paying attention. I have voluntarily made a covenant with God. That's what makes me a man. Now I've become a different kind of man.

While we wait for the subway train, Frank says, "Nice work, Fred."

"Now teach me the rules for that game you were playing in the park."

"Nothing to it," said Frank and by the time we arrive at our station, I've learned the rules.

* * *

Mutti gives me a note for the rabbi telling him I would miss three lessons because of school. I deliver it on Thursday. He frowns.

On Monday after the bell rings, I show up at Mr. Halvorson's office. I study the ASSISTANT PRINCIPAL sign on the door. I knock and enter. He leads me to a desk, asks if I have #2 pencils and explains that I have until ten minutes after five o'clock. "Miss Miklos will be typing some reports until you're done. Give your papers to her before you leave." Then as he puts on his hat to leave he adds, "I'll see you here tomorrow at three."

The secretary's typing is annoying and disrupts my concentration. She types like mad, pushes the return lever and starts on the next line. I can hear the rhythm change as she comes to a short line that ends a paragraph. Now and then she rustles papers. She rarely makes mistakes but twice I hear her say, "*Szar*." My limited knowledge of Hungarian includes "Szar." Shit.

I'm happy that I have good erasers on my pencils. Once, after putting a black mark in the wrong circle, I yell, "Szar." Miss Miklos bursts out in uncontrollable laughter. She knows not to talk to me. Her laughter becomes a quiet giggle and then she returns to her typing.

By the second day, I'm used to the sound of the typewriter and I work efficiently. On this day most of the questions require paragraph answers. I'm great at filling space with words. Wednesday's test is mostly about grammar rules and I'm feeling insecure. I can't fake my way through these questions. I make guesses as best I can. I finish the short essays quickly, hoping that whoever reads my words can decipher my handwriting. Once Miss Christie said, "Fred, you ought to be a doctor."

"You think I'm that smart?" I asked.

"Maybe, but I know your handwriting is bad enough." Apparently physicians are known for bad handwriting.

I'm done by 4:30. Reviewing my answers for a third time won't help. I did my best. I know that I did pretty well on reading and writing skills.

Will the grammar rules fail me? I don't know German grammar rules either. No one ever taught me how to structure a sentence. I just do it by ear. Like playing the piano by ear.

I say goodbye to Miss Miklos. We've not said many words to each other. One word, however, binds us. We have our secret.

The twelve-block walk to my street helps calm me down. I see Josephine sitting alone on the steps of her tenement playing jacks. I'm usually reluctant to go near "Little Italy" for fear that Albert's relatives will come out to kill me. I feel for the switchblade in my pocket—just in case. I sit next to her but a step below. I want to be able to break away if "they" show up. Josephine offers to teach me to play jacks. She's apparently forgotten that I've played with her before and I pretend I'd like to learn. As we play, I tell her about my three-day testing ordeal. She sympathizes and asks if I'd like to go to church. She goes to church when she's upset. I tell her that I'd like to go sometime. I have to go in for supper in a few minutes. But one day I'd like to see the inside of a church. We make a date to go tomorrow after Hebrew school. We'll meet at her steps at about 4:30. Is this my first ever date with a girl? We're going to a Catholic church.

On Thursday, I run home after Hebrew school, tell Omi that I'm going out to play and that I'll be home for supper.

Josephine is waiting. We walk to Saint Somebody's church. It's a long walk and Josephine tells me about her school located next to the church. Her father works hard to pay her tuition. She's an only child, but not by choice. Most of her uncles and aunts have large families. Josephine's mother was very sick during childbirth, almost died, and a doctor tied her tubes when the baby was born. Then she adds that everyone was very angry about what the doctor did. Catholics, I learn, don't tie tubes. Women should have lots of babies, no matter how much pain and risk to life. God decides when pregnancy is difficult and when it's easy. According to Josephine, God decides almost everything and we are quite powerless. God and the Devil. "It was the Devil that got into Albert," she tells me. "And then God saved his life." That's not how I remember it. I remember that Albert was really mean and the passerby who slapped my face saved Albert's life. If Josephine knew about my switchblade, she'd argue that the Devil decided that the switchblade should fall into my pocket. The rabbi wouldn't agree. He teaches that Jews are responsible for their behavior. I point this out to Josephine without mentioning the knife.

We mount the steps to the church. Huge, heavy doors stand between me and whatever is inside. I open one door and hold it for Josephine. We enter a lobby before another set of tall doors. Our synagogue also has a double set of doors, but they're not as tall and we have less ornamentation. I open the second door and Josephine steps into the church. She gets down on one knee, crosses herself and stands up.

Mutti has told me never to enter a church. "Why?" I asked. "Because God doesn't want you to." She must have been talking about the Jewish God.

Inside, the church is bright with a white light from windows in the dome and from the reflection off the white walls. I'm enveloped in museum calm. A hush pervades the sanctuary. A few stained glass windows tell stories I recognize. Abraham's binding of Isaac. Adam and Eve and the serpent and the apple. Noah and the flood. Josephine points to several stained glass stories about Jesus walking from one station to another. And then we come to the front of the church, the *bimah*, and there, instead of an ark to store the Torah, is a sculpture of Jesus on his cross with nails in his hands and feet. It's grotesque and I want to throw up. I've seen paintings like this in the art museum but this three-dimensional crucifix is too realistic for me. I turn away.

Josephine is sitting in an aisle seat in the fourth row. I walk over to her and she scoots in a little. I'm sitting closer than I've ever been to a girl. Our thighs are touching. I forget Jesus and wonder what this 15-year-old woman can teach me. We sit in silence for several minutes. Then Josephine interrupts our reverie with, "Isn't this peaceful?"

"Too peaceful," I say. "Let's walk." On the way out, Josephine tells me about the candles and she lights one with a little whispered prayer that I can't hear. As we meander home I report that I find the crucifixion story as grotesque as the binding of Isaac. Josephine admits that the crucifixion is scary and used to keep her awake when she was a little girl. She doesn't know the binding of Isaac story. I tell it in great detail and my date is wide-eyed. She loves children and cannot understand how Sarah could forgive Abraham. "Do you like children?" she asks. I shrug. Perhaps that's a girl thing.

* * *

I look up "crucifixion" in the Britannica at the library. At first I can't find it because I didn't spell it correctly. I tried looking for "crucifiction" as if the story were acknowledged "fiction." Miss Orlofsky laughs when I tell her about my spelling error. "Well, some people believe the story is true and others think it's a myth." She doesn't let on what she believes. However, she explains that evidence exists that criminals actually had been nailed to a cross. Pictures of human skeletons from Dachau and Buchenwald and Auschwitz come to mind.

* * *

After several weeks, Mr. Halvorson reports that I passed the English tests with flying colors. While my score was not perfect, I was happy to pass. Now Mr. Halvorson wants me to take some math tests and gives me two books. "You can take the tests right after the Christmas vacation. That will give you plenty of time to study. Mrs. Ziolkowski has promised to help in any way she can. She'll be waiting for you during the lunch period so that you can introduce yourself."

Mr. Halvorson has just spoiled my Christmas vacation. I'll have to prepare for tests. I like the Christmas and Chunakah season. I like the music on the radio and singing songs in school. Mutti won't let me go to church, but she helps me sing *Ave Maria* in three languages.

I walk to Mrs. Ziolkowski's room and check the spelling of her name on the door. I had it right. Mrs. Z turns out to be the big bosomed lady I met at orientation. She's really friendly and tells me to drop by any time so that we can arrange to talk about my mathematics work.

* * *

As fall turns to winter, my wardrobe changes. My favorite winter coat is a forest green Mackinaw with wooden buttons and a hood. It's just like the one Papa wore when he was the Chanukah man back in Germany. Josephine and I take some long walks and talk about school and what we want to be when we grow up. Josephine wants to be a mother with many children. I don't know what will become of me. My mother wants me to be a doctor but I hate the sight of blood. Josephine—she doesn't like to be called Josie—talks about her 10th grade Catholic school classes which I find quite interesting except that her teachers seem to mix God into everything. Josephine loves to talk about God and the Devil.

To bring our conversation to a more interesting level, I persuade her to go to the art museum with me. When I explain stuff, she tells me how clever I am. She loves paintings of the baby Jesus and of Mary. Nude bodies seem to hold her attention the longest, but she doesn't comment at all and I don't know what to say either.

Time with Josephine convinces me that my curiosity about romance is not being satisfied by medical books. I think I'd like to try romance stories—the kind I saw at the five and dime with the covers showing half naked men and women. I can't borrow them from the library because I don't want my true love, Miss Orlofsky, to see that I read trash. So I go back to the store and browse. I have no money. I can't even afford a quarter for an inexpensive paperback book.

Somehow one of the books slips under my coat and stays there until I'm out on the street. On the way home I think, "That was easy."

I read the book quickly, skipping the boring parts. I focus on the romance and the touching. A week later, I "borrow" another book from the store and soon I'm feeling quite expert. However, I also feel dirty as a thief and as a voyeur. Am I sharing the Devil with Albert? Has the Devil replaced God? Being a man is more difficult than I thought it would be.

* * *

In January I learn that I passed the math tests. Again not perfect, but Mr. Halverson is pleased. He has some other tests for me and an interview with some VIP at the school administration building. The outcome is that I don't need any summer school. I'll be in ninth grade next September. Mutti and Papa are proud. I have greater freedom. When I go out with my new friends, I just tell my parents I'm going to the library. No one checks to see if the library is actually open.

Occasionally I sneak out with Josephine. I try to keep up her interest in museums so that we don't talk about Jesus too much. One Sunday afternoon we decide to go to a movie. We tell our parents that we're going to a show with a crowd of friends from school. We meet at the corner and walk down Second Avenue to 72nd Street.

The Postman Always Rings Twice is playing. I saw the book on Mutti's shelf and I gleaned it in hopes of finding some sexy sections. I didn't like the book, but today I don't really care which movie we see. I'm not a cinema connoisseur.

In the lobby, I help Josephine off with her coat. I've watched Papa do the gentleman routine. I take a close look at my first date to a movie. Smooth olive skin, straight black hair three or four inches past her shoulders. We're about the same height. She's full figured. I don't mean that she's fat or even plump. She's just not skinny. She has a body. Hips and breasts are clearly part of Josephine. She's wearing a tight sweater and a calf-length plaid skirt. And a shawl that, she tells me, her grandmother knitted. It's the sweater that catches my attention. If her parents are so strict and so Catholic and so afraid of the Devil, why would they let her wear a tight sweater that shows two cones? I don't comment except to admire her shawl. I touch the wool and it feels soft. I rub it against my face. Josephine smiles.

The movie has already started when we find our seats. We watch some of it and I'm pretty bored. I look at Josephine and she seems absorbed. After a while there is some smooching on the screen and Josephine touches my hand. Wow! I'm holding hands for the first time. The movie still bores me. I'm busy thinking about what I should do next. I see that some guy a few rows toward the front has put his arm around his date's shoulder. That's worth a try. When Josephine shifts position I release my hand from hers and place it around her shoulder. She leans toward me.

As the plot becomes complicated, I forget about Josephine for a moment. I feel a kiss on my cheek. Unexpected. I look over and our lips meet. She holds the kiss for several seconds. Lips touching. I'm excited, but don't know what to do. I feel Josephine snuggle closer and we kiss again. We watch the movie as it draws to its climax. Josephine, who hasn't read the book, probably never reads books voluntarily, wants to know what happens to the characters. My arm is stiff from stretching it around Josephine's back. I bring it back and touch her hand. She holds tight. The drama has infected her. The movie ends, the credits scroll down the screen and Josephine leans over and we have a long kiss. We stand up and Josephine puts her arms around me and gives me a hug. We walk out hand in hand.

As we come closer to our street, we keep a respectable distance from each other. She wouldn't want her parents to find out that she was out with a boy. Going out with a Jewish boy makes it a double crime. And

I certainly don't think that my parents would approve that I went out with a girl—a Catholic girl who really loves Jesus.

* * *

Mr. Halvorson said I won't be able to take non-required courses if I want to skip eighth grade. That's why I'm surprised that typing is on my spring semester schedule. Mr. Halvorson says it will be the most useful course in junior high. He also signs me up for the traffic safety squad. This is a group of kids who use flags to control traffic before and after school. We wear armbands that say AAA because we're sponsored by the Automobile Association of America. I volunteer for the morning shift because I have to go to Hebrew school as soon as we're let out from public school.

I'm also selected as one of two flag bearers, the color guard. Each week we have an assembly and after everyone is seated, someone plays *America, The Beautiful* while I walk down an aisle with a flag in a holster that I wear like a belt. The actual flag holder sits in my crotch. Another boy marches his flag down the other aisle. We approach the stage from opposite sides and stand tall while the principal leads us in the Pledge of Allegiance and *The Star Spangled Banner*. Then everyone has to remain standing until the other boy and I return the flags to their stands in the back corners of the assembly hall.

While I'm on stage I feel very patriotic. Each week I think about my coming to America. I picture the Pennland, the boat I took across the Atlantic. I remember that I'm now a citizen of the United States of America—a Jewish citizen. When I tell Papa that I'm a flag bearer, he says, "A Jewish flag carrier." Then he adds as he often does, "We're in America now."

The Safety Squad is OK, no big deal. Typing class is a burden for two reasons. First, I can't seem to learn how to type. My fingers won't obey my brain. I memorize QWERTYUIOP and other parts of the keyboard, but that doesn't seem to help my fingers. Secondly, I'm in a class with several of my Friday afternoon friends. They're not enamored by school and our typing teacher can't control their behavior. There is lots of talking and giggling in class, which makes the teacher yell in a squeaky voice. That generates even more laughter. I cut class several times, which doesn't enhance my typing speed. When I'm in class, I don't behave like the goody-goody student that I am the rest of the day.

One day, about three weeks into the term, the teacher has a scream-ing fit and sends me to the principal's office. Instead I go to see Mr. Halvorson—ASSISTANT PRINCIPAL. I explain that I'm in real trouble. He offers to intercede with the teacher if I promise to work hard from now on. I argue that I can't believe that typing is a required class. Fur-ther, I argue that I have no respect for the teacher and can't develop respect for her. Finally I tell Mr. Halvorson that I seem to have a brain/finger miscommunication and can't seem to learn to type. I offer to take a summer typing class if I really have to learn this skill. He smiles. My guess is that I'm not the first student who wants to get out of Miss Screamy's class. "Come to my office tomorrow during your lunch peri-od." I thank him.

When I return the next day, he says, "Well, you must have been very bad. She won't let you back in class and she even screamed at me. She's really upset with you and some other boys in class."

I can't imagine a teacher yelling at an assistant principal, but I reply, "I'm sorry to cause you this problem. You've really done a great deal for me. I let you down."

"We no longer spank students with rulers," said Mr. Halvorson. "So let's just solve this problem. Typing is useful, but not required. You have three choices: First, you can take typing in summer school. Second, I can get you into a different typing section now, but you'll have to catch up with the other students. Third, I can get you into a mechanical drawing class, but here too you'll have to catch up."

"Mechanical drawing," I announce without hesitation. Anything but that accursed typing. Then I say to myself, "Girls choose typing. Boys take mechanical drawing." Of course, I have no idea what mechanical drawing is all about.

The boys are pretty proud of me when they learn that I was kicked out of typing. I become a minor hero. I tell my parents that I am too good for typing and have been promoted to mechanical drawing. I be-come a hero to them as well, particularly because they don't know what mechanical drawing is either. It sounds important.

I like my new teacher, Mr. Bogaccio, instantly. He's a big man with a name to match. He tells me that he also came to the United States as a youngster. He served as a translator in Italy while in the U.S. army during World War II. He promises to help me catch up to the other students and challenges me with hard work. I'll have to read all the handouts that the students have received so far. I'll have to read the first third of the workbook. I'll have to do all this by the next day.

While I'm not spectacular at drawing, I learn the concepts quickly and I'm willing to work on weekends to practice drawing skills. We learn to draw three-dimensional objects such as file cabinets and cups. I design a chair and a park bench. Ferguson, my after-school friend, designs a car. We're not allowed to use colors so he uses the side of his pencil point to create shading. The car looks silver.

Once I'm caught up with the other boys in the class (as I predicted, there are no girls in Mr. B's class), I go to see Miss Orlofsky at the library. I want mechanical drawing books but she doesn't have any. She gives me beginning architecture books instead. I try my hand at a few introductory architecture drawings and hand them in to Mr. Bogaccio with a note thanking him for his help and understanding. Another top grade despite my late start in the class.

Spring comes and goes quickly. It's been a busy time with lots of unexpected introductions to manhood. School keeps me busy and I try for excellent evaluations so that I can stay in Mr. Halvorson's good graces. Since the typing fiasco, I've come to really trust him.

* * *

Mutti has found a summer job for me at a tool and die company that manufactures metal parts. I work some kind of press that uses heat to shape metal. I also learn to use a grinding tool. Most of all, I sweep up. I'm the boy who fills in wherever needed. I feel useful. The metal shavings require wearing a mask part of each day and the general dirt sends me home to a bath every evening before supper. There isn't much time for play.

During the last three weeks of summer, I go to Camp Solidarity, a children's camp run by a German socialist organization that earns money by selling life insurance via an organization called The Workman's Benefit Fund. I love being away from home. I love being a kid allowed to play all day long. I love making new friends—girls included.

While I'm still not very good at sports that require two functioning eyes—tennis and baseball—I discover that I'm an awesome swimmer.

During my first week at camp I set several camp records including swimming two miles. That wins me points with girls and I flirt a great deal. I even try kissing a few, but none are as bold as Josephine. Of course, she's an older woman.

Kenny Kessen is my best friend at camp. He's also my enemy. We compete for the same girls and the same positions on teams. He's Jewish and somehow we find each other. Why is finding a Jewish friend important or even of interest? I ask Kenny these questions. He lives in a Jewish neighborhood in Queens and doesn't think about it much. He thinks I'm a nut case. I agree. Perhaps the war, the Holocaust and the "Jew boy" epithets have made me a nut case.

One counselor is talented in music and theater. She leads the camp in songfests and performances. She announces tryouts for Gilbert and Sullivan's *The Mikado*. Many of the campers rush to read the libretto and music. I decide to try out for the part of Nanki-Poo, the character who sings the best songs and wins the pretty girl at the end, a role played by a girl whom I covet in real life. Kenny wins the part because he's handsome and a tenor. I'm assigned the part of the Mikado. Since my voice finished changing, I sing bass or baritone. I get lots of laughs and it's a fine character part, but Kenny gets the girl. Damn those handsome tenors.

On the bus ride home from camp, I think back-to-school thoughts. I also think about the lessons I've learned that are introducing me to a manhood much more complex than my bar mitzvah.

I've learned to be a thief, a talent that I can't tell the world about. I can't tell my parents or Mr. Halvorson or Josephine. I won't even tell my "brother" Morris.

I've had my first kiss, again an event that I can't share with family. After that movie date, Josephine and I had a few more trips to museums with occasional kisses behind buildings or in dark doorways. With the spring, after we could go without coats, we had some full frontal hugs. Somehow I feel that I need to know more about sex and romance (two different topics for study) in order to move forward with the relationship. The year included my first unsuccessful class, typing. While I do hope for more kisses in future years, I am not anticipating any more disastrous courses.

I had my first real job with a weekly pay check and serious responsibilities.

And I had my first experience starring in an operetta. Although our run lasted only three performances, we played for many campers, their parents and for citizens from small towns near the camp.

As the bus approaches the city, my recollections start to frighten me. Manhood is more complicated than I've anticipated. Convinced that there is little left to learn, I vow that I will now correct my errors and enter the path of righteousness.

The camp bus drops us off at the offices of the Workmen's Benefit Fund. I say goodbye to Kenny and a few others. I give my address to one of the girls, Barbara, who suggests we keep in touch. I promise to call her. She's agreeable to my proposal that we visit a museum together—sometime. Barbara even introduces me to her parents—Jewish. Papa is waiting and together we *schlep* my luggage home on the subway. I am not altogether happy to be home. I feel that if I am now truly a man, I should be living on my own, unencumbered by parents.

XXVI. SMOKING, SKIN AND SIN

I ARRIVE HOME FROM CAMP on a Sunday afternoon. School starts on Monday morning. Mr. Halvorson has a ninth grade schedule ready for me. I'm ready to be a perfect student—even a scholar. Mr. H. suggests I think about high school selection and gives me a small brochure. At lunch time the boys have a reunion. Chuck, who graduated and now attends high school, is missing. Frank, my knife-stealing cohort, is now in eighth grade and doesn't understand how I jumped to ninth. A few new boys hang out with us. I ask some of the older boys about high school plans. All look puzzled. Of course they'll go to the neighborhood high school to which they're assigned.

On Monday evening, Mutti takes me to the five and dime store to buy some school supplies. It's the same shop from which Rich stole a can of oil. It's the same shop from which I "borrow" paperback romance novels with sexy covers. I'm pretty nervous and stay close to my mother. Visions of MASTER THIEF keep me from focusing on the task at hand. As soon as we're out in the fresh air, I feel better.

My mid-September birthday coincides almost perfectly with the start of school. I turn 14 with little fanfare. The 19th of September, my birthday, falls on a Friday. The family goes to Friday evening services. As usual, I sit with Papa in the men's section. Mutti and Omi sit in the balcony with the women. After we're home from synagogue, Mutti makes coffee for the grownups and pours cold milk for me. She serves a surprise apple pie. I wonder if I should be drinking coffee now that I'm a man. I've tried it and don't like the taste.

173

Out come the presents. The same as almost every year—clothing. I've stopped being disappointed. I do like the blue-gray plaid flannel shirt which makes me feel very manly. A gray wool pullover sweater is OK except that I muss my hair when I pull it over my head. Papa and I share Wildroot Cream Oil to keep our hair in place and give it a shine. Like Papa, I've become fussy about my hair. Like Papa, I carry a small pocket comb.

Tante Beda and Uncle Ernst visit on Saturday night as does Uncle Max, my wonderful bachelor uncle. Beda gives me a great hug, holding me against her soft bosom before she strokes my cheek. I'm still "little Freddy" to her even though I'm a head taller than everyone in our family. After dinner, she gives me a birthday gift, a box of kosher bonbons, "Because you're such a sweetie." I don't like sweets but I know Omi will enjoy them. Uncle Max, my favorite human being in the whole world, gives me a pipe and a tin of tobacco. Mutti is furious and tries to take them away. No one in our family has ever smoked except Uncle Max. I protect them, although I'm as dumbfounded as I was with Josephine's first kiss.

Uncle Max fills his own pipe and then fills mine. He removes a dollar from his wallet. "I'll give you this dollar if you can smoke a whole pipe-ful." Mutti hisses at Papa, "Tell your brother to stop this nonsense." Papa is so amused he can hardly keep from laughing. Mutti stomps out of the room to join Omi, who is doing dishes.

"Watch me," says my Uncle Max. He holds the pipe stem in his mouth, strikes a match and positions the flame over the tobacco. He inhales, then exhales, then inhales again. A few more tries and the tobacco glows. With a flick of his wrist, he extinguishes the flame. Now it's my turn. Pipe in place, I strike the match, inhale a few times and blow the flame out. I don't trust my wrist to kill the flame. I can see that the tobacco isn't glowing like Max's. I try again and it works. I cough a little and everyone laughs at me. Smoking is another new experience and I puff at the pace that Max has set. Not too fast. Occasionally, Max puts his pipe down and then I do too.

I daydream of growing up and becoming a jolly, mischievous uncle like Max. Then I realize that as a solo child, I can never become a bachelor uncle. I take a long, thoughtful drag on my new pipe.

I had planned to write a paper for school while the relatives visited. However, now I'll have to stay so that I can be the center of attention. I need to earn that dollar. And if I can pass this test, I'll have taken another step in my quest toward manhood. I understand now that my bar mitzvah wasn't the end of the road.

It's 1947. World War II has been over for only two years and, as it frequently does, the conversation turns to the people who aren't here. The Holocaust is central to all our conversations—even at birthdays. Tante Beda, Uncle Max and Papa are siblings. Their father died of war wounds

Tante Bertha with Sitta (top center), Karola (right) and Käthe (bottom)

after World War I, but their mother, Oma Jettchen, lived long enough to meet the Nazis. She died at the age of 70 in the Riga Ghetto shortly after we left Germany. There, among the many Germans transported to Latvia, she was one of more than 25,000 Jews murdered there.

Mutti, who has returned to the living room, bemoans the loss of two sisters. She tells their stories in a whisper and with deep sighs. Tante Käthe, her husband and their three-and-one-half-year-old daughter, my only cousin, died in the gas chambers of Auschwitz. Tante Karola and her husband died in the Riga Ghetto a few months before the end of the war. Mutti points out that they didn't just die. They were butchered. There are others. Uncle Max and I smoke our pipes and listen.

Uncle Max changes the subject to discuss the quality of smoking pipes. Mine, he explains, is a high quality Meerschaum made of a porous clay that filters the nicotine and cools the smoke. He points out the carvings on the bowl. Much to everyone's surprise, I don't gag, choke or barf. I almost enjoy the taste. I walk to a full length mirror and admire the look of me smoking a pipe while wearing my new flannel shirt. My mustache is starting to grow. I return to Uncle Max to collect my dollar. He grins. Mutti scowls.

* * *

I haven't seen much of Josephine during the summer. On Sunday I go out to skate with the boys and to visit Morris. Josephine, sitting on the steps of Little Italy, is chatting with a few cousins who live in the same building. I catch her eye, fasten my skates and start rolling slowly toward First Avenue. I'm guessing that she'll find an opportune moment to leave the conversation and follow me.

When I reach First, I turn around and slowly glide west again. I see Josephine approaching so I turn back east and wait at the corner, practicing tricks on my skates. When she reaches the corner, I skate a loop around her, stop in front and we hug. She's now 16 and looks quite pretty. Still no makeup. Just that fabulous body. She's wearing patent leather shoes, short socks, a skirt about three inches below the knee and a thin, loose-fitting blouse. I remove my skates so that we can walk together toward the East River. Josephine wants to know all about camp. I report selectively.

When it's her turn to talk about her summer, she tells me she may be moving. Her father and three of his brothers have bought some land in New Jersey and they plan to each build a home for their families. She's been out to see the land and finds it disappointing. Apparently the land is a beautiful wooded area far from any city-type activities. No shops, no neighbors. She doesn't want the isolation. She doesn't want to leave the city. Josephine starts crying. She tells me that two of her uncles have a good start on their homes and one will move in before Christmas. Hers will be the last because her father works in New York and he can only work on their house on weekends. She may have to join him often to help with the building.

I try to put a positive spin on her plight. She'll be with all her cousins and have great family get-togethers. This makes her more depressed. She doesn't want family. She has to keep secrets from the family gossips. She wants the excitement of big city life. More quiet tears. I have a clean handkerchief and I hand it to her. I read about a scene just like this in one of my "borrowed" romance novels. The hero produces a hanky at just the right moment and the girl in distress falls all over him. It works. Josephine dries her tears, gives me a tiny smile and then one of those full frontal hugs. I kiss her forehead, another hint from the romance novels.

We walk hand-in-hand along the river. We stop under a tree to study the water. A tourist boat comes by. We wave at the passengers.

"Do you know about casting sins upon the water?" I ask.

"Yes. Our priest talked about it a few Sundays ago. He read a Bible passage."

"Next week will be Rosh Hashanah," I continue. "That's when we atone for our sins. My parents and I will spend most of the day in the synagogue. However, during the afternoon, we'll walk to the river with some bread. We'll say some prayers in which we ask forgiveness for our many sins. Then we'll throw some crumbs into the water and we'll watch some fishes jump up, fighting for our sins."

Josephine doesn't get the joke. Quite seriously she says, "I can't imagine that you have any sins. Fred is sinless."

Then she goes on to tell me how she prays to the Virgin when she has sinned. She tells me about the Virgin's statue at her church. She visits it often and shares some of the Virgin Mary prayers with me. Josephine is fully convinced that the Virgin listens to personal desires and answers prayers. We arrive at a bench and Josephine sits and points to a spot for me. I sit and almost automatically put my arm around her shoulder. She snuggles close. She still has the hanky and tries to hand it back. "Keep it," I encourage. "You may become teary on the way home."

We kiss a long kiss. I hold her close as if to protect her from her relatives. Another long kiss. This time her tongue touches my lips. I part my lips and her tongue enters my mouth. She explores with her tongue. As soon as I dare to meet her tongue with mine, she guides my hand to one of her breasts. I can't help but wonder if she learned more this past summer than I did.

My life is full of NEW. I'm ill at ease, yet happy. Josephine becomes flushed and starts to breathe unevenly. I stroke her face. I suggest we go to a movie matinee next Sunday. Josephine gives an eager "Yes."

We need to go home for dinner now so we head back to our block. At First Avenue we share a quick kiss and Josephine heads west toward "Little Italy." I don my skates and zip toward my apartment. I wave as I pass Josephine.

On the following Sunday, I leave my apartment building at the appointed hour and see Josephine across the street. She's trapped in conversation with her cousin Albert—the kid I almost killed. I go back into my lobby and watch through the glass door. I see Josephine start toward Second and then turn back as Albert keeps her engaged in conversation. Albert sits on the stoop. Josephine stands, shuffles from foot to foot and turns toward Second Avenue every few seconds. After ten minutes I decide to take action. I walk slowly across the street in *High-Noon*-cowboy-movie fashion. I reach into my pocket and palm my pocket knife. Just as I get close enough for Albert to see my hand clearly, I press the button. The blade pops out with an audible zzzzp. Albert is up the steps and inside his building before I can replace the blade.

"I'll be around the corner," I announce as I start walking.

"Soon," answers Josephine.

But before she can get ten steps away, Albert's mother, Josephine's aunt, is at a third floor window, curlers in her hair, yelling for Josephine to explain why Albert was frightened.

"I don't know," Josephine shouts back. "Some kid came over and Albert ran away."

"Who was the kid?"

"I don't know."

"You're supposed to take care of your little cousin."

Then they start to talk in Italian, shouting three floors down and three floors up. I'm crouching behind a parked car and can see everything.

Eventually the aunt disappears and Josephine and I meet around the corner. Josephine immediately begins to reprimand me for having a switchblade.

"The Virgin would not like that you frightened poor Albert."

"Would not like? What do you mean by 'would?' She either knows or she doesn't. She either likes or she doesn't."

This fine grammatical point slips by Josephine. There is silence while she tries to figure out what I meant. After a minute or two, Josephine starts to giggle. "Anyway, it was a funny scene, you chasing Albert with your knife. You're really bad." And with that she takes my hand. I hope that she has forgiven me for making fun of her Virgin.

In the lobby I help Josephine off with her sweater. "Knitted by my grandmother," she says. I rub it against my face. She smiles, just as she did when I rubbed her shawl against my face.

Josephine is wearing a man's blue work shirt and a dark blue calf-length skirt. Clean white sneakers and white socks complete the outfit. She must have changed after church.

This week's matinee is *Desire Me*. Sounds sexy. Actually it turns out to be an awful, post-war love story. The war flashbacks frighten me. Gun fire and grenades remind me of the bombs over Hannover. However, the love scenes seem to be of some interest to Josephine. Greer Garson is lovely to look at, but today I'm totally focused on Josephine.

We watch the movie for a while. During a tense war scene, Josephine reaches out for my hand. After my switchblade routine, I'm feeling very daring. However, I don't know if Josephine wants to be distracted from this movie. At a part of the movie when the camera is exploring the French countryside (I think it's the French countryside), I put my arm around Josephine's shoulder. She leans close and we kiss. A second kiss, longer and sexier than the first. On my own, I reach for a breast. A loud noise on the screen captures Josephine's attention and we're distracted for a few minutes. Then she leans in for more making out. She kisses my hand, then another kiss on the lips. I feel daring enough to undo one of her shirt buttons. No protest. I undo another button and then another. Now my hand is inside her shirt and I touch Josephine's breast. More accurately, I touch the cotton bra covering her breast. Suddenly Josephine buttons up and whispers, "I'll be right back."

Several minutes later, she slips back beside me, pushes my arm around her shoulders and places my other hand on her breast. Holy bananas! No bra! What would the Virgin say?

Josephine snuggles close and we kiss. I work up the courage to undo her buttons, reach into shirt—and touch naked breast. I stroke gently. I wish the medical books had given me more guidance, but Josephine's uneven breathing suggests I'm doing something right. Touching real flesh is altogether different from seeing pictures in a medical book. Reading is interesting. Stroking is dramatic.

After a few minutes, Josephine takes my hand out of her shirt and kisses my palm. Then she kisses my lips in a way that feels romantic, not just sexy. I've read in my "borrowed" romance books that one can kiss more than lips. I kiss an eye and then an ear. Josephine sits quietly, her head close to my chest. Is she sleeping? Are her eyes focused on the screen?

While Josephine is snuggled close, I check out the end of the movie. Greer Garson's husband, presumed dead in the war, returns. She and her new lover must work things out. I stop paying attention. I focus on what happened today. What comes next? I wish I knew more. I'm glad that I'm learning from an older woman.

As the credits scroll down the screen, Josephine fusses with her hair. I hand her my pocket comb. She strokes it though her lovely hair. I hope that a few strands will stay on the comb for me to keep.

In the lobby, Josephine asks to borrow my comb again and goes to the ladies room. As I wait in the lobby I see several boys from school. We chat a moment until I see Josephine. I excuse myself and meet her half-way, happy to know that the boys have seen me with a pretty girl. She returns my comb and clasps my hand. We walk toward home.

Since celebrating my 14th birthday, I've learned to smoke and I've touched Josephine . I feel like a sinner. I'm filled with shame. And pride.

XXVII. TODAY
I AM A MAN—REALLY

ABOUT TWICE A MONTH, when I'm walking home from Hebrew school, some big kid, never the same kid, steps into my path. With a scowl he asks, "Are you a Jew?"

I'm carrying my books with Hebrew writing on the cover. That should be a hint, but no bully ever notices the books.

"Who, me?" I ask back, stalling for time, checking for an escape route.

"Yeah. You look like a Jew."

"How does a Jew look?"

"Are you some kind of Jew wise ass? We don't want no Jew boys around here."

Before the kid can think of his next line, I'm ten steps away. I run. Always toward groups of people. There are always people in New York City. Sometimes the bully chases. I can outrun anyone.

Hitler came to my bris. He chased me out of Germany. Now, little Hitlers in America continue to plague me.

* * *

Hebrew school is mostly rote memory work. The rabbi is boring, mean and smells of yesterday's sweat. I see no reason for learning more Hebrew language skills or Bible stories. The classroom is dark and depressing. When I question the rabbi about the meaning of stories he gives rigid answers like, "Because God said so."

I can't master Hebrew grammar as quickly as the rabbi demands. One day while I'm supposed to be working out a tricky problem in the grammar workbook, I fall asleep at my table. The rabbi hits me on the back of the head and says, "If you're not interested, you shouldn't be here." I gather my books and papers and walk out.

As I randomly wander some neighborhood streets, trying to contain my rage, I find myself admiring some shop windows on Lexington Avenue. In a pharmacy window I see DELIVERY BOY WANTED. I walk into a clean, well-lit store with a counter and display cases on one side and a soda fountain on the other. I step up to the display counter and wait my turn.

A tall man, about 35 years old, with a clean light-blue lab coat asks, "Can I help you?"

"Tell me about the delivery boy job."

"How old are you?"

"14."

"Grade?"

"Ninth grade at Yorkville Junior High."

"Wait over there," pointing to the soda fountain. "Joe," he shouts, "give the boy a Coke."

I don't like soda, but I sip while I wait. I doubt that drinking Coke is a job requirement. Twenty minutes pass, my glass is empty and, except for two teenage girls sipping malts, the whole store is empty. The pharmacist calls me over.

"Sorry about the wait," he says. "Customers come first." He asks about my grades and work habits and references. I persuade him that I'm a stellar student—DAR Award—that I work hard and that all my teachers will vouch for me. He asks me to name one. I name the assistant principal, Mr. Halvorson.

We agree on 40 cents per hour plus whatever tips I receive. "When can you start?"

"I have to ask my parents first. I'll come back tomorrow after school."

At dinner, I announce that I have found a part-time job. I speculate how much I can earn if I work 15 hours per week. My father is impressed. Mutti is concerned that my grades will suffer. I drop the bomb: "Well, I'd have to quit Hebrew school." Her eyes open wide. Her fork drops into her lap. She's upset. Why would I give up an important learning experience? For the hundredth time, she tells me how her father was wounded in World War I. Left for dead on a battlefield, he promised to give his life to God if he were to live through this experience. He was saved and became a leader in his synagogue and devoted much of his life to God. I don't fall for the guilt trip. It occurs to me that I might try a similar strategy.

I point out that I'm good at everything I do. I'm an excellent student. The best. And then I fib that Hebrew school is making me sick. I describe excruciating headaches that appear only when I'm in the shul. I describe dizzy spells. Mutti, one of the world's leading hypochondriacs, responds to my descriptions. Almost immediately she feels a headache coming on. Indeed, I've learned the symptoms from her. I use her exact words.

"What do you think about this crazy idea?" she asks Papa.

"Let me think about it," he says.

When we're alone, he asks quietly why I want a job. "So that I can save money for college," I begin. Then I change my tactic. "So I can get out of Hebrew School," I answer honestly.

He nods and goes back to his newspaper.

Later, as they're getting ready for bed, I overhear Papa explain to Mutti why I should take the job. I can't hear the whole discussion. I do catch, "He's a man now."

The next afternoon I return to the pharmacy and say I'll take the job as long as it doesn't interfere with my studies. Fred agrees. Fred is the pharmacist. He insists that we can't have two Freds in the shop. Because he's older and the boss, I'll have to pick another name. "What's your middle name?"

"Michael."

"OK, Mike. Why don't you start by sweeping the basement?" He gives me a broom and a dustpan and I go to work. He shows me a ledger where I'll sign in and out whenever I work.

I'm about halfway done with the sweeping when Fred shouts down the steps, "Mike, come here please."

I run up the steps. Fred has two small packages behind the counter. "Whenever you see a package here, deliver it at once. People need their medicine. If you're on Park Avenue, remember to use the service entrance to buildings."

The names and addresses are clearly marked on the packages. I find my jacket and dash out the door. I run to the first address on a side street two blocks away. It's a fancy building, not on Park Avenue, but the doorman still won't let me in. He points to the service entrance. When I'm inside, I take a service elevator to the sixth floor. I find the back door to the apartment and a maid answers. I deliver my package and receive my first tip, one dime. Hooray.

The second delivery is on Park. Again I find the service entrance, take a service elevator and find the service door to an apartment. An ancient woman with a cane opens the door. She's clearly not the maid. I ask for Mrs. Gross.

"I'm Mrs. Gross."

"Here's your medicine from the Lexington Pharmacy."

"How nice. You're a fast one, aren't you?"

"I ran all the way," I lie.

"Just a moment, please." And she toddles off. She comes back and presses a quarter into my hand. Then she hands me a cookie. "Thank you, young man."

I return to the pharmacy and Joe, the soda jerk, gives me a glass of milk to go with my cookie. After sweeping some more, I run another delivery for a dime tip. When I return, Fred says to sign out. "Come back tomorrow and finish your sweeping."

I run home, do some homework, and when Papa arrives, we have dinner. I tell about my 45 cents in tips, cookie and free milk. "And I'll be paid 80 cents for two hours work." Papa says that pretty soon I'll be earning more than he brings home.

On my second day of work, Fred has some forms for me to fill in. Something about child labor laws. One form is for my mother to sign assuring that she gives me permission to work. I don't mention that she wants me to die in Hebrew school. I promise to return the signed form on the next day.

I sweep until the basement is really clean. I ask for a cloth so that I can dust. Fred is impressed. I have only two deliveries that day but on the next day when I arrive at the shop, there are six packages behind the counter. I arrange them by location. I deliver the two nearest first. Then I come back for two more that require me to go east. The final two packages are for apartments on Fifth Avenue. I'm getting to know the neighborhood. One of my delivery stops is another rich old lady who asks if I can go shopping for her. I agree but tell her I can only do it after I'm done at the pharmacy. "I'm not going anywhere," she says.

When I return to the shop, I tell Fred about my six adventures. I also point out that I swept and that the basement probably doesn't need sweeping more than once each week. He tells Joe to teach me the art of being a soda jerk, "Just in case you ever need a backup," he tells Joe. I have noticed that Joe never gets breaks. I wonder when he goes to the bathroom.

I make one more delivery before Fred sends me home. Then I do the grocery shopping for the old lady. I spend most of her five dollar bill. When I ring her doorbell, she's happy to see me. Again I lie that I ran all the way. It's a good line that I plan to use often. I show her the bill and give her $1.33 change. She keeps the dollar bill and lets me keep the coins.

"Call whenever you need me."

I run home to count my loot: $1.33 plus pay for two hours. Even Mutti is impressed.

Because I don't have regular hours yet, Fred tells me to take Friday off. Come any time after lunch on Saturday.

On Friday I meet the boys after school. We go to an empty lot to play Territory. Ferguson is there and I try to find out what he knows about girls. The word that I was seen at a movie with a pretty girl has already made the rounds. Ferguson seems reluctant to talk intimately about girls with other guys around. I need to find a better opportunity. I tell about my job and everyone wonders if I'm ready to quit school. "Not till I'm 16," I lie. The idea of quitting school sounds preposterous to me. I want to be like Pharmacist Fred or a school teacher. I want the "good life," although I don't know what that means except that I've learned that poverty and cockroaches go together. Perhaps I can own a house in Jersey on a wooded lot. And I'd own a telephone, maybe two.

* * *

I'd like to see Josephine, but I don't know how to make contact. I can't just walk into the Little Italy building and say, "I'm the guy who almost killed Albert and I scared him with a switchblade and I touched

185

Josephine's breast and I'm Jewish and I don't believe in the Virgin. Can Josephine come out to play?"

Nor can Josephine ring my doorbell. Well, I suppose she could, but then I'd have to answer a lot of questions. Mutti would want to know everything about the girl and finally she'd ask, "Is she Jewish?" Besides, how many 14-year-old boys have 16-year-old girls call at their apartment?

On Sunday, I go downstairs while everyone from "Little Italy" is in church. I bring chalk. I study the six steps that lead to the wooden front door of Josephine's tenement building. I write "2 p.m." on the third step.

At 2, I'm inside the glass door of my building. I watch for Josephine. Perhaps she didn't understand the message. Perhaps she's not allowed out. Perhaps she's in Jersey with her father. After 20 minutes, I give up and visit Morris.

On Tuesday, I come home from work as the sun is setting. I hear a klunk as I near my building. Another klunk is followed by the sound of something rolling. I look around, but see nothing. Then another klunk and I see a stone rolling in the middle of the street. I walk over to pick it up. Perhaps it's a coin. In our neighborhood it's quite common for a mother to holler from a third or fourth floor window, "Tony."

"What, Ma?"

"Pick up 5 cents soup greens."

"Aw, mom."

"Do it now if you want supper. Your father will be home soon."

Tony's mother then throws a nickel wrapped in newspaper into the street.

But this time someone was dropping stones, not coins. I look up and there is Josephine at her window. I wave and wait. When I see the brown door of Little Italy open, I start walking toward Second Avenue. Josephine follows. It's too cold to stand at the corner so I walk into the neighborhood candy shop.

"Do you want some licorice?" I ask as Josephine walks in.

"Red," she whispers. She likes licorice. I spend two pennies on two sticks.

The clerk gives the licorice to Josephine. I don't like licorice.

"Can you come out for a little while tonight?" I ask.

"Not 'til after supper."

"Could we meet at 8:15? I'll tell my parents I'm going to the library. We'll go to the Horn & Hardart. I have money."

"Wonderful. *Arrivederci.*"

Right on time, Josephine comes out and I walk out my door. I race to the corner, turn and walk more slowly. When Josephine catches up to me I say, "*Ciao.*" She's been teaching me Italian. Josephine grabs my hand and tells me how happy she is that we made contact. I immediately tell her about my new job and how much I love it and how I'm free of Hebrew school and that she looks pretty.

We place our coats at a table in the Automat before we go to the little windows to select our goodies. I select coffee ice cream, drop my coin into a slot, the little window opens and I pull out a dish. Josephine selects pie from another window. I put in coins and her little window pops open. I have a pocketful of coins from tips. We walk to a counter where a woman wearing a chef's hat and a white apron pours drinks. I order hot chocolate. Josephine orders coffee. We put our sweets and drinks on a tray. Josephine carries it to our table and serves us. She lays out napkins.

Josephine was in Jersey last weekend with her dad and saw their new house growing. She's very sad. She bemoans the potential of moving next summer. However, she says that I've given her an idea. At the end of the school year, she'll be 17 and she'll quit school to get a job and then she can live in New York. She lists possible jobs. She'll work until she marries a man who promises to live in New York City and who wants lots of children.

As she talks about her home in Jersey she starts to cry. I take out a hankie. She sniffles.

"Where do you want to live?" she asks.

"New York City," I lie. Actually, I want to move far away from my parents. Soon. Certainly when I go to college.

"How many children do you want?"

"300," I joke.

I turn the conversation to the important stuff. When and how can we arrange our next rendezvous? I need to explain "rendezvous."

Josephine describes a loose brick on a building next to mine. She discovered it last year while playing jacks with a girlfriend. We can leave notes. We agree to alternate movie and museum dates as long as the cold continues.

As we walk home, Josephine returns my handkerchief. Apparently her mother found the one I had given her. "I had to lie to stay out of trouble. Then I had to pray to the Virgin and then, at confession, I told the priest that I had lied."

Confession is a new topic and it puzzles me. I ask about a hundred questions. What does one confess? How often? Does the priest tell your parents? What are the punishments? I make Josephine promise that the next time we go out she'll show me the booth in which one confesses.

* * *

Between my job and Josephine's weekends in New Jersey, we don't get together often. Our next movie date doesn't occur until almost Christmas. Our movie dates are no longer about movies. They're a place to make out in the cold weather.

As usual, in the lobby I help Josephine off with her coat. She's wearing a man's shirt again. She goes off to the ladies room and when she returns, we find seats in the back row. The theater isn't crowded and we place our coats on seats next to us.

"It's been a long time," Josephine whispers. Then she kisses my ear. I wonder if she also reads romance novels. Or does she learn from older boys in her Catholic high school? I'm feeling a little shy until Josephine starts kissing. Slowly at first, then more vigorously. I hold her in a passionate embrace. I reach for a breast. She's not wearing a bra! Timid at first, I open shirt buttons and my confidence returns. Josephine looks around. No one is near us. She puts her hand between my legs. Startled, I jump and she pulls her hand away. I bring it back and she opens my fly. She plays with my circumcised manhood! We kiss. I explore her body and she strokes between my legs and all the world is good.

As the movie ends, I can feel my face glowing and Josephine, too, seems especially warm. I button my pants and Josephine buttons her blouse. We stay in our seats for a moment and share a long kiss. Josephine goes to the ladies room with my pocket comb. When she returns she looks clean and polished. I help her on with her coat and we leave. A group of my friends from school are entering the theater just as we hit the street.

"How was the movie?"

I'm tempted to say, "I don't know," but I don't want to embarrass Josephine. Instead I say, "It was great. Terrific! Really great!" Josephine and I smile.

We see each other so rarely that I ask, "Do you have time for a cup of coffee or a soda?"

"What time is it?"

I look at my watch, an expensive extra bar mitzvah present from Uncle Max. We have almost two hours before dinner. But I have some homework to finish. I can afford at least an hour. By the time we've made a decision, we're standing in front of a cafeteria. We enter, select two pieces of pie, a cup of coffee and a hot chocolate. Josephine carries the tray to a table. She serves the pie and drinks, sets out forks and pulls napkins from a dispenser. I think that she'll be a good wife for someone. But I just say, "Thank you."

After I finish my pie, like a magician, I pull out my Meerschaum and tobacco tin. Josephine's jaw drops and her eyes open wide. I fill the bowl and light the tobacco. Then I tell her about the Uncle Max challenge.

Josephine has an Uncle Francis who smokes the same Granger Rough Cut tobacco and she loves the smell. She tells me she's impressed that I have a job and that I skipped a grade and that I smoke a pipe. She leans over and gives me a peck on the cheek. I take her hand. She then tells me that she's glad I'm interested in her church. I remind her that I only wanted to see the confessional. I'm not ready to confess.

We did stop at her church a few weeks back and she explained the booth where the priest sits on one side and the sinner sits on the other. I still have questions, but I don't know how to ask them without offending. She truly believes that confessing a sin cleanses the soul. I finally dare to ask, "If Hitler or Goering or Goebbels confessed their sins against the six million, would Jesus forgive?"

Josephine needs some explanation before she understands the full impact of the question. Once she understands she answers without hesitation. "Absolutely. If they truly confess and truly accept Jesus they would be forgiven. The priest would assign them many prayers and some difficult tasks. They would have to do good works. But Jesus accepts all those who accept him."

Then Josephine blows my mind. She asks, "Can you forgive them?" The last of the gas chambers was turned off two and a half years ago. The last of the ovens was turned off two and a half years ago. I mention my aunts and my uncles and my cousin and my grandmother and I say, "I don't think so." We sit silently for a few moments. Then I say, "Perhaps one day I can learn forgiveness." Then I add, "Perhaps it's easier for God to forgive than it is for people." That seems to please Josephine.

When I finish my pipe, I tap the remains into the ashtray and make sure that the bowl is cool just as Uncle Max would do. I return everything to my coat pocket. I leave a small tip for the busboy, help Josephine on with her coat and we leave hand-in-hand.

* * *

During our Christmas vacation I spend more time with Morris. It's pretty certain now that the UN will create a new country, Israel. We argue. I contend that it may become a theocracy, that the Orthodox will try to rule and that it could split the Jewish people. Morris asserts that we need a homeland of our own. Morris, who, coming from the area feels that he has some firsthand knowledge, predicts that the Arabs will protest and that wars will follow the creation of Israel. Current skirmishes between Arabs and residents of the kibbutzim give the predictions credibility. Will other nations take sides? Will the Muslim nations fight the Christian nations over a Jewish nation?

Morris, who, like me, started school a year late, also skipped eighth grade. We talk about high schools. His counselor wants him to go to Stuyvesant, the elite liberal arts school named after Peter Stuyvesant, the last governor of a Dutch colony, New Netherlands, renamed New York by the British. Mr. Pearlstein tells us that the 17th century Peter Stuyvesant hated Jews. Nevertheless, the Pearlsteins agree with the counselor. They want Morris to have a liberal arts education, study commerce at college and join his father's business. Morris and I eliminate Brooklyn Tech, an engineering prep school, because it's too far away. We eliminate Music and Art because we don't plan to become performers. Mr. Halverson wants me to go to the Bronx High School of Science, the most elite of the "special" schools for gifted kids. Perhaps he thinks that one day I'll become a great scientist.

I like Stuyvesant High because it's in Manhattan, a short ride on the subway from my home, and I'd like to be with Morris. I have no idea what kind of career I want. Zero. My parents want me to become a doctor but that's the only career I've eliminated. I hate the sight of blood. Mutti wants me to go to Science High because she wants to brag about her son.

In January, I take the tests for Stuyvesant and Science High and barely pass both. Mr. Halvorson predicts that one day I'll be a huge success and that I ought to go to the best school. He arranges an interview at Science. I attend and I'm impressed. However, I want to go with Morris. What a choice: Morris or Mr. Halvorson. I pick Mr. Halvorson.

My job is fabulous. I'm now putting in about 15 hours each week. Christmas tips are fantastic. My boss—I call him Pharmacist Phred—is quite flexible about hours and when I've done my work, he lets me read in the basement on work time.

One day, early in January of 1948, my buddies invent a contest. Which of us can steal the largest item from the local five and dime store? Four of us agree to the pact. I'm wearing my Mackinaw which allows me to hide quite a bit. We wander around the store. I see lots of stuff that's too fat and lots of stuff that I can't even identify. Quite a challenge. After half an hour we meet at a location about two blocks from the store. Frank claims to be the winner. He has a legal size writing pad. I open my coat to display a two-foot fluorescent bulb.

A few days later I return to the store to "borrow" some books. I've got the technique mastered. And I have two large pockets on the sides of my Mackinaw. Just as I'm ready to leave, a tall man in a suit grabs my arm. "Come with me." Without letting go of my arm, he takes me to a back room where a security guard is waiting.

"Empty your coat pockets."

Life is over. My career as a scholar has ended. No high school for me. I'm on my way to jail. The tears start flowing.

"Empty your pockets."

I empty my coat pockets. They contain only two items, two books with covers that show shirtless muscular men and helpless women with large rips in their blouses. I try to collect my thoughts, but I'm in a panic and crying hysterically.

"What's your name?"

"Mike," I answer, using my store name.

"You were stealing these books."

I admit my crime, but I add to the sin by lying. "I don't know why. I've never done this before. I'll never do it again." I'm babbling. How can I talk my way out of this predicament? I even promise to go home to get money to pay for the books.

The man in the suit says, "We'll have to take you in and check your fingerprints."

I'm beyond hysterical. My parents will be shamed by having a thief in the family—their only son. Mr. Halverson will make a speech at the next school assembly. A member of the color guard has let the school down. Shame from all corners.

I beg. I promise. I'm incoherent.

The security guard suggests, "Perhaps we should let him go this time. We'll see if he can reform himself."

Pause. A pause that seems to last for hours. Finally the man wearing the suit says, "Well, OK. But," looking straight at me, "don't ever let me see you in this store again."

He walks me to the door and repeats his command.

I run. I run *away* from home. Not toward it. Surely they're following me. Surely this is a trick to see where I live. I turn west and run a few blocks. Then north. East and north and west again and then south. I have to confuse these people lest they find my parents. After an hour I arrive home. En route I've made some decisions. I'll never steal again. I've cast Josephine's Devil out. Never will he enter my body again. I'll never lie again.

I wonder if I should see the priest in the confessional booth. I've sinned. The sin has stained my soul. How can I atone? I confuse Josephine's God with my God.

During the next night I count my sins. There is one that puzzles me. Is lusting after Josephine a sin or a sign of God's love?

* * *

One day as I'm making deliveries for the Lexington Pharmacy, shortly after my commitment to give up the sinful life, I see a group picketing a neighborhood restaurant. A sign reads, "End Racism." Another boldly proclaims, "Negroes Have Equal Rights." I chat with a few of the picketers, both black and white, and learn that they're protesting some discriminatory act by the restaurant. Apparently some black people were not permitted to eat there. The details are fuzzy. The group is boisterous, chanting slogans and singing songs. *Go down Moses* and *Michael Row Your Boat Ashore* distract me for some time until I remember that I'm on the job.

I return after work and befriend some of the protesters. I learn other places they will picket and other causes they defend. I decide to attend some of their other events. It certainly seems more virtuous than shoplifting.

Over the next few weeks, I learn that some members of this loose group are supporting Henry Wallace for U.S. president; 1948 is an election year. Thomas Dewey, governor of New York State, is running on the Republican Party ticket. Harry Truman, who became president after FDR died, is running for re-election. Henry Wallace is running on the Progressive Party ticket.

Miss Orlofsky finds some books which teach me that Wallace was once Secretary of Agriculture and served as vice president under Roosevelt during most of the war years. While he is best known for innovations in crop development, a foreign concept to this city slicker, he wants to end racism and poverty. He wants to create more jobs so that the divide between rich and poor is diminished.

I attend some Wallace rallies and learn that he supports closer ties to the Soviet Union and an end to the Cold War. He wants to end segregation. Wallace refuses to speak to segregated audiences and will not eat in segregated establishments. He regularly has people of color on the platforms from which he speaks. Most controversial is his advocacy of universal health care. Endorsed by the American Communist Party and vilified by both major parties, Wallace is the anti-establishment candidate to excite a teenager.

I become active in the Progressive Party campaign, attending meetings and handing out leaflets. I quickly achieve some leadership positions with responsibility for organizing rallies and for inventing ways to
involve young voters. The fact that I'm years away from voting seems
inconsequential.

Mutti is appalled that I spend my evenings at meetings and rallies. "Why you? Why should you stick your neck out? Haven't the Jews
had enough trouble? You should be quiet and stay out of trouble." She's
concerned about my safety—and hers. I think she pictures an American version of a concentration camp. We'll be hauled away as political
trouble-makers.

"It's the Jewish thing to do," I argue. "We have to look out for our
neighbors lest they, too, face a Holocaust. We should promote justice for
all."

Mutti cries. Papa simply says, "Be careful." I think he is secretly
proud.

I read books by Henry Wallace and meet many of his campaign staff.
I generally enjoy my new life as an activist. At one large rally, Glen Taylor,
Progressive Party candidate for vice president, senator from Idaho and
country western singer, plays his guitar while sitting on a horse. I'm introduced to Taylor and to his horse. I'm escorted past the police guard so
that I can pet the horse. The first horse I ever touched.

Politics becomes my social life. Sometimes I lie about my age because
I'm the youngest member of my new circle. None of the girls is as sexy
as Josephine, but all of them have read books and can participate in an
interesting conversation without mention of Jesus or the Virgin Mary.

* * *

In 1947, the UN proposed two nations, Israel and Palestine. Most of the
Arab states rejected the resolution. On May 15, 1948, the UN declares
that Israel is an independent nation. Borders are clearly specified. A new
Israeli government proclaims independence on the 14th day of May because the 15th falls on the Sabbath.

In New York, Jewish communities hoist Israel's blue and white flag
with the Star of David in its center. Every synagogue and many homes
display Israel's symbol. There is dancing in the streets on the Jewish

Lower East Side of Manhattan and in Brooklyn's Jewish neighborhoods. My new left-wing friends are generally supportive because it seems Israel will become a Socialist nation. President Truman recognizes the new State almost immediately.

That evening I visit the Pearlsteins. They're happy and pensive at the same time. They know the territory. "Wait," cautions Morris. "Hope," says his father. They've picked up an Israeli station on their short wave radio. We hear a tinny version of the Israeli National Anthem, *HaTikvah*. I foolishly translate for this family whose first language is Hebrew, *The Hope*.

HaTikvah was not written for this occasion. Rather it stems from 19th century Europe where the hope for an Israeli nation was already blossoming.

> *As long as the Jewish spirit is yearning deep in the heart,*
> *With eyes turned toward the East, looking toward Zion,*
> *Then our hope—the two-thousand-year-old hope—will not be lost:*
> *To be a free people in our land,*
> *The land of Zion and Jerusalem*

On the 15th of May, less than 24 hours after Israel's declaration of independence, five Arab nations invade the new state. Morris's warning was prophetic. He explains that the Arab countries are fighting Israel to avoid a massive influx of Palestinians, generally perceived to be a potential drain on growing economies. The UN Secretary General characterizes the invasion as the first armed aggression since World War II.

Each day we pore over newspapers and listen to radio reports in hopes of learning that the tide had turned. At first Israelis respond bravely, but haphazardly. After about ten days, Israel has organized an army and begins to centralize its war effort. Eventually an air force is mobilized. The Israeli government is able to buy planes mostly from Communist Czechoslovakia. By the end of May, Israel has recovered from the surprise attack and is ready to fight and win a war. Morris and I wonder if we should volunteer to serve in the IDF, the Israeli Defense Forces. Of course we're much too young.

* * *

Spring passes quickly. School, my job and my exciting activities with the Civil Rights Movement keep me busy. I visit with Morris when I can and occasionally meet my junior high friends after school.

My trysts with Josephine have become infrequent. However, the occasional visits to movie theaters become ever more passionate. I wonder where Josephine learned the moves she teaches me.

As the time for her departure to New Jersey comes closer, Josephine becomes more depressed. She counts the days until the school year ends. Then, she promises herself that she'll find a job and leave home. "After all, I'm 17 now."

One day in early June, we walk west. Our goal is the Central Park Zoo. I reason that I have to take Josephine somewhere beyond the local museum and the movie theater. It's a sunny day and Josephine thinks a walk in the park would be fun. It's finally warm enough for short sleeves. As we enter the park I tell Josephine that I know a secret spot where I occasionally read.

"Would you share your secret with me?"

"I'd like that."

"Will we have to read?" she asks as if that would be a punishment.

"We can daydream." My imagination is racing.

We climb a hill to some bushes. I lead us through a little opening to a grassy spot surrounded by low bushes. I rest on my back and wait. Josephine walks around the circle of bushes and then kneels next to me. "This is beautiful. May I come here when I need to be alone?"

"Of course. I don't own this spot. I only found it—like Columbus finding America. Now it can be our secret."

Josephine smiles and lies down beside me. A moment later we're kissing. Long, deep kisses. Josephine's loose silky blouse hangs over her skirt. I reach underneath. No bra! I lift her blouse and see her breasts This is so much better than the pictures I've seen in medical books. Josephine smiles when I kiss her mouth. I kiss wherever I choose and wherever I choose seems to please her. I've never really seen Josephine's face when we make out in the movies. Now I can see the glow. Her cheeks have reddened, her lips are parted. We kiss and hug some more, clinging to each other in the fresh air.

I reach under her skirt. No panties! My mind is in disarray. Thoughts are bumping into one another. Does she enjoy my touch? May I look? Will anyone come to bother us? Has the Devil come back? What next?

Josephine lies with her eyes closed. She seems totally relaxed and happy. We kiss some more. She opens my zipper. I can't believe how her gentle touches make me feel. She shifts her weight and now she's straddling me. I'm engulfed in waves of ecstasy.

We spend the entire afternoon in our secret spot—secret has a new meaning now. The zoo can wait for another day.

On the walk home we stop at an ice cream cart and each select a flavor. I treat, now that I have a steady income.

That evening, much to Mutti's chagrin, I light my pipe. I puff slowly thinking, "Today I am a man—really."

XXVIII. A BRONX CHEER FOR NERD HIGH

JOSEPHINE DISAPPEARS into New Jersey just before I start at the Bronx High School of Science. I never see her again. Never hear from her again. I have no forwarding address, no city, not even a photo.

Morris attends Stuyvesant High in lower Manhattan and I rarely see him. He's busy with studies and soccer.

I'm busy with subway rides. Forty minutes in each direction. From my Manhattan home, 315 East 77th Street, I walk two blocks west to the subway station on Lexington Avenue. Down the steps into the tunnel, I select the correct train. An empty seat means I can study. The Periodic Table for chemistry, laws of physics, important scientists for history, the intricacies of calculus—all interspersed with novels and poems. I'm drowning in stuff to memorize.

When the train arrives at the station near school, I climb the steps to street level and run. I sprint. It's important that I not arrive late. More important is that the track coach sees me gasping for breath.

"Good man," he says. "We need you at your best on Saturday morning."

"Yes sir. I'll have wings on my feet."

At our first assembly, the principal, Dr. Meister, has us chat with kids sitting near us. Most of the kids I meet have names like Ginsberg, Shapiro and Rubinowitz. After five minutes, Dr. Meister asks for our attention. "You're no longer the smartest kid in class. You'll have to learn to live with that," he counsels. "Your teachers, many with Ph.Ds., expect each student to be a genius."

Dr. Meister says he wants to teach us humility. I'm humbled. I'm so terrified, I'm ready to wet my pants. He lectures some more, "Some call our school Bronx Science. Others say Science High. Most of us simply say we attend Science. Whatever we call our school, we're all convinced that we're part of the premier and most selective science high school in the country."

He's quite right. Most of us have recently graduated from junior high schools to attend Science for three years, grades ten through twelve. Almost every student admits to being a nerd. We carry slide rules from day one and during lunch, students relax by playing variations of three-dimensional chess. Rumor has it that there was once a graduate of Science High who didn't attend college.

I'm no longer special. Principal Meister claims we're all special, perhaps equally special. Special is the new normal.

As part of our orientation, a guidance counselor and a social worker encourage us to visit if we have personal or career questions. We're told to again form small groups and each student is to tell one problem one might ask a counselor. A tall boy in my group can't decide if he wants to be a dermatologist or a neurologist. A girl with dark eyes says that her parents will kill her if she doesn't get into Radcliffe. Her father and grandfathers went to Harvard. Her mother and grandmothers went to Radcliffe. Papa finished the fourth grade. My mother finished high school. I'm in a different league. I admit my terror to those around me, "I'll probably flunk out in the first month. If I don't, I'll need my personal full time counselor." Just then Dr. Meister dismisses the assembly and we're off to class.

A biology teacher with a Ph.D. from Michigan, begins his first class: "This is a college level biology course with a focus on genetics. We will breed variations of *Drosophila*. What do you know about *Drosophila*?"

Sure enough, a sixteen-year-old budding Nobel Laureate raises his hand. This kid looks pudgy and pale as if he doesn't play outdoors much. He's wearing a brownish tie with paisley design. "*Drosophila melanogaster* is the common fruit fly. It is included in the family of Drosophilidae." There isn't much you can teach a Science High student. They know it all. I don't know and I feel really dumb.

Each biology student shares a lab station with a partner. The station includes a super microscope with a fancy name that mystifies me. Because I'm half-blind, all I can see is what James Thurber calls a "lacteal substance." Fortunately my partner, the son of an ophthalmologist, aspires to be a nuclear physicist. He describes what's on each slide under the scope and I pretend that I see it too.

Dr. Hovde's classes are often a learning adventure. Dr. Hovde teaches languages. He's the stereotype of an absent-minded professor. His brown suits don't fit and he speaks in long obtuse paragraphs. One day he walks into class and starts discussing a Roman play, "Great friendships can spring from bad beginnings." He's lecturing about a Terence drama in Latin. The students let him talk. Many know some Latin and the others are amused. Finally, several students poke me and point to Dr. Hovde. They want me, his favorite student, to tell our teacher that this is German class. Finally, in German, I interrupt to say, "Excuse me, Doctor. This is German class and we're ready to speak German."

He smiles, "*Ja, gut*" and the students applaud. He leads the class in a discussion about last night's homework assignment, Goethe's *Faust*. German is my first language, but I can barely keep up with the discussion.

I'm not special any more and I want to be. I've spent all my life being special. Being normal feels weird. Feeling below normal hurts.

Even being Jewish isn't special. Almost all the students are Jewish. Science High is closed on Jewish holidays. They say it's not worth turning on the lights for the few who would show up.

* * *

The Bronx High School of Science has no football team. No soccer team. Hardly any sports at all except tennis, swimming and track. Apparently nerds don't do competitive sports. There's a chess team and a debate team and some kind of quiz bowl team. I try out for track and make the team.

Mike Levinson, Black Mike—because he's so grumpy, and only behind his back—is a math teacher, assistant principal for discipline (discipline at Science High?) and the track coach. Black Mike is tough and gruff. Everyone in the school is so afraid of him that we address him as "sir" and we stand at attention when he speaks to us.

We have no track near school so it's another fifteen-minute subway ride further north in the Bronx to our practice oval in Van Cortlandt Park. More time to study.

Coach Levinson is discouraged with the track team. The members would rather solve math problems or play three-dimensional tic tac toe than train for running, pole vaulting or jumping.

One afternoon, soon after I join the team, Mr. Levinson sends everyone except the team manager home early. The manager is in charge of equipment and is always the last to leave. He drives a station wagon that displays the New York City Public Schools logo.

"Amram, you stay." Why me?

"Amram, I'm going to see what you can do." And he does.

"How far is a mile," he asks.

I don't know what answer he wants. "5,280 feet?" I try.

"How many laps?"

"Four, sir."

"How fast can you run one lap? How fast can you run four laps?" He's looking directly into my eyes. I feel challenged as if he wants to pick a fight. I look at my feet, trying to avoid his stare.

"I don't know sir. A four-minute mile would be a record." I've been reading about track.

"Let's see what you can do." He's challenging me. "Run one lap." He holds a stop watch that always hangs around his neck. "Now. Ready. Set. Go."

When I return, my chest hurts and I can barely breathe.

"OK," says the coach. "Now three more laps."

"Now?"

"Now!" I run, although my pace slows with each lap.

At the end of the last lap my chest hurts worse and tears are streaming down my cheeks.

"OK. Rest a minute." I want to rest for three days. I collapse onto the grass. Coach talks to the equipment manager who starts unpacking a pole.

"Now I want to see how high you can vault."

"Now?" I've only had a few lessons on the pole and hated vaulting.

"Now! Try this pole."

I fly over the bar at three feet, four feet, five feet. I land on the mats badly and I think I've broken my neck. Coach checks me out, tells me I'm OK and wants to keep trying until I vault ten feet.

At 5½ feet I don't make it over the bar. Each time I slam the pole into the vaulting box I rise a bit and fall to the ground. Coach says I'm balking just like a horse that won't jump a hurdle. I've lost my nerve.

While I'm pole vaulting, the manager has set up three hurdles. I knock the first hurdle down and take a hard fall. I explain to the coach that I'm blind in one eye. I lack binocular vision. I can't judge distance. Mr. Levinson understands, but I can see he's disappointed. I'm not his perfect specimen.

We try broad jumping, but, by now, I'm totally exhausted. My calves hurt. My thighs and shoulders hurt. My chest hurts. I'm ready to cry. Coach and I sit on a bench while the manager packs up. "I like your attitude kid. You can really run and you've got stamina. You don't know anything. I'll teach you how to work your legs, to pace, to use the starting blocks. I'll teach you to become a runner if you work hard. And I'll keep you away from vaulting and the hurdles. You don't have the nerve. You might be the star I've been looking for." If it means this much pain, I don't want to be a star.

Mr. Levinson and I build a relationship. I don't like him because he's too grouchy. He, on the other hand, loves me because I work hard and I learn what he knows. I become Black Mike's star, which at Science High isn't saying much.

I anchor middle-distance relay teams. Coach teaches me to handle the baton, the little stick that relay runners hand off to one another. He teaches me to sprint past the finish line—not just to the finish line. I run long distances. The coach teaches about pacing: "There's no such thing as a third wind," he advises.

We compete against other city high schools where the students value sports. I learn that serious athletes stretch and do push-ups and run everywhere. I rarely win. Occasionally a third place or an honorable mention. But I represent our school in national competitions like the Penn Relays and I watch real athletes. Tall boys with long, strong legs leave me discouraged, but I receive brass medals—no gold or silver—simply because I attend. I collect variations on a winged brass foot with a loop at the top—made for a charm bracelet or a necklace or, best of all, to give to a girlfriend. First and second place winners receive a full statue of Mercury. I'm content with Mercury's foot.

No parents show up for meets. They seem to value Nobel Prizes more than track trophies.

Nevertheless, I wear a green and gold Science High letter-jacket and each year I earn another letter in a school where scholarship, not athletics, is valued. I'm special, but not very.

* * *

The 86ᵗʰ Street station is the first subway stop after I get on. Gene, a student in the same grade, starts his morning trip at this station. Every now and then he finds me and we ride to school together. We become friends. Gene, my height, more broad shouldered, regularly wears dress shirts and cardigan sweaters—he must have a closet full of sweaters. Gene is the son of the Consul General from the newly formed South Korea. Is Papa the only peddler parent at Science High? Other parents are doctors and scientists and lawyers, even judges.

Gene is special. He's Asian. More Asian than the Asian-American students in our school. Like me, he's foreign.

Gene invites me for dinner at his home—the Consulate. Gene's English is flawless with the slightest accent. Gene's parents speak English perfectly. At dinner, the Consul General discusses Shakespeare as we eat in a book-lined room. Two long walls are lined with floor-to-ceiling dark wood bookshelves. The two short walls made of the same dark wood have doors that slide into the wall. Servants bring food. Servants clear dishes.

"No, I haven't read all of Shakespeare," I admit to Gene's parents. "Yes, I like the sonnets although I don't always understand their meaning."

Gene's dad catches me off guard with, "What would you change in any Shakespeare play?"

I'm flustered. No one has ever given me the power to change a famous play. Then, "In Hamlet, I wouldn't have Ophelia die. I'd strengthen her character so that we could see a contrast to Hamlet's indecisiveness."

I want to ask what the Consul General would change in Shakespeare, but I don't dare.

Gene's dad, I'm instructed to not address him as His Excellency, wants to know about my father's work. I describe Papa going from farm to farm, from door to door, in New Jersey. I avoid the word "peddler." I can't imagine Gene coming to dinner at my home, sitting at my metallic kitchen table, listening to the conversation in German or in broken English because there's an American guest. Papa doesn't know "from Shakespeare." I picture Gene eyeing the books in our living room. *The Razor's Edge* and *The Postman Always Rings Twice* in paperback editions. A few prayer books in Hebrew and a German newspaper.

Gene invites me to another dinner. His parents like me and are happy that Gene has such a nice friend. Gene's dad wants to talk with me about my coming to the U.S.A. Gene warns that I should dress in a suit. This is a formal dinner with other guests.

I walk the ten blocks to the Consulate. As I come around the corner I see people stepping out of a handsome chauffeur-driven car. Another handsome black vehicle appears. I watch the driver run around the car to hold the door open for a woman in fur. In the foyer, Gene's mom tries to put me at ease with a friendly greeting. I hand my coat to a butler. I'm the last to arrive.

A waitress offers me a drink but I decline with a "No, thank you." If I were to request scotch, Gene's mom and Mutti would probably have a long talk. I don't like water or coffee or soda. Wouldn't I look silly with milk?

Aside from Gene's family, there are two Korean couples and two American couples. As I join the party, conversation centers on belligerent acts by the North Korean government. The Consul General assures everyone that a war is out of the question. At dinner I learn that the American men are U.S. merchants. One of the Korean men represents the Korean toy manufacturing industry. The other represents the textile industry. Both hope to expand markets in the United States.

Gene is seated across from me between the two American women. I am seated between the two Korean women, both dressed in beautiful dresses with what I assume to be Korean designs. They're bedazzled with jewelry from head to toe—literally. Both wear glittering diamond earrings and bracelets that tinkle as they lift their forks. The woman to my left is wearing a red dress with gold geometric patterns and has reflective colored stones on her slipper-like shoes. She is interested in American politics. I find myself defending Henry Wallace and the benefits of a third party, the Progressive Party, in American politics. The woman seems quite aghast with the potential of an unstable U.S. government. Perhaps she has never before met a teenage radical.

I'm invited for dinner at the homes of other Science High students. Not all have maids and butlers. Nevertheless, elegant apartments and thoughtful dinner conversation are the rule.

Papa is no longer my idol. When asked, I refuse to go for walks with him. I rarely bring colleagues home. I'm ashamed of having uneducated, unworldly parents. I have a chance to join the elite, but I'm a boor.

When Mutti asks, "Why don't we see you anymore?" I want to answer, "Because I'm ashamed of being an Amram, ashamed of you, ashamed of my history." Instead I say, "I'm so busy and between school and track and work, I barely have time to sleep." But the real reason is, I'm avoiding the life of an Amram. In a Social Studies class, we study the Holocaust. I don't mention to anyone that I was a witness to that event. I want my father to be a highly sophisticated, wealthy merchant, perhaps a Consul General.

But it is also true that homework and track and work at the Lexington Pharmacy really don't leave much leisure time. I don't even have time to go on dates—and I'm afraid that I'm not classy enough anyway. Am I an outsider again?

Occasionally I see Barbara, the girl I met and tried to impress at summer camp a while back. She's a year ahead of me. She's interesting to talk with and we occasionally chat at lunch. A rare trip to a museum describes our dating. Mutti wants me to marry Barbara because she's Jewish and friendly and smart and comes from a good family. Mutti likes that Barbara's father is called doctor. He's an optometrist.

I work up the courage to invite Gene to our apartment on East 77th Street, but not for dinner. I'm totally embarrassed. Our tiny, dingy apartment embarrasses me. No library or elegant dining room. No private place to study. My parents are too unsophisticated and can't even speak proper English.

I feel embarrassed whenever Gene stops at my apartment after school. One day, on the subway ride to school, I tell Gene about my parents' history. I confess that I'm ashamed of being ashamed of my parents.

"Your parents are typical of the working poor," he says, "while my family is atypical of families in the U.S. and Korea. My family is pretty rich and extremely well educated."

"Your parents have given you a tremendous head start by being wonderful models," I point out. "How can I be a 'somebody' if my models are the working poor?"

Gene leans close. "Listen Fred, you already know that Jews have to work a little harder to succeed. Asians in white America also have to work a little harder. The poor have to work a lot harder. Look how far you've already come. You've got an open-ended future."

"But I'm embarrassed when I bring you to meet my parents in my dumpy apartment."

As we arrive at our destination, Gene sets me straight. "That's your problem. Not your parents'. Your parents are doing their best."

In the spring of our senior year, 1951, Gene and I, we two foreigners, treat ourselves to a trip to Washington, D.C. Gene, from his generous allowance, and I with my earnings at the Lexington Pharmacy, have accumulated enough money for bus fare, food and three nights at the Washington Young Men's Christian Association. We don't tell the registrar that neither one of us is Christian.

Touring the White House and walking through the halls of Congress are not the highlights of our travels. The take-way from our adventure confronted us as we stepped off the bus in D.C. "Colored Only" water fountains and "White Only" bathrooms stop our happy conversation in the bus station.

As if with one voice we ask each other the same question: What color does "Colored Only" mean? White is clear. I'm white. I pass. However, I'm reminded of "Nur für Juden."

"Colored" probably refers to people with African heritage. Black. Gene is Asian. "People call me 'yellow,'" he says.

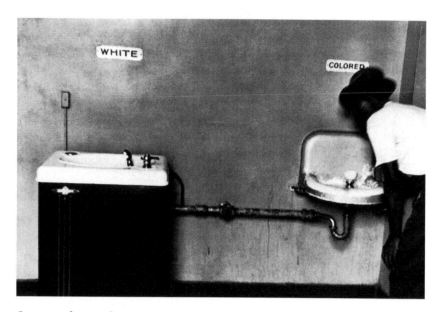

Segregated water fountains

We find segregated drinking fountains and toilets throughout the city. Gene claims to be eligible for both bathrooms so, on our second day in Washington, he decides to inspect. He reports that the bathroom for people who appear African is dirty, lacks toilet paper and most of the faucets leak. We both enter the bathroom for people who look European. It's about as clean as one expects a public toilet to be. Toilet paper is adequate and we find no leaking faucets. We choose to use neither bathroom. Looking around nervously, Gene uses the "Whites Only" drinking fountain.

Three years at Science High introduced me to the elite. A short trip to the American capital with an Asian student reminds me where I come from and who I am. "White only" is too close to "Juden verboten."

XXIX. COLLEGE DAZE

THE EARLY 1950S treat me well. Syracuse University welcomes me with academic scholarships and freedom from home—250 miles from Manhattan. Far enough from my conservative Jewish home to let me taste pork and to carouse with both kosher and non-kosher coeds.

I'm enrolled in the New York State College of Forestry, a public college affiliated with a private university. Forestry students wear flannel shirts year round. When the weather turns warm, we roll up our sleeves to create pockets for our cigarettes. A compass and calipers hanging from a wide leather belt with brass buckle add to the macho image. Identifying every tree on campus by genus and species makes a hit on dates—at least the first date. We establish that we're real men, outdoors men, hunters and fishers—even though I'm a city slicker from the east side of Manhattan, miles out of character. Chemistry labs and botany field trips conflict with beer and girls and jobs and sleeping late. I muddle through most classes.

My trysts with Sarah, Rachel, Rebecca, Leah and the occasional Mary are interrupted by periodic visits to Professor Henry Leventhal's home. Uncle Henry and his mother, Aunt Nanette, are distant cousins with whom my mother maintains a sporadic correspondence. Aunt Nanette responds to one of Mutti's letters by calling to invite me for dinner. I reluctantly agree to meet these strangers who, I'm told, share my mother's bloodline—the "good" side of the family.

My mother insists that I address them as "uncle" and "aunt," even though they are neither. Mutti also insists that I address Henry as "doctor." While on the bus I try various combinations: "Doctor Uncle Henry." "Uncle Doctor Leventhal." "Herr Doctor Professor Uncle Henry." "Uncle Henry" works best when I'm at his home and "Professor Leventhal" seems appropriate on campus.

At dinner, a stew followed by chocolate pudding, Aunt Nanette asks lots of questions, certainly posed by my mother.

"Yes, I'm quite healthy."

"No, I haven't seen a doctor."

"Yes, I study every evening."

"No, I don't drink or smoke."

"Yes, I've met some nice girls." Mutti's ambitions for me are first that I meet a rich, Jewish girl (of which there are many at Syracuse) and second, that I gain admission to medical school.

After dinner I take the bus back to campus with the packet of "nutritious," food forced on me by Aunt Nanette. She insists that I visit at least weekly for a healthy meal. We compromise on weekly phone calls and monthly dinners "because I need to spend all my time studying"— or so I lie.

On the bus ride home, I wonder why I don't like Aunt Nanette's nostalgia for the old country and the old days. She speaks German in her home, just like my mother. Aunt Nanette reminds me of my former German life and brings back the guilt of a survivor.

* * *

I don't need Physics I and II because it duplicates advanced courses at Science High. Physics III is required. I manage to attend most of the sessions because the lectures are in the afternoon and because the teacher is Uncle Henry who knows my face and my name. I even raise my hand now and then to show Professor Leventhal that I am alive and well.

The physics labs, however, are scheduled in the early morning and taught by graduate students. I rarely attend because I need my beauty sleep after nights out on the town. Toward the end of the semester, a classmate warns me that lab workbooks are due in one week and will be personally graded by Dr. Leventhal.

By then I've joined a fraternity. A more experienced student introduces me to the file cabinet that holds papers and exams representing most of the courses currently taught at SU. Sure enough, there is a Physics III Lab Workbook that has a "B" grade on the first page. I copy everything into my blank book with occasional embellishments and grammatical corrections as needed. I attend the lab session at which the workbooks are collected. During finals week, I receive a call from a secretary in Dr. Leventhal's office. At her request I make an appointment. Perhaps he wants to say, "Goodbye," before I leave for the winter break. (With "Jewish" encoded in my DNA, there can be no "Christmas holidays" for me. I continue to experience a central conflict. Am I Jewish or American. No. I cannot become a Jewish-American. I'm guessing that people who witnessed the Holocaust can't live with a hyphen.)

"Fred," begins Uncle Henry in his quiet monotone. I want you to know that you've summarized the physics experiments extremely well."

"Thank you, sir." I add the "sir" in hopes of raising my grade a notch.

"Your workbook went beyond expectations."

Perhaps my embellishments really helped.

"You even described an experiment we didn't do this semester."

Disaster!

The syllabus warns that I will be assigned an "F" for cheating. However, Uncle Henry suggests that because we have a common bloodline, he will let me drop the class with the understanding that I take it again in the spring semester. I almost argue that he is being dishonest and unfair to other students. But, given the circumstances and my desperate need for scholarship funds, I simply say, "Thank you." I add an extra, "Sir."

I don't feel bad about cheating with the physics workbook. I feel stupid that I've been caught. I should have been more cautious and checked with classmates. I should have foreseen this disaster.

However, I do feel guilty about the outcome. I feel dishonest about my light punishment. Because I'm "special," because I'm a relative of the professor, I cheated other students who, under the same circumstances would have been kicked out of school.

I can't stop thinking about *Genesis*. The rabbi taught how Jacob fooled his dying father, Isaac, into bestowing the birthright that belonged to his twin brother Esau. Esau was the firstborn, but Jacob became one of the "fathers of Israel" despite the fact that he cheated. Does our Bible teach us to cheat?

The workbook incident is not my first taste of privilege. When I attended high school, I'd ride the subway from my Manhattan apartment to the Bronx. Oftentimes, at the final subway station, I'd meet my friend, Barbara, and together we'd walk the last few blocks. Lively and interesting conversation occasionally caused us to be late to school.

Mike Levinson was the vice principal in charge of discipline and my track coach. On those occasions when Barbara and I were among the last stragglers to arrive, Coach Levinson slapped my butt and encouraged me to run to school more quickly. "We're counting on you in Saturday's meet." Then he'd scold Barbara and assign her to after-school detention.

Science High is a school for geeks, also known as "gifted students." Nerd Academy. Athletes are rare and precious. During my senior year I was assigned to Coach Levinson's math class. Toward the end of the year we had a surprise quiz. When Mr. Levinson returned the tests, every one of my solutions had a big check. We reviewed the quiz in class. After class I visited with our teacher.

"I wasn't prepared for this test and despite all the checks on my paper, only one question had the correct solution. You may want to adjust my score."

The coach's response: "You let me worry about teaching this class. Saturday's all-city meet is the race of the season. Science High is counting on you."

I won a few medals for the school, but somehow the world doesn't seem fair—in the Bible, at Science High or now at Syracuse.

* * *

Forestry students are enrolled in math, chemistry, physics, biology, botany, silviculture and the like—not a regular hangout for female students in the early '50s. Almost every course includes long hours in labs. Saturday field trips teach us to identify trees by their scientific names. Look at the leaf or the bark and every student should be able to tell everything about the tree including its name, age, health and preferred environment. Some of us even assign fake social security numbers to each tree as we record descriptions into our log books.

My goal is to study pulp and paper chemistry, forest products and plastics, a hot field in the early '50s. When, in the 1967 movie, *The Graduate*, Mr. McGuire tells Ben, "There's a great future in plastics," he was repeating a mantra of the'50s.

Unfortunately, endless hours in organic chemistry labs and all-day Saturday forestry field trips did not capture my soul. My personal interests are embedded in the humanities. While many Jewish scientists, several of them graduates of Science High, have won Nobel Prizes, I am not destined be one of them.

All School of Forestry students are required to take an oral communication course in their senior year. The class description promises improvement in interpersonal communication and public speaking. While none of us are afraid of bears, with only one exception, every senior is petrified of public speaking. I am that exception.

Most of the guys complain that the interpersonal communication activities are sissy and that public speaking is useless. "I'll never give a speech in the real world," is the general grumble. I don't seem to fit the forestry student mold. I love learning about rhetorical theories and the psychology of relationships.

During my last semester, just shy of graduation, I replace several required courses with additional communication courses. Not only are communication classes loaded with girls, but I begin to understand the dynamics of group behavior and the history of language. Most wonderful, I enroll in my first theater course. I enter a fantastic new world of learning where I apply ideas every day and do more than memorize the names of trees and bugs. Teachers even welcome disagreement and self-expression. Without a thought about earning a living with a communication degree, I abruptly change majors and move from the physical sciences to the humanities.

My new advisor, fiftyish Miss Allison (she prefers the title of "Miss" to that of "Professor"), informs me that all speech majors are required to minor in English. I want a minor in Psychology. With all my science training, I am ready for a scientific look at how personality works. Miss Allison is adamant.

During the first few months of 1955, she and I have several get-acquainted sessions. She likes to guide our conversations toward a rhetorical analysis of the president's latest speeches: Dwight Eisenhower, who as Supreme Commander of the allied forces in Europe during World War II, liberated the concentration camps. Now in the White House, he focuses significant energy in seeing to the resettlement of close to 20 million people who were displaced by the Holocaust. Not quite a decade since the end of the war, several Displaced Persons camps are still receiving American aid. The horrors of the Holocaust, thanks in part to Eisenhower's speeches, are still in the news and are tugging at Miss Allison's heart.

When my new advisor learns my history, I can curry almost any favor. I tell a personal experience, see Miss Allison wipe her eyes so that I won't see the tears and, in effect, place several more tokens in my bank of favors. One day, when *The New York Times* has a particularly moving photo of a concentration camp, I pop the question. "It seems to me," I argue, "that Hitler's rhetoric can only be studied with a psychological perspective." Then I add, "I'll need a psychology minor, to study the Holocaust."

I have come to Syracuse to be far from my parents, to escape the Holocaust, to become American. Eating non-kosher food and dating non-kosher girls helps me feel American. And yet I seem to date more Jewish girls. The Leventhals speak German and eat German and remember the Holocaust and are, in my view, foreign. Syracuse University promises me the freedom to be American, the freedom to not be different and freedom to not feel guilt.

I want to not be special. I want to dissolve into the melting pot. I reject the special of being Uncle Henry's relative. I reject the special of being Dr. Levenson's favorite. And now I am using special to manipulate Miss Allison.

Deciding on a major or a minor program of study is, suddenly, not my most urgent problem. Finding my place in the world is the priority. Living with hyphens requires all my attention. German-American, Jewish-American, Jewish-German (or is it German-Jew or American-Jew?), victim-survivor (survivor-victim?), boy-man...

XXX. HOME AGAIN

IN 1956, I stun the world by 1) finally receiving a baccalaureate degree, 2) marrying Barbara (the same Barbara I met at camp in 1948 and who I knew at the Bronx High School of Science) and 3) being accepted to the Graduate School at the University of Minnesota specializing in Communication.

I return to New York City, work at Louis Marx Toys briefly in statistics and briefly in toy design. In the fall, my new wife and I travel to Minnesota, she with a job as a social worker in a prestigious clinic and I to become a fine graduate student and to learn the teaching and research trades.

By 1959, I've finished a master's degree. I'm working on a Ph.D. degree and I've been selected as advisor to 15 students from diverse Minnesota colleges who will spend the summer of 1960 doing research in Austria. Barbara and I have an opportunity to travel for 13 weeks with all our expenses paid by the Student Project for Amity Among Nations (SPAN)—my first opportunity to visit Europe since I immigrated to the United States as a six-year old escaping Hitler and Nazism.

***

In August of 1960, my wife and I are standing on Goethe Strasse in Hannover, Germany. We face a parking lot that was once the site of a five-story building, number 25. I draw the building in the air with my finger and point to where the fourth floor might have been. I describe the balcony from which I watched the beginnings of the Hitler catastrophe.

The parking lot reflects the massive bombing by the British. They bombed during the day and during the night. They bombed so much that by 1945, the end of the war, Hannover was mostly flat, as flat as the parking lot where my home once stood. Some of the new streets don't even follow the old city pattern. A new beginning. Burying the past. Forgetting.

Had I stayed a day, a week, a month, a year longer than I did, I would almost surely be dead. Killed by the Nazis for being a Jew or killed by the British for being German.

"How does it feel?" my wife, Barbara, asks.

"Mixed. I'm glad I'm an American. I'm glad I survived. But this is my birthplace. My childhood memories point to this street. I even had a different name when I played on this street."

We've just arrived in Hannover from a visit to the Dachau concentration camp, located a short distance outside Munich. This scene, the parking lot, adds to our sadness. We recall Munich.

As we boarded the bus in Munich, our bus driver had warned us not to settle in too comfortably. "The ten miles to Dachau will take only minutes."

My wife and I sat in the front of the bus to better see through the big, clean windshield. We didn't want to miss a single scenic wonder along the way. After all, we were Americans in Germany.

It's true that I could translate at will. My command of the German language was still excellent, but on this day I felt American to the core. Even the German food was now "foreign." I had been away from *Deutschland* for 21 years and from German home cooking for nine.

The guidebook, written for the American tourist, encouraged us to visit the Dachau art museum and the art galleries. Dachau was an interesting art colony until 1933, the year of my birth and the year that Hitler became Chancellor. The book asserts that painting outdoors was invented in this beautiful Munich suburb. It may be that landscape as an independent motif was invented here. However, I always thought that France and Holland moved painting from the studio to the open air—*en plein air* painting.

On the next page of our guidebook, I found our real destination: the concentration camp that was built in, and named after, the charming city of Dachau.

The driver was quite correct. We arrived at the camp in minutes. The bus stopped 20 paces from the entrance, directly in front of the first information sign. I translated for my English-speaking wife: "Dachau, the first concentration camp, was opened in March of 1933." A group of tourists gathered to hear my translation. I pointed out that the grand opening happened just weeks after Hitler became chancellor and six months before the day of my birth.

"It didn't take Hitler long to get started on his dirty work," Barbara noted

I continued to translate aloud. "More than 200,000 people were imprisoned here and over 40,000 were murdered in this camp. At first only political prisoners were housed here, then Jews, Roma, Jehovah's Witnesses, homosexuals and the crippled."

The tour guide arrived and began the official translation. We moved away. Over the iron gate of the main entrance to the camp we read, "*Arbeit Macht Frei*." Work will make you free. That's a joke. Perhaps death will make you free at Dachau. We walked under the sign.

"See the barbed wire fence," my wife said as she backed away. I touched it, knowing that it was no longer electrified.

An information kiosk predicted that Dachau would soon be converted to a tourist-friendly memorial. The camp will have a museum so that visitors can see what happened here. Displays will be built so that visitors can "enjoy" a walking tour. Apparently we arrived before the place was cleansed of its horror.

Grass was growing on both sides of the walkway. It had been recently mowed, perhaps this morning. I could smell the sweet cuttings. Ten thousand Jews were sent to Dachau on Kristallnacht. After the Anschluss in 1938, Austrian prisoners arrived followed in '39 by Czechs and Poles. Soon Dachau became international.

We visited the admission building where prisoners were stripped of their clothing, their possessions and their identities. We saw the building where prisoners had their initial showers, where their heads were shaved and where they were issued uniforms. Next door was a series of tall poles designed for the daily hangings of inmates. All around the poles we saw splotches of bright yellow. Dandelions. New life.

We didn't talk much as we fought back our tears. Really, we couldn't talk. The aura of death surrounded and choked us. The acrid smell of burning flesh was overpowering, even though its odor was only in our imagination. Gray skies and still air set the stage.

Thankfully we were not allowed into the building where political prisoners were tortured. "Repairs" said the sign. I really didn't want to see where people were tortured. I think how easy it would have been to make me confess whatever the SS wanted to hear. A sign assured that one day this building would be open with educational displays.

The barracks, mostly built by prisoners, leaking cold air in the winter, now stuffy in the August heat, have clearly been neglected since liberation in 1945. A sign promised reconstruction soon. Another beautification project.

We skipped several buildings to ensure that we'd meet our return bus on time. The barracks all looked pretty much alike.

Finally we found the crematorium far distant from the central square. Signs informed us that the death camp was purposely designed to be a little distance from the slave labor barracks. The crematorium building was unlighted and dirty, making it feel as cold and ugly as the activity it housed. Several bricks around each of the ovens were loose

Dachau crematorium

and the iron doors were open. I looked inside an oven to see where the bodies of human beings, the bodies of men, women and little children, were burned to ashes and black smoke. I looked inside another oven and another. Was I searching for relatives? My skin tingled. I was chilled. I gagged. I rushed outside into the fresh summer air.

We returned to a very quiet bus just as the driver was ready to depart. Our front row seats were filled, but it didn't matter. In our heads we were still seeing the insides of the ovens.

Back at our tidy bed-and-breakfast room we tried to wash Dachau off our skin and out of our systems. We changed clothes. Then we walked into the kitchen to visit with our hostess, Frau Finster, busily making dinner for her husband.

In German, my first language and my hostess's only language, I asked about Dachau. "Yes," she said, "isn't it a lovely town?"

"I mean the *KZ* camp."

"I've never been there."

"What did you think about it during the war?"

"We didn't know the camp existed."

"You're just a few miles away. Didn't you see the smoke from the enormous chimneys? Didn't you see the smoke blocking the sun and the moon?"

"Oh yes. The ashes fell on our window sills. And it smelled awful."

"What did you think about that?"

"We thought it was a factory."

That evening Herr Finster gave us the same unbelievable story, "We thought it was a factory."

* * *

The next evening we visited the celebrated 400-year-old *Hofbräuhaus*. Mozart and Lenin enjoyed its beer and we wanted to assure that Freddy did too. Here one drinks beer by the liter.

We entered just as a group dressed in *lederhosen* was singing the famous *In München steht ein Hofbräuhaus*. In Munich stands a courtyard brew house. We joined in the chorus. Noise everywhere. Friendly, raucous. happy. No memory of a world war here. No notice that Munich was bombed to smithereens by American airpower just fifteen years earlier. No memory of the 40 million Europeans who perished in the war. We smelled hops and malt and cigar smoke and found two seats at the end of a long table. A waitress dressed in a dirndl came almost immediately. I ordered beer for two. The man sitting by himself just across from us ordered a refill and introduced himself. I introduced my wife and myself and then translated for my wife. I explained to our new friend, Rolf, that my wife speaks little German.

Rolf raved about the pork knuckle he was eating mostly with his fingers. The smell of the sauerkraut tempted my appetite. We chatted in German about the beer and the weather. I translated for Barbara. We guessed that Rolf was about ten years older than us.

"You have a pretty wife. Is she British?"

"She's American," I explained.

He apologized that he speaks no English. Then he added, "Your German is without accent."

"I was born in Hannover." I didn't mention that I'm Jewish and that I left to escape Hitler.

"I was born and raised here in Bavaria. Haven't traveled much. Except during the war." Then he wanted to know when I left Germany.

"I left at the very end of '39."

"Oh, I was in the *Hitler Jugend*, in '39." The Hitler Youth, I translate for Barbara. He probably had been 16 or a little older then.

"Why did you join the Hitler Jugend?" I asked.

"Because they promised to give me a motorcycle." I wondered how many Jews he beat and how many Jewish-owned store windows he broke. I wondered how he fared when the Russians and British and Americans started winning the war, when boys in the Hitler Jugend had to fight in the streets to protect the Fatherland. My questions were answered with "I really didn't like the Hitler Jugend very much."

"So why did you stay?" I asked.

"Because they let me keep the motorcycle."

As we left the Hofbräuhaus I wondered how many American teens would beat up Jews if they were offered a motorcycle.

The next morning we boarded a plane to Hannover. My first trip "home." During the short trip, Barbara and I talked about the three denial monkeys who hear, see and say no evil.

During three months traveling through Austria and Germany we meet very few who take responsibility. Only 15 years after the war ended and we meet very few who think they did anything wrong. Few who feel guilty about having been a bystander or even a perpetrator.

XXXI. POLITICAL UPHEAVAL

AUGUST 23, 1968, is almost over. I'm enjoying a rare quiet evening at home with Barbara. I have a budding career at the University of Minnesota and I'm deeply embroiled in Minnesota politics.

Papa and Mutti have now spent a decade in the lovely seaside community of Red Bank, New Jersey. After I left for college, Papa finally persuaded Mutti to move closer to his work and out of New York. I'm glad that Papa can enjoy his semi-retirement in more pleasant surroundings.

My children, Susan and Michael, are fast asleep and we adults are ready for bed. Friday night means sleeping late on Saturday. The telephone rings and promises that this night will be different from all other nights.

Papa is dead. His heart gave out.

I am in the throes of preparing for the 1968 Democratic National Convention, scheduled for Chicago from August 26 through 29. I am an elected Minnesota delegate to that event. Minnesota offers two candidates, Vice President Hubert Humphrey, the favorite and Lyndon Johnson's legacy, and my hero, Minnesota Senator Eugene McCarthy. There are other candidates, but they are of no consequence to me.

I'm preparing physically, packing and making transportation and housing arrangements. I'm preparing emotionally for the highlight of my political life. I came to America as a refugee to find freedom. Now I'm to be part of the process for selecting the Democratic Party candidate for president of the United States. Papa planned to watch for me on television. He had cancelled all appointments so that he could sit by the TV.

Now joy and pride turn to sadness—and a hectic overnight trip to Red Bank to bury Papa and to comfort Mutti. Truly, two small grandchildren sitting on one's lap can comfort, even cheer, a distraught grandmother. I don't dare cry. I forbid myself to feel.

While Barbara and the children console Mutti, who has been called Oma since she became a grandmother, I watch television news. People are gathering in Chicago for the Convention. Protesters against the war in Vietnam are blocking streets. Radical groups are threatening to poison the Chicago water supply and police respond with batons and tear gas. The TV announcer lists familiar names of men organizing demonstrations throughout the city. Abbie Hoffman, Bobby Seale, Tom Hayden and Jerry Rubin are among the spokesmen riling up the protesters. Mayor Daley calls on the National Guard to supplement the Chicago police. Meanwhile, supporters of Eugene McCarthy for president are trying to "be clean for Gene." Candidate Hubert Humphrey and Mayor Daley are specific targets of the protests while the war is a more general target. Some radical groups such as Students for a Democratic Society (SDS) and the Black Panther Party, lack specific goals. They are attacking "the system." Reporters predict that we will see worse when the convention starts.

Papa's funeral is drab. The funeral home is dark. The room assigned us clearly had a recent dose of air freshener to mask cigar smoke and sweat. A makeshift platform and folding chairs decorate a Spartan room. Perhaps 35 people attend including Tante Beda, Papa's older sister. His older brother, Uncle Max, died several years ago. Beda and my family are Papa's only living relatives. A few friends, also émigrés from Hannover, chat in a cluster. I am pleased that some of Papa's customers attend. He would want his family of clients to remember him. How did they learn of his passing so quickly?

The rabbi obviously doesn't know Papa and says some bland stuff about Milton being a refugee in a new country and that God has called him. Mutti has decreed that no one but the rabbi will be allowed to speak.

My mother has organized an efficient event with adequate snacks and no real celebration of this important life that was my Papa.

Martin Luther King had been shot in April and Bobby Kennedy in June. Their funerals were national events. Where were the crowds to mark the passing of this peddler, this ordinary working stiff, this no-one-special "everyman?" Hundreds, thousands, millions should know about this good man. I feel that Papa has been cheated.

I don't believe in a soul, but "generous soul" is the tag that should appear on his grave. No one asks me.

I have no memory of the burial at the gravesite. None.

* * *

Papa died on August 23rd. I arrive in Red Bank on the 24th. I arrive in Chicago on the 27th, one day late for the convention.

Alpha Smaby in her encyclopedic book, *Political Upheaval: Minnesota and the Vietnam Anti-War Protest* (Minneapolis, Dillon Press, 1987) discusses the convention, quoting from a letter I had written:

Fred Amram, also a Third District delegate, came to Chicago from New Jersey on the second day of the convention: "I took a taxi directly to the convention site, struggled with my luggage, and started toward the main entrance. As I approached the door, two non-uniformed officers lifted me by my armpits— suitcase, briefcase and all—and carried me for a considerable distance from the building. They set me down and, belligerently, began their questioning. How does one explain that one is a legitimate delegate, and that one's credentials are inside the building? Ultimately I was permitted to call into the convention hall and have a fellow delegate deliver my credentials.

That night a few members of the Minnesota delegation were milling about in the Hilton lobby, listening to the news of the police tactics, and [Congressman] Don Fraser [Minnesota 5th district] led some of us across the street to Grant Park, where we joined in singing with Peter, Paul and Mary. The air was rich with tear gas, but we stayed and sang. We could see that beyond us were young people who were worse off than we were; those who broke through the barricades were beaten and gassed...

The trip home was painful. I had come to the convention from the funeral of my father and my personal loss was intensified by the political loss of the convention—Gene McCarthy, my hero, had not won the nomination. But the pain was mixed with pride at that important event; a Jewish refugee from Hitler's Germany had participated. Papa would have been proud." (pp. 296-297)

Hubert Humphrey is nominated for the presidency. The riotous Chicago convention is a disaster for the Democratic Party. In November, Nixon wins the election. He manages to end both the war in Vietnam and the war against poverty.

Papa would have looked at the bright side. He would have reminded us that democracy, even when it doesn't go our way, is better than what happened in Europe some 25 years earlier. He would have looked at his Jewish son and said, "Only in America." Then he would have said his favorite prayer, the shecheyanu:

> *Baruch atah adonai eloheinu melech ha'olam shecheyanu*
> *v'kiy'manu v'higyanu lazman hazeh.*

Blessed are you, our God, Creator of time and space, who has supported us, protected us and brought us to this moment.

XXXII. TANTE BEDA DIED LAST NIGHT

TANTE BEDA COULD LOVE. Five feet tall and fleshy with a happy face. Her rosy cheeks needed no rouge. My aunt's big bosomed hugs were always welcome—especially when I was a teenager. While other adults pinched my cheeks, Tante Beda stroked gently and smiled. She always smiled.

My mother mocked Tante Beda behind her back. Mutti chuckled that Tante Beda hadn't read the latest novels—and never would. Mutti was right. With little education, my aunt had difficulty deciphering words in print. Uncle Max, the oldest in a family of three children, and Papa, the youngest, each finished the fourth grade and were then apprenticed in the dry goods trade. Beda, the middle child, a girl born in 1899 to a poor Jewish family in a small German rural community, would surely need little schooling.

She made her way to the big city, Berlin, where she married Ernst Lustig. Uncle Ernst was the only tall man in our family. At perhaps 5'10", he towered over the rest. Yet he was an unimposing figure. He was as untutored as Tante Beda; his face was passive and he said little. Lustig is the German word for cheerful, jovial. He belied his name. In my playful learning of the English language I joked, "Uncle Ernst is earnest." Even when I was still a child he shook my hand as if formally greeting an adult.

He loved Tante Beda. Unlike my parents who rarely touched, Ernst and Beda held hands as they strolled outdoors or when they sat on our living room couch. Uncle Ernst was protective of his little wife. Every time they left our apartment for the long subway ride back to their

Tante Beda and Uncle Ernst

tenement on New York's Lower East Side, Uncle Ernst asked Beda if she had forgotten something important. Always, as if her doting husband had invented a new mathematical concept, her face brightened. "*Na, klar!*" "Of course," she said in German, as she dutifully trotted off to the bathroom.

My aunt always spoke German. She and her beau (my child's imagination always saw my aunt and uncle as lovers) had come from Germany to New York City via Southampton, England, in January of 1939, 10 months before my family did. Yet neither of the lovers learned much English and seemed to need only the bare minimum in their Jewish neighborhood.

Unlike Tante Beda's unending warmth, Mutti was cool, formal and correct. To Mutti, major sins included bad breath, dirty fingernails and not being in the right social circles. She used *two* bath towels and *two* wash cloths. One for "up" and one for "down."

Mutti's hair, piled in a perfect bun on top of her head, was never to be touched by anyone. Indeed, she rejected touch. Often, when she was dressing for an event, standing before a full-length mirror in her slip, Papa would step close to stroke her behind. "Stop that. The boy will see you," she'd protest.

When visitors came, they might receive a quick peck on the cheek from Mutti. Papa, like his sister, was a serious hugger and kisser.

Dressed in tight-waisted, broad-shouldered clothes, Mutti tried to accentuate her figure. She boasted to friends that she had been to a museum or befriended someone who knew Eleanor Roosevelt. As a curious youngster I thought that *knowing* Mrs. Roosevelt would be really cool. The value of a second-hand friendship puzzled me.

"What's so big a deal about knowing someone who knows a president's widow?" I inquired.

"That shows my friend travels in the right circles," Mutti explained.

When the Hebrew Immigrant Aid Society called to say that a new refugee to the United States needed to see a friendly face, just as we had when we first arrived, she would say, "My own family keeps me much too busy" even though I, her only son, was at school most of the day and she quit her job as soon as Papa was able to provide adequate support. She grew her fingernails quite long to show that she was not employed. Tante Beda worked in a factory.

When she didn't want to visit Tante Beda, Mutti would respond to an invitation with "We're already busy that evening." Then her vanity might invent a bookbinder or businessman whom she knew from the old country. These sometimes fictitious visitors were more valued than a loving aunt.

As part of Mutti's status-seeking, her first goal for me was to become a physician, even though the sight of blood made me sick. Secondly, I was to learn tennis so that I could meet a rich girl. Her plan totally ignored the fact that I have only one functioning eye—hence limited depth perception—a handicap that creates severe problems on the tennis court.

Mutti did not like Tante Beda. So far as I could tell, Mutti did not care much for any members of Papa's family. When we first came to the United States, Mutti worked diligently to rescue her mother from Hitler's clutches. The grandmother I called Omi joined us in freedom just weeks before Pearl Harbor Day, the day most gates to the U.S. closed. On the other hand, I recall only minimal efforts to rescue Papa's mother, the grandmother I called Oma Jettchen—perhaps a call to the Red Cross. Nothing more. Of course, I was just a small boy and didn't have access to all the details. However, small boys can sense relationships. German National Archives record that Oma Jettchen was transported to Latvia where she died in the Riga Ghetto in December, 1941.

* * *

My mother barely tolerated being with Tante Beda and only when Papa insisted. Aunt Beda, according to Mutti, was ignorant, tasteless, boorish, overweight and generally lacked "class." Uncle Ernst was a notch lower.

Mutti thought that the Lustig apartment was appalling. I loved it.

Our apartment had a glass coffee table which, as an over-active youngster, I broke occasionally. Glass-fronted display cases were not conducive to active indoor play on a rainy day. High-gloss on all furniture meant fingerprints, food smudges and many scoldings. Imitation Persian area rugs invited tripping for a careless boy. Ours was a home for show designed by a house-proud "lady."

Tante Beda's design formula included overstuffed everything, great for curling into corners. She allowed feet on all furniture. Her wall-to-wall carpeting was so inexpensive that no one minded a spill or two. And Tante Beda couldn't allow her only nephew to be without food. He was permitted to eat in the living room with a new toy and a loving embrace.

Uncle Ernst was a laborer in a cigar factory and explained in great detail the art of making cigars by hand—fascinating to a young boy planning one day to become a serious cigar smoker.

Tante Beda was devastated when Uncle Ernst died in 1961. As much as she missed Ernst, the greater loss was not having someone to love. "Bursting with love" had a new meaning for me.

Papa insisted that Mutti join us at the funeral.

Each year when I light a *Yahrzeit* lamp for Uncle Ernst, I think about cigars and my second-hand expertise in their manufacture. In both Yiddish and German "Yahrzeit" means "time of year." For Jews a Yahrzeit commemorates the anniversary of someone's death. At sunset before the Yahrzeit day, one lights a 24-hour candle or oil lamp. I like to recall favorite memories and say a prayer or two. I like to begin with the words, "I pause for thought in memory of my beloved ..." At this time of bereavement I give thanks for memories and for the companionship I once enjoyed.

When I recite prayers at the annual remembrance of Uncle Ernst and other family members, I become a little teary eyed. At my Papa's Yahrzeit, I become so choked that my wife holds me and finishes the prayers on my behalf.

Although each year I light the lamp and say the prayers, I shed no tears at Mutti's Yahrzeit.

* * *

A few Yahrzeits for Uncle Ernst passed before Tante Beda remarried. The widower, Chill Davis, came into our family with an adult, sickly daughter. Beda could now give full-time love to two new people in her life.

Chill was super-Orthodox, a trait my mother disliked. To Mutti, people were either not observant enough or too "*frum*," a Yiddish word meaning religious. Clearly Chill was way too frum.

Uncle Chill and Tante Beda

While Mutti had not liked Ernst's company, she hated Chill's. However, I was fascinated. Chill's Judaism included a mystical, Eastern European component based on learning as well as *shtetl* tradition that included magic. In the small Eastern European Jewish community, the shtetl—visualize *Fiddler on the Roof*—one spoke directly to God. The Jewish mystics I had met in books now became real. I could ask questions. I could debate. I could learn first-hand.

Beda, who had never been more than Jewish in name, learned to keep a kosher home, learned to support Chill's morning and evening prayers, learned to appreciate the mystical beliefs that Chill had brought with him from the Polish shtetl.

Mutti's hierarchy of humanity placed Polish Jews somewhere below *goyim*—even below Polish goyim. When Mutti said "goyim," the Yiddish word for non-Jews, her face contorted just as it did when she tasted a dish gone sour. "Polack" was not foreign to her vocabulary.

Once, as a teenager, I dared to inquire why someone who had escaped the concentration camps and the hatred of the Nazis wouldn't be accepting of differences—particularly Jews of different beliefs and heritages. Mutti's response included phrases like "the right people" and "unclean." Apparently she—and by extension I—was better than "them."

When Papa died in 1968, our small family—those few not killed in the Holocaust—attended his funeral. Tante Beda was there with comfort for everyone. Chill took me aside and explained his version of the meaning of death, the spirits that lingered and those that traveled into the "other life."

* * *

One day in May of 1977, Mutti calls long distance from Red Bank. I am now a professor at the University of Minnesota as well as a husband and a father.

"Tante Beda died last night," she announces.

She tells me that Beda died peacefully in her sleep having loved life for 77 years. Mutti claims Chill is hysterical. In keeping with Jewish tradition, the funeral is 24 hours away.

"I'll see you at the funeral," I say, assuming that my mother will be pleased to spend time with me, even on this sad occasion—at least sad for me.

"I won't be at the funeral. That Polack will behave without dignity. The service will be too frum. I won't know anyone there." She uses short abrupt sentences. All in German, our native tongue, the language of the Gestapo.

There is a moment of awkward silence while I catch my breath. That gives her time to gather more thoughts and to add, "There is no reason for you to go either. You're busy at work. Your children need you. And Beda is not worth the expense of flying all that distance."

I quietly interject, "You owe it to my late father to attend his sister's funeral."

Her response: "I won't go."

And that is that! Case closed!

I call colleagues to cover my classes, arrange the purchase of an airline ticket to New York, call Chill and bid farewell to wife and children. Within six hours of my mother's call, I am on my way to the airport.

Chill, a small, thin, nervous man, has everything under control. The funeral has been arranged. His daughter, Mona, sits on a couch staring straight ahead in her melancholy, mourning the loss of her second mother.

All the mirrors are covered with towels. To make conversation I ask why, although I already knew that Orthodox Jews believe that there should be no vanity in a house of mourning. Chill provides a second reason, reflecting his mystical beliefs. The mirrors hold Beda's spirit which, he believes should stay in the mirrors until she is buried. To assure that she will be transported to the next, happier life, her spirit, her soul, should not be tempted back into this world.

We walk a few blocks to the funeral home where Chill wants me to see Beda. I don't know what he means by "seeing" Beda. Once inside he takes my arm and leads me to an open casket. Jews *never* have an open casket. NEVER! Everything I ever learned in religious school forbade viewing the deceased. I have no experience viewing a dead person.

Reluctantly I look into her pudgy, smiling face. Her cheeks are pink and I sense that she wants to hug me. Chill stands on his toes, leans over the casket and kisses Beda. A heartfelt kiss. Then he looks at me and at Beda indicating that I, too, could give her a last kiss. Suddenly I am 12 years old and feel her soft bosom pressed against my chest and that gentle stroking of my cheek, always the right cheek. I smell her special perfume. I burst into tears.

I cry again at the funeral. Beda has no remaining living relatives other than Chill and Mona and me—and the sister-in-law who refuses to attend this last event with Tante Beda. Chill has no living relatives other than his daughter. Some of their friends attend. Barely a *minyan* of the ten men needed, according to Jewish law, for the official prayers. I cry because I will miss my Tante Beda's hugs and because so few attend her funeral. She deserves more. Can I ever forgive my mother for not attending?

The hearse leads three vehicles to the cemetery. Chill and I are in a small limousine with two of his close friends and his daughter, who says nothing. Three other cars follow with more friends.

When we arrive, I am surprised that we are next to Uncle Ernst's grave. Chill decided to have his Beda buried next to her first husband. He explains that he has already bought a plot for himself and another for Mona next to his first wife. As much as he loves Beda, he believes that God prefers her to rest with her first husband in the next life.

It is a clear, warm day in May. None of us wear coats. Chill whispers to me that the pleasant weather is a bad omen. "Days like this are for weddings. Beda's burial requires a storm."

The rabbi recites all the relevant prayers with Chill mumbling along. Chill knows all the Hebrew. Perhaps he could have been a superb Orthodox rabbi had he been allowed an education and had the Nazis not chased him from his shtetl home.

The grave attendants begin to lower the casket which is braced on two straps. In keeping with Jewish tradition, it is an unadorned, rectangular wooden box. As the coffin starts its descent into the pre-dug hole, Chill begins to panic. He shouts for the workmen to be careful. He uses a Polish word that could be translated as "beware." Apparently he has a premonition. Chill's observation about the fine weather comes to mind. He believes in omens.

Suddenly one of the two straps holding the wooden box snaps. One end of the casket drops into the hole. The box stands on end. A moment of silence, of awe. None of us has ever seen such a disaster. Then Chill, at full voice, demands that the casket be raised and opened to check on his beloved. The rabbi, carefully selected by Chill because he shares similar mystical beliefs, asserts that the body should not be raised again. Rather, he argues, it should be leveled while still in the hole. Chill and the rabbi debate mystical law and lore. I understand very little of the argument based on their unique belief system. Much of the debate uses Hebrew, Yiddish and Polish language far beyond my understanding.

Suddenly the discussion stops. Chill asks me, a professor and presumably a wise and all-knowing person, which end of the coffin is down. Although I don't know the answer to his question, I know the response that will be most reassuring. "The casket fell feet first," I declare with as much authority as I can muster through my tears. With that, the rabbi apparently wins the day and Beda's coffin is re-adjusted while still in the hole.

Jewish tradition suggests that each of the bereaved throw some dirt on the coffin to symbolize closure and letting go. Using the back of the shovel to hold the loose earth suggests that one buries the loved one reluctantly.

The rabbi holds the shovel in front of Chill. The trauma of the slipped casket has been too much. Chill is frozen in place. He makes no motion to grasp the shovel. The rabbi hands the shovel to me and

I pick up some dirt and throw it into the hole along with a small bottle of Tante Beda's distinctive sweet-smelling perfume. Mutti called it "cheap." Chill lets out a scream and becomes inconsolable. As the casket is covered by the workmen he sobs with great cries. He tears at his jacket, his shirt, even his prayer shawl. Meanwhile Mona cries quietly, embraced by one of the women in attendance.

The rabbi speaks gently to Chill for perhaps 20 minutes. Finally Chill is able to walk to a nearby bench and sit calmly for a while. The rabbi gently holds his hand. Meanwhile, I speak with the other guests and thank them for attending. One of Chill's neighbors says she will take Mona to her home for a few days. Another neighbor, understanding that I will be returning to Minnesota in the morning, promises to look in on Chill often. The neighbor's wife promises to see that Chill eats home-cooked kosher food until he can again care for himself.

Our little caravan makes its way into the city and I spend the night with Chill. The next morning he thanks me for coming to be with him. He kisses me on both cheeks. Chill never asks why my mother did not come to the funeral.

On the flight home, I think about fervently religious Chill. I have never believed in omens and magic and souls in mirrors. I do, however, admire Chill's depth of feeling, his passion. The contrast to the façade that is my mother's life becomes clear.

I think of sweet Tante Beda and the men who had loved her dearly. Her two brothers, my Papa and Uncle Max. Her two husbands, Ernst and Chill, who both loved her with complete adoration. And, of course, the boy that I once was, as well as the man I had become and who had helped to bury her.

* * *

A few days after my return home, Mutti calls. She wants to hear about Beda's funeral. After I describe the events, including the casket disaster, she declares that she is happy that she hadn't attended. My story proves to her what a boor Chill is and Beda had been.

Suddenly I am no longer the dispassionate observer. "Who," I ask, "Who do you think will want to attend *your* funeral?"

"Don't be fresh to your mother," is her response.

Many years later, when we bury my mother, only those who need to be at her funeral attend: my wife and I, our two children and their spouses, our two grandchildren and a rabbi—not even the minyan, the quorum of ten, required by Jewish law.

EPILOGUE:
MY CHILDREN AND MY CHILDREN'S CHILDREN

"Tell your children about it,
And let your children tell theirs,
And their children to the next generation!"
Joel 1: 3

I WROTE THIS BOOK to demonstrate that the Holocaust didn't begin with Auschwitz. By September of 1933, Jewish women were not welcome in public hospitals. Consequently I, a Jewish baby, was born in a Catholic Infants Home under the supervision of nuns. Slowly "Nur Für Juden" led to "Juden Verboten" followed by Kristallnacht in November of 1938. Auschwitz did not receive prisoners until 1940 and did not become a fully functioning death camp until 1942. Auschwitz sneaked up on us slowly. Genocide develops in stages.

We arrived in the United States to witness some name changes and some culture shock. Papa taught me to be grateful that WE'RE IN AMERICA NOW.

I became a citizen and soon started participating in American politics. Supporting candidates and causes from Henry Wallace to Eugene McCarthy with others in between and afterwards, I became an American. I AM AN AMERICAN.

I raised an American family always trying to teach the values I learned from my experiences as a Jew in Nazi Germany. I built a career, wrote a few books, many articles, some stories.

Fred and his "babies," Susan and Michael

I divorced, remarried and glow with pride in response to my adult children and grandchildren. I had brilliant successes and made dramatic mistakes. From my bris to my retirement, nothing can be undone. Only reported.

Of course there are more stories to tell. I want to tell a story about my Oma Jettchen, my grandma, Papa's mother. I was a young boy when I saw her last. I sat on her lap when she read Rotkappchen and Rumpelstilzchen and let me turn the pages of her books. She was murdered by the Nazis in the Riga Ghetto. I grew up without my Oma.

As a survivor, I can tell my life story. I can write a memoir. Oma Jettchen didn't survive. I have no Oma story. I can't paint an Oma portrait. Just an empty frame.

My friend Alice Musabende witnessed the genocide in Rwanda. One day she arrived home from an errand to find the dead bodies of her mother and father, her twelve-year-old sister and her nine-year-old and two-year-old brothers. Alice was fourteen.

Alice survived and grew to be a successful adult. Like me, she writes about her life and her assimilation into a new culture. But her siblings have no story to tell. Her parents can't boast about their children or Alice's wedding or the day Alice's first baby was born. Just empty frames.

How many families, mother, father, children, walked into the Auschwitz gas chambers? Only the smoke from the crematoria chimneys can tell how many whole families died with not a single survivor. Dead children have no story to tell. Dead parents and grandparents and uncles and aunts. Millions of frames forever empty.

Jews leave a stone when visiting a grave. I don't know where to leave my stone for Uncle Jacob or Aunt Karola or Cousin Aaltje. Can I leave a stone in an empty frame?

I dedicated this book to Cousin Aaltje whose ashes were shoveled out of an Auschwitz crematorium when she was only 3½. I wrote this book for Oncle Isaak and Tante Käthe and for Oma Jetchen and the other six million who can no longer speak for themselves.

I have been telling these stories to my children throughout their lives. I hoped that they could, through me, meet a few of the relatives they might have known. Uncle Jakob might have given them their first driving lessons, an activity that bonded him to me—even though I was only five years old, my feet didn't even come close to the accelerator pedal and I only helped with the steering. Tante Karola might have read stories to them as she did to me. She might have hugged them too tight, just like she hugged me too tight, because she never had children of her own.

As they blossomed, my children heard my pleas to be alert to injustice—in all places and at all times. I hope this book will help my grandchildren and great-grandchildren understand that genocide begins slowly, first with an insult followed by a seemingly meaningless unjust law. And then the ball gathers speed. And then the Holocaust. And then Rwanda or Darfur or...

My stories must have had an impact on my children. Could there be genetic influences? After all, not only was their father a witness to the Holocaust, their grandparents, my parents, were witnesses as well. My food shortages were my parents' food shortages and my fears were also theirs. Might one expect a genetic impact on my children and my children's children?

Some plants, confronted with great stress, perhaps drought or excessive rain, struggle successfully to adapt. They survive. Their offspring are often immediately able to grow and prosper under the stressful conditions. To explain this phenomenon, biologists are exploring epigenetics which suggests that, while the DNA sequence of the stressed plants is not changed, chemical changes to the DNA surface modify the way genes express themselves. Chemical changes activate or repress expression. These epigenetic changes can last through several generations.

When female mice are artificially stressed by deprivation or other uncomfortable manipulations of their environment, they produce offspring who immediately display unusual behaviors even though the new generation has not experienced the stress and has not learned behaviors from its mothers. The next generation of mice, for example, may have an aversion to whatever caused the mother's stress. Similarly, dietary modifications in one generation can impact fur growth in future generations.

Biologists are working to further document epigenetic behavior modification. The nature vs. nurture conundrum persists. One wonders how stress impacts the children of war veterans or survivors of genocides. Can chemical changes in one generation impact how genes in future generations express themselves?

Certainly there must be learned behaviors based on conversation and modeling. Might there also be behavioral changes based on chemical modifications of genetic expression—and, if so, for how many generations might those changes last? I leave the answer to these questions for future scientists. I can, however, speculate and I can ask what my children and grandchildren think about the impact my Holocaust experiences had on them.

My "babies" have now each passed their fiftieth birthdays. They're both perfect. Isn't that what parents think of their children? Consequently it's difficult for me to judge whether daughter Susan or son Michael have taken on symptoms reflecting Holocaust stresses experienced by their father and grandparents.

Susan, when learning about epigenetics, noted that her Oma, my mother, must have had remarkable stress during pregnancy. Susan notes that Hitler became chancellor on January 30, 1933. Her Oma would have confirmed that she was pregnant at about that time. I was born on September 19 of that year. Hence, Hitler's anti-Jewish policies were infecting Germany while I was growing in my mother's womb. The fact that I was born in a Catholic infants shelter illustrates what my mother was experiencing during that period. What other Nazi policies impacted the lives of Jews? Could the surface of my DNA have been chemically changed even in the womb? Could those changes have affected Susan?

Susan agrees that behavior and attitude don't tell us if they are expressions of epigenetics or simply growing up under the tutelage of family. She acknowledges that while part of her behavior may reflect that her grandparents and father experienced the Holocaust, she adds, "I might also be responding to the fact that I had two socially conscious, politically active parents." Who can say? We do know that Susan became an educator with a focus on Jewish education. She teaches about the Holocaust and trains teachers to understand genocide.

Susan earned certification for teaching children with nontraditional needs and, in her teaching and supervision of teachers, insists on adapting educational and counseling opportunities to these children. She likes to point out that every child has distinctive needs. She believes that each of us is unique.

Both of Susan's children, my granddaughters, expressed interest in their *zayde's* history. When, in public school, teachers asked them to interview a grandparent, each granddaughter, Ari and Zoe, wrote heavily illustrated reports about their grandpa's experiences in Germany and his growing up as a refugee in the United States. Teachers lauded them for exceeding expectations with most interesting presentations.

I recall my visit to the New York World's Fair in 1940. When Papa and I discussed the DuPont mural, "Better Things For Better Living Through Chemistry," I promised Papa that I would dedicate myself to tikkun olam, repairing the world. Both granddaughters have also selected careers focused on tikkun olam.

Ari has a degree in environmental science. She currently tests water samples and works toward assuring safe water ecology. Zoe, a college senior, has plans for a graduate degree in special education.

Ari, the older, writes,

When I read books—history or memoir—I don't really know the author. But I know Zayde and therefore his stories about his history, especially about the Holocaust, seem more meaningful. I'm more interested and more involved in stories about history my zayde has experienced. When we talked about the Holocaust in middle school, high school and religious school, I felt a bit more advanced. I knew a little more because of the family stories I had heard and read.

I feel that I've become extra sensitive. When people mention the Holocaust in an offhand way, I think that one might have said that differently.

In college I registered for a course about the Holocaust. Family stories piqued my interest and I wanted to become even more informed. I expect that I'll continue my interest and hope that I can be an upstander in opposing all genocide.

My second grandchild, Zoe, celebrated her Bat Mitzvah on March 17, 2007. The Bar or Bat Mitzvah is a "coming of age" celebration for Jewish boys and girls, when, typically at thirteen, they make their covenant with God just as Jews have done since the time Abraham made his covenant.

Zoe decided to partner with "Remember Us: The Holocaust B'nai Mitzvah Project" to honor a child, one of the 1.5 million, who did not survive the Holocaust. Each B'nai Mitzvah youngster is assigned a child who perished in the Shoah. Zoe, like other program participants, integrated her chosen child into her own ceremony and said Kaddish, the mourning prayer, on the day of her Bat Mitzvah and will again, each year, on the anniversary of that day as well as each year on Yom HaShoah, the day of Holocaust remembrance. When she read from the Torah, Zoe spoke with two voices: her own and that of the child she honored on this special day. Zoe has given her selected child the gift of Bat Mitzvah.

Zoe specifically selected a Dutch child named Aaltje Wurms, my only first cousin—a child who was murdered in Auschwitz at age 3½. Zoe's congregation, Temple Emanuel of Worcester, Massachusetts, provided a bracelet with Aaltje's name, a bracelet that honors Aaltje and reminds Zoe of my cousin—and Zoe's cousin, although several generations removed.

Zoe writes,

I don't truly understand most history I've studied nor do I remember all the details teachers have thrown at me. Studying the Holocaust and World War II is different. Having you and your stories as part of my life has made this piece of history real. I know that the six million were real people who had active lives and real families just like ours.

I act differently at times knowing I'm a third generation Holocaust survivor. I am more hurt by anti-Semitic jokes; I am more heartbroken when, in the National Holocaust Museum, I see a little rocking chair that could have belonged to my cousin, Aaltje. I am more passionate in teaching kids about not being a bystander. I am more proud when I am asked about my heritage... Even though it's a devastating story, knowing this piece of my roots so well helps me know and understand who I am and where I came from.

Son Michael is a mixed-race, chosen child. He was adopted when he was just three weeks old. Consequently, there is no expectation that his genes would reflect my stresses or those of my parents. Whatever impact I had on Michael is not genetic. Might my post-Holocaust stresses have impacted Michael's DNA as he was developing into adulthood?

Michael has expressed enormous aversion to bigotry. While still a youngster in grade school, Mike walked out of classes when films were shown about American slavery or about the Holocaust. Indeed, almost all scenes of violence caused distress and he left the classroom. We quickly arranged that Michael would be excused from classes when he experienced stress from movies.

Michael writes,

A clear example of the influence my dad's experiences had on me is my decision to study German in high school rather than French or Spanish. When my high school German class went to Munich, we made a day trip to Dachau, the medieval town outside of Munich now known for its concentration camp. Knowledge of the deaths of Dad's aunts, cousins and uncles impacted that visit. I was the only one in our class who literally could not stomach the barracks museum at the camp. I had to excuse myself after a few minutes of seeing black and white pictures of the dead and dying. I could relate on a personal level. I'm adopted, but the stories I'd heard through the years from Dad and his mother became part of my life.

After high school I furthered my German study with an intense course at Carnegie Mellon University. That course was followed by a two-week class at the Goethe Institute in Luneburg, Germany. It was on this trip that I visited the area where the Amrams lived in Hannover.

Like Dad, who was bullied for being a Jew (and also for being a German), I went through junior high school enduring daily hazing for using crutches. One of the stories in this memoir bears similarities to my experience. As I read a scene in which Dad comes close to killing a bully named Albert, I saw a past demon of my own, a kid who tormented me mercilessly for walking with crutches. One day I was the aggressor and the kid's life was literally in my hands. I let him squirm a while, extracting every ounce of vindication, and threw him back into Bully Lake. Of course this incident and my dad's story are decades apart, but that forgiving trait, that idea of not descending to the bully's or bigot's level, worked its way in me. The "'special' (I prefer 'different') is worth defending" mentality was part of me long before I read this memoir.

Clearly my personal history has impacted my children and grand-children. Susan's and Michael's dedication to tikkun olam reflects both their parents. Their commitment to being activist upstanders reflects both parents.

The Hebrew word mitzvah refers to a good deed. Mitzvah also trans-lates as a commandment. To do good deeds is a commandment. Perhaps intimate images of the Holocaust and its after-effects have provided my family extra incentive to lead a life of mitzvah. I hope that this memoir has the same effect on my readers.

ACKNOWLEDGMENTS

Ellen Kennedy and Steve Campos started the process by alerting me to my responsibility to tell my story as a vehicle for teaching about genocide.

I owe enormous gratitude to the Loft Literary Center for providing mentors and colleagues, instruction and inspiration. Specifically, the members of my writing group, Anika Fajardo, Katy Jensen and Mary Jane LaVigne have each earned a thousand and one thanks for not permitting me to avoid the hard stuff. They continually push toward honesty of feelings. They force me to probe my joy and my pain. And they let me test wild ideas.

Sandra Brick, a visual artist, helps me think like an artist. Her constant "what if" challenge, pushes the creativity buttons. Thank you!

My son and daughter, Michael and Susan, have grown up as second generation survivors with stories of their own to tell. Both have suggested additions and corrections.

Jim Perlman, guru of Holy Cow! Press, helped make the tough decisions: which chapters to drop from the manuscript, where to add and how to end the book. Of course, he made the big decision to publish my manuscript.

Most of all, my eternal gratitude goes to Ellen Weingart, who fixes my grammar and puts the commas in the correct place. More important, she questions every detail to assure that I come as close to the truth as possible. And then she takes my awkward phrases and replaces them with lively language. She molds my sentences into what I really meant to say. Ellen is much, much more than an editor.

Several of these chapters have appeared in altered form in diverse publications. I thank these editors for giving my stories a wider readership and for permission to retell my experiences in this book.

- "Unjust Desserts," *Poetica Magazine*, Special Holocaust Edition, Fall 2014.

- "Tante Beda Died Last Night," *Prick of the Spindle*, Vol. 7, No. 4, 2014.

- "The Outsider," *Hippocampus Magazine*, March 2012.

- "The Reluctant Grown-up," *Hippocampus Magazine*, January 2012 (reprinted in *Poetica Magazine*, Special Holocaust Edition, Fall 2014).

- "Kristallnacht: The Night of Broken Glass," *Marking Humanity*, Edited by Shlomit Kriger, Toronto: Soul Inscription Press, 2010.

- "The Brownshirts Are Coming," *Prick of the Spindle* (Literary Journal), Vol. 3, No. 2, 2009 (reprinted in *Marking Humanity*).

- "Two Butchers," *Whistling Shade* (Literary Journal), Vol. 7, No. 3, Fall 2007.

- "Bat Mitzvah with Cousin Aaltje," *The Jewish Chronicle* (Worcester, Mass.), vol. 81, no. 9, May, 2007 (reprinted in *Remember Us*, Spring, 2007).

- "My First Seder In America," *American Jewish World*, April 2006 (reprinted in *Jewish Transcript* and *Jewish Chronicle*, 2006).

- "The Chanukah Man," *American Jewish World*, December 2005 (reprinted in *Jewish Chronicle*, December, 2006; reprinted in *Turtle River Press*, Issue # 68, November - December 2007).

ABOUT THE AUTHOR

FRED AMRAM spent his early years in Hannover, Germany, where he experienced the Holocaust from its inception in 1933. He witnessed Kristallnacht and the Gestapo invading his home. He watched the British bombers from his balcony when Jews were banned from air raid shelters. The loss of uncles, aunts, a grandmother and many more relatives has motivated him to share his experiences in hopes of ending genocide everywhere.

Although the transition to a new language and culture was difficult, the alternatives were worse. Consequently, the United States truly became a land of opportunity where one could build a new life and become more than a "Holocaust survivor."

Amram has spoken about the Holocaust and other genocides at Clark University, Carlton College, William Mitchell College of Law and many other educational institutions, churches and synagogues. He frequently leads workshops for government agencies, including the U.S. Army and Air Force. He has testified about his Holocaust experiences at the Minnesota legislature. Amram is admired for his scholarship as well as his story telling ability.

With degrees from Syracuse University and the University of Minnesota, Amram is a retired professor of communication and creativity who served in many administrative capacities including Director of Academic Affairs for the University's General College. He has authored several books as well as many articles, essays and stories. He has been a visiting lecturer at many universities and has curated several exhibitions about inventing. Amram's consulting and public speaking services have been utilized in Europe, Asia and North America. In presenting Professor Amram the Patent and Trademark Office's prestigious Excellence in Education Award, the Commissioner of the PTO referred to Amram as "excellence in education personified."

For more information, please visit *www.fredamram.com*.